Appalachia to Dessau

Appalachia to Dessau
Letters of a Tank Commander in World War II

JOHN GOODIN

Edited by Sandy Laws

McFarland & Company, Inc., Publishers
Jefferson, North Carolina

Frontispiece: John D. Goodin in a World War II officer's uniform with tank battalion pin.

ISBN (print) 978-1-4766-9445-0
ISBN (ebook) 978-1-4766-5369-3

LIBRARY OF CONGRESS AND BRITISH LIBRARY
CATALOGUING DATA ARE AVAILABLE

Library of Congress Control Number 2024039764

© 2024 Sandy Laws. All rights reserved

No part of this book may be reproduced or transmitted in any form or by any means, electronic or mechanical, including photocopying or recording, or by any information storage and retrieval system, without permission in writing from the publisher.

Front cover image: John Goodin was mayor/military governor in Germany after the pullout from Dessau in April 1945 (John Goodin Papers, Archives of Appalachia, East Tennessee State University).

McFarland & Company, Inc., Publishers
Box 611, Jefferson, North Carolina 28640
www.mcfarlandpub.com

To the World War II families and their descendants,
of which I am one;
to all veterans who have selflessly served their country
so that the rest of us might enjoy freedom;
and especially to the family of John David Goodin
for so graciously donating his invaluable papers,
photographs, and letters to the Archives of Appalachia.

Table of Contents

Preface	1
Introduction	3
List of Goodin's Family and Friends	5
ONE. Basic Training: May 1941–June 1942	7
TWO. Dog Biscuits and Dust Devils: July 1, 1942–September 14, 1943	34
THREE. England "Somewhere": September 15, 1943–December 30, 1943	71
FOUR. Somebody's Johnny: January 1944–June 1944	99
FIVE. Normandy—Baptism by Fire, the Spearhead Is Born: June 23–September 14, 1944	118
SIX. "Still Rollin'": Rhineland, Germany, September 15, 1944–March 21, 1945; Ardennes, Belgium, December 19, 1944–January 25, 1945	151
SEVEN. Dessau: Victories and Atrocities: March 22–April 25, 1945	193
EIGHT. The Fatted Calf: April 28, 1945–September 10, 1945	209
Epilogue	252
Chapter Notes	253
Bibliography and Further Reading	257
Index	259

Preface

In 2019, as the new assistant archivist at the Archives of Appalachia at East Tennessee State University, I was assigned the task of inventorying the collections. This task required that I compare shelf content with the inventory listings. While some may find inventorying thousands of boxes an intimidatingly arduous and tedious task, the librarian in me found this quite fascinating and exciting. I launched into this treasure trove with exuberance and enthusiasm.

One day, while slowly perusing shelves and peering into boxes, I came across an unprocessed box stuffed with hundreds of letters mainly from the 1930s and mid–1940s. Being the curious soul that I am, I simply could not resist opening the discolored, and sometimes fragile, 80-year-old envelopes with fascinating stamps, to see what the letters were about. Little did I know that I had just launched into a project that would carry me through the next three years.

I meticulously began to organize and catalog the letters by date. Reading these letters was like reading a novel with all the necessary elements: setting, characters, plot, conflict, resolution, point of view and theme. There was mystery, romance, history, horror and realism all woven into the life story of John David Goodin. I became absorbed and a bit obsessed.

I was immediately drawn in by the articulate and eloquent writing of John Goodin. After reading only a few letters, it was obvious that he had a close relationship with his family. The letters revealed a hard work ethic, which came from his dad who was a railroad conductor for fifty years, and who was always encouraging him to stay away from the girls, work hard, go to church, and get a good education to avoid hard, physical labor such as railroading. Goodin's talent for storytelling came from his mother, a hilariously funny homemaker and part-time dabbler in real estate, who told humorous stories about shocking the Women's Auxiliary with outlandish hats and dangly earrings. The close relationship between Goodin and his parents is palpable. They loved one

Preface

another, but they were not a perfect family and were not afraid to state the hard truths.

Excited and eager to share these letters with the general public, an idea began to formulate. I had spent so much time immersed in these letters, I felt that I had become intimately acquainted with the Goodin family. I wanted to share this rare and important story of daily life in Appalachia, which would evolve into a global story of life in Europe, and also bring Europe to the small town of Erwin, Tennessee.

Unless otherwise noted, all of the information in this book is taken directly from the John Goodin Papers, housed in the Archives of Appalachia at East Tennessee State University. The John Goodin Collection contains over 300 letters exchanged between Goodin and his family and friends. Due to length constraints, only 170 of those letters are included in this book. All 300-plus letters, including some wonderful letters exchanged between Goodin and his mother and father, have been transcribed and scanned in date order, and the John Goodin Papers/John Goodin Collection may be accessed online at the East Tennessee State University Archives of Appalachia.

A digital exhibit titled "A Soldier's Letters Home—World War II" is also available online through the East Tennessee State University Archives of Appalachia. This exhibit contains additional material that could not be incorporated into this book including numerous photographs, memorabilia, postcards, stamps and currency, Goodin's field book, and a map detailing the movements of the 32nd Armored Regiment, 3rd Armored Spearhead Division.

Introduction

John David Goodin was born in South Carolina on May 1, 1917, to Thomas Elliott (1877–1963) and Glenna Hall Goodin (1882–1974), but his familial roots were in East Tennessee. T.E. was the son of John C. and Cordelia Price Goodin, and the great-grandson of Benjamin Goodin, who settled in Greene County, Tennessee, in 1783, when the county was first established. T.E. married Glenna Lee Hall on November 30, 1901. Glenna was the daughter of David F. and Ella Lucas Hall. T.E. and Glenna had three children: Thomas Elliott Jr., Ellene Cordelia, and John David.[1] T.E. served the Clinchfield Railroad for 51 years and was presented his 50-year pin in 1956, having never had a demerit or personal injury on the railroad. Referred to as Captain Tom, T.E.'s 58-year career on the railroad led him away from East Tennessee temporarily, but he soon brought his family back to his Appalachian roots.

John grew up in the Appalachian region of Erwin, Tennessee, situated in the foothills of the Unicoi Mountains. After graduating from Unicoi County High School, Goodin attended East Tennessee State Teacher's College in Johnson City, Tennessee. Encouraged by his father to get a good education that would allow him to obtain a less labor-intensive career, from 1936 to 1939, Goodin attended Washington & Lee University and the University of Kentucky, both at Lexington. He graduated from University of Tennessee Law School in Knoxville, Tennessee, in 1941.

After graduation in May 1941, Goodin began his law career at the office of William J. Carter in Johnson City, Tennessee. Only one month later, on June 28, 1941, Goodin received his acceptance letter for military service from the United States Army. Little did he know that he was about to become a tank commander in one of the most notorious and prestigious regiments in World War II, the 3rd Armored Spearhead Division, the 32nd Armored Regiment. This unit would earn the name "Spearhead" early on because they were the leaders of the pack, forging

Introduction

the way across Europe with single-minded dedication and unstoppable determination. Their motto was "Victory or Death."

Goodin was miraculously able to save most of the letters he received from home. There are over 300 letters in the John Goodin Papers housed in the Archives of Appalachia at East Tennessee State University. Goodin advised his parents early on that it might be a good idea to save the letters and other items he sent home, because he was not allowed to keep a diary for security reasons. His family, and many friends and neighbors, faithfully kept the letters they received. Spanning a period of four years, from basic training beginning in June 1941 to VE Day in 1945, these precious and priceless letters relate not only the experiences of a young man leaving home and country for the first time, but also the experiences of a soon-to-be soldier with close-knit relationships to family, friends, an extended Appalachian community, and the cost of separation and service. Goodin's transformation from greenhorn (rookie) to seasoned soldier is played out in uncensored and sometimes emotional letters that familiarize his Appalachian family with his military family, and expounds upon his pride of the men under his command. This is a refreshingly open and honest story of the life of a young man, what he gained, and what he lost in the harshness and hard realities of war.

This book focuses on the correspondence of John Goodin, his experiences as tank commander, and the movements of the 3rd Armored Spearhead Division, 32nd Armored Regiment. Due to strict censoring, Goodin could not be explicit about his location or activities, but the movements of the 3rd Armored Division were published in a detailed map of the Combat Trail of the 3rd Armored Spearhead Division, 32nd Armored Regiment by Ravenstein's Geographical Publishing House, and in a book titled *Spearhead of the West—The Third Armored Division 1941–1945*, a publication of the United States Army. These two sources are taken directly from official records and are accurate and reliable.

List of Goodin's Family and Friends

Goodin exchanged letters with more than 30 people while he was in the service. Many of the people mentioned in his letters are friends and neighbors.

Dad	Thomas Elliott Goodin
Mom/Mo	Glenna Goodin (Witch of Endor)
Glenna Sawyer	John's niece, daughter of Ellene and Reginald
Sis	Ellene Goodin Sawyer, wife of Reginald Sawyer, sister of John. Lived in Maynard, Massachusetts, until 1942, then returned to Erwin
Bill Carter	Friend and employer—attorney-at-Law, William J. Carter
Art Meyer	Roommate at Western and Lee University
Margaritte Carter	Friend, daughter of Bill Carter
Pyott Hall	John's uncle, Glenna Goodin's brother
Reginald P. Sawyer	Brother-in-law, Ellene Goodin Sawyer's husband
Jean Briscoe	John's girlfriend when he entered the service. Many letters were exchanged; however, she eventually wrote to tell him she was marrying someone else. There are 21 letters from Jean in the collection
Kat Morgan	Friend
Lou Baker	Fiancée. There are 118 letters from Lou in the collection

List of Goodin's Family and Friends

J.R. Goodin	Brother, Tom Goodin Jr. (wife Carolyn Dickenson Harris, children: Betty, Jean, and Tom III)
C.D. Moss	Manager, Clinchfield Railroad (Charley)
Anne Carter	Close friend, daughter of Bill Carter. There are 14 letters from Anne
George Mattox	Clinchfield Railroad employee and friend
L.H. Phetteplace	General manager of the Clinchfield Railroad, Erwin, TN
Joe & Ruby	John's maternal aunt and uncle, Glenna's sister
Bubber	John's first cousin, son of Joe and Ruby
Paul and Liz Duncan	Friends from college in Louisville, KY
Tommy Goodin	John's nephew, son of Tom Goodin, Jr.

Chapter One

Basic Training
May 1941–June 1942

John David Goodin was a disciplined, structured individual long before he ever entered the United States Army. Raised in the rural town of Erwin, Tennessee, Goodin learned about hard work and responsibility from his father, T.E., or Captain Tom, as he was referred to on the railroad where he maintained a 58-year career. Gardening, raising cows and chickens, and training hunting dogs were an established part of Goodin's life. He was a faithful church attender and played the piano. He had a plethora of friends, as his family was involved in the community through organizations and church. The family was tight-knit and respected.

Before leaving the University of Tennessee, Goodin inquired about volunteering for the U.S. Army, but was told his order number had passed. While disappointed, he decided to spend what little time he had left with his family. He did not have long to wait. By June 28, 1941, he had received his notification to report for duty.

```
May 17th, 1941 Postmarked Knoxville, TN
Excerpt
Dear Dad, Mom and all:--
```

Thanks for your letter of this week, which I received along with my notice of expiration of deferment and that I would be called sometime between June 15th and 25th.

I had written Mr. Miller the day before asking about volunteering, and today have a letter from Mr. Sugg, advising me that I cannot volunteer, since my order number has been passed in selecting men, because of the deferment, and so cannot be accepted as a volunteer. So, private wishes or no, it looks as though I go as a draftee. I have just written and told him unless I could go as a volunteer the 10th of the month, I would wait until I was called, as it will give me a few more days at

```
home, and in the second place, I'll get to see a little of
Sis before I leave.
                    Love to all, as always, Johnny
```

John Goodin was a handsome man who wore the uniform well. He had gray eyes, brown hair, stood 5'10", weighed 155 pounds, and had just turned 24 years old in June 1941 when he entered the Army. Goodin began basic training in Camp Wheeler, Georgia, where he expressed in letters to his parents the grueling schedule, extreme temperatures, K.P. (Kitchen Police) duties of washing dishes and mopping, and also lack of sleep. But in light of this, Goodin maintained a positive attitude, assured his parents all was well and counted his blessings, one of which was getting his milk every day. Throughout the war, Goodin longingly spoke of "sweet" milk and was so appreciative when he was able to get it. (In Appalachia, regular fresh milk is called "sweet milk" to distinguish it from buttermilk.)

In the beginning, Goodin's letters were all handwritten. Sometime in July 1941, Goodin told his parents that he had "resurrected this portable typewriter and now maybe I can get a letter or two written. My fountain pen is on the blink and until I find time to get it fixed, I guess you all will suffer." After the "resurrection" of this typewriter, many of Goodin's letters are typed.

By December 1941, Goodin was transferred

John D. Goodin in uniform, 1941–42.

One. Basic Training

John D. Goodin in uniform, 1941–42.

to Fort Knox, Kentucky. Over the next two years, he would move six times: Camp Wheeler, Georgia; Fort Knox, Kentucky; Camp Polk, Louisiana; Rice, California; Camp Pickett, Virginia; Indiantown Gap, Pennsylvania; and finally, in 1943, Codford, England.

The geographical locations of basic training were strategically chosen to expose soldiers to every type of climate and terrain. The 3rd Armored Division engaged in rigorous and brutal training. Goodin mentioned dynamite, rifles, and tanks. By the time they shipped out in September 1943, they had been exposed to every possible element they would encounter in Europe: insect-infested bogs and sweltering humidity in Georgia and Louisiana, extremely hot, dry temperatures and fierce dust storms in the Mojave Desert, mud and rain in Virginia, and cold, wet, mud, snow and icy roads in the mountains of Indiantown Gap, PA.[1]

Goodin was no stranger to writing letters. From the time he entered college in 1936 until he graduated from the University of Tennessee Law School in Knoxville, Tennessee, in May 1941, Goodin and his parents frequently exchanged letters. It is no surprise that he wasted little time getting in touch with his family to let them know he was well, and that

Appalachia to Dessau

CAMP WHEELER, GEORGIA

Monday a.m.
9:30.

Dear Folks,

Have 10 minutes off & will write a couple of lines. Wanted to write yesterday but caught K.P. (washing dishes, mopping, etc.) and had to get up at 5:15. I had planned on getting off yesterday & catching up on my sleep and correspondence, but I didn't make it!!

This 5:30 a.m. business is getting me down. I got "sick call" this morning & went over & had some work done on my teeth. He took my false one out & won't put it in till Friday. & I'm going to an invitation dance tomorrow nite. I won't dance much — I'm too out of sleep. But, well, that's the army.

Reg is crazy as h---, talking about only working 4 hrs. We are on duty from 5:45 till 6:30 at nite. Drill, lectures, details (all kinds of work - I'm even a cement mixer now, & we do all kinds of work). We never have more than 10 minutes off at any one time. Saturday, we're supposed to be through at 12:00. But most of the kids worked till 3:00 & then a bunch worked till 5:00. I finished my cement job at 2:00 & quit.

Our 13 weeks of "basic training" starts today, & I'm missing part of it. I worked too d---hard last week, & I'm coasting this week all I can. If only I could get about 18 hours sleep once.

When are you all coming down? I had a nice letter from Jean. I thought you all would be down yesterday, but glad you didn't, since I had to work all day. I took a ½ hour nap yesterday a.m., & a short one yesterday afternoon, but I could still sleep about 14 hours!! I haven't been able to even write cards for the last week.

I sure appreciated Sis's letter – but I'm going to need one of my 2 checks. (I should have a retail credit) pretty soon. My expenses have run about a $1 a day since I've been here – I've left home with $21, + I have about $6.25 left. I've bought a few odds + ends, necessary to army life which aren't furnished. I'm going to buy some shoes, + a shirt or two yet.

I got my fill of milk + drinks yesterday. I had about 6 or 7 ½ pints, a quart of grapefruit juice, a couple of gallons of grape juice, and so on. I really went to the toilet yesterday. Usually, all I go is about 2 or maybe 3 times a day – it just sweats out of you. It sure gets hot here, + I don't mean maybe!

If I had time to think + were awake enough, I could write an interesting letter, but I can't quite make it today. So maybe sometime next week I'll be able to make it for you.

If you all should happen to come down, + Jean can't come, why couldn't you bring Kat or Lou? I haven't had a date in about 3 weeks now, and I'd love to have one!!

I'm supposed to meet a girl from Randolph-Macon Tuesday nite, if I make it to the dance. But I may sleep instead. Thursday nite, the Macon lawyers are giving all the camp lawyers here a barbecue – and I'm hoping to make that, too. ⅔ of this "intelligensia" is lawyers, ⅓ teachers, + the rest a dub's mixture. But they're nice kids – they're from Pa., N.Y., Tenn., Fla., + all Southern states. Some brilliant, and others medium, + rest of us dumb like me.

Well, my outfit is not back yet, and I got to finish this. Best of luck, + write when you can.

Love,
John

Opposite and above: Many of John Goodin's letters were handwritten, but once he found a portable typewriter, the letters were typed. Here is a sample of one of the early handwritten letters written while stationed in Camp Wheeler, Georgia.

Appalachia to Dessau

his life in the Army had begun. His law training only strengthened his command of the English language, which is apparent in his letters. He is well-spoken and eloquent, frequently writing long and detailed letters to his family and friends. His training as an attorney, and his communication skills, would serve him well in the U.S. Army.

Goodin's military career began at the induction and processing center in Fort Oglethorpe, Georgia. He describes the process in detail for his parents and jokes that "anybody who could see at all got in." Physical examinations, intelligence tests, drills, uniform assignment, and kitchen police were all a part of the introduction to military life. Goodin did so well on his intelligence test that he was told he would be placed in the legal department.

While not thrilled with the food, he describes it as "balanced" and always mentions that he is getting milk. Goodin's love of "sweet" milk reappears throughout his letters for the endurance of his time in service. He also excitedly reports that several people from home and college are at Camp Wheeler, stating this will ensure that "my stay here won't be lonesome."

Goodin maintains a cool demeanor in his letters, appearing to take it all in stride: intense heat, wet beds, rising before dawn, endless drills, exercises and inspections. It didn't take long for him to prove he was his father's son when it came to discipline and hard work. He writes about the men acting like "babies" and griping about the situation. Echoes of his father's instruction and training to study hard, work hard, and be a "good boy, try to do the right thing, and make a good soldier," stayed with him. This would prove to be good advice.

```
Envelope to:
Mr. & Mrs. T. E. Goodin
Mr. & Mrs. Reginald Sawyer (Sister)
Miss Glenna Sawyer (Niece)
Erwin, Tennessee
July 2 1941 FORT OGLETHORPE GA

Tuesday Night [July 1]
Dear Folks,
```

   Just got some stamps this afternoon & decided to write while I can. Course, I haven't heard from you, but a J. C. boy who is in charge gets the J. C. Press Chronicle, & I read it every day.
   Friday nite we came on out in trucks, & I had my 1st nite of Army life. My bed was wet as it had rained & they hadn't closed the tent, but not bad. Sat. morning we

One. Basic Training

started exams, physical mostly, only they could hardly be classed as that. Anybody who could see at all got in, unless they had some obvious defects.

Which I didn't. Sis will remember the boy whose sister & girl were crying over him. Well, he was sent back, as all the arteries in knee had been severed once upon a time. He was the only reject in my group.

I've met more people here I know. - Dr. Harvey (Tammy Ratcliff's husband) was one of the 6 doctors who examined me. M. L. Bailey, David Silvers, the Register (county) of Carter Co.; one boy with whom I graduated at U-T [University of Tennessee] last month; dozens from Knoxville, Johnson City, Elizabethton; as well as a dozen or so with whom I used to go to TC [Teacher's College] with 5 & 6 years ago. So at least my stay here won't be lonesome.

Sat. afternoon we took our intelligence tests - 150 questions, out of which I scored <u>142</u> - class <u>I</u>. As a consequence, they have <u>promised</u> to place me in the Legal Department at the end of my 13 weeks basic training. But - one can never tell <u>what</u> they intend to do until they've done it. Heaven only knows where I'll be sent to. But I wouldn't be surprised if I go <u>anywhere</u> in the U. S. - most of the kids have gone to Ga. (south - oink!!!) & Camp Lee, Va. - 25 miles from Richmond, Va. at which place, I wouldn't minded being sent!!! Oh, well! One never knows!!

On Sat. afternoon, I happened to be looking at a Chatta. [Chattanooga] paper, when I saw Art's girls' picture in it!! Well - you know me!! I called up the people with whom she was staying, & talked to her and later she drove <u>out</u> to see me. She is really a nice kid - and somewhat Art's type. It was really a pleasure to meet her and talk to her.

Sunday, I slept all afternoon - it was 105° & the tents were not very good shade. I weighed in at 141 Sat. & I don't think I weigh <u>135</u> now. It's too hot. I'm learning fast not to drink <u>cold</u> water - two guys who had been drilling & were hot, drank too much & caught <u>cramps</u>.

The food is sloppy, but well-balanced. Breakfast seldom varies from eggs & 1/2 <u>pint</u> of <u>milk</u>. & you may guess how I love <u>that</u>!! At any rate, I have had about 2 good meals since I've been here. But as I say it's balanced & not too bad.

Funny, all my clothes fit me - even to the <u>9-E</u> shoes. And some of the boys have awful fits with their clothes. I've been fairly lucky so far, and I can't complain.

Yesterday we got our uniforms, drilled a little bit, & back to bed. Then up for 1st inspection - O.K.!

Today, Tuesday, we took exercises, & learned the

Appalachia to Dessau

fundamentals of marching steps. (I just ran out of ink & went over to the top sargent's [sic] tent & filled my pen. - I doubt if I get another one as nice as he has been - bet I catch Kitchen Police in the morning) after about 3 hours of alternate drilling & resting, we came in. Nothing this afternoon.

One is really surprised at some of the illiteracy & brilliancy floating around here. Several flunk out because they're too dumb. But the brilliant boys - wow - if they can see with 6 lens glasses they stick in here.

I was surprised at the lawyers in here, & they're thick as fleas. Some of the top - kicks here are lawyers, & all of them cuss at the fees they're missing. Oh - well!!

Some of the kids tickle me - such babies. So particular about their eating & drinking, dress, and so forth; others griping in general; mostly, though grinning & making the best of it.

I don't suppose I'll see you before I'm stationed, so I'll call as soon as I learn when I'm to be shipped & talk to you all - it may be a couple of days & it may be 2 or 3 weeks. But I'll call some night, just for the heck of it.

Love to each & all, & all my girls - I'd sure like to see all of you!!

Love, Johnny

After Fort Oglethorpe, Goodin was sent about 200 miles south to Camp Wheeler in Macon, Georgia, for basic training. Camp Wheeler was an army training camp in World War I but closed after the war ended. It was reopened for World War II.[2]

The timeframe for basic training was thirteen weeks. In this undated letter in July, Goodin says, "Our thirteen weeks of basic training starts today." Goodin writes about the busyness of his daily life in training and the long hours, saying they never have more than ten minutes off at any time.

Goodin took nearly one hundred pages of meticulous notes in a personal field notebook dated July 21, 1941, through October 2, 1941. The notebook includes detailed drawings of positions, tactics, layouts of division headquarters, infantry regiments, divisions, scales for aerial photography, symbols, codes, and mathematical equations. There are instructions on the use of cover, anti-tank lookouts, marches, squelching noises, weather, map reading, weaponry, uses of intelligence, photography, combat decisions, command intel, organization of units,

One. Basic Training

observation duties, camouflage, etc. Goodin notated nine pages of symbols with drawings, totaling over 100, which had to be memorized.[3]

Basic training conditioned mind and body. Soldiers learned to think as a unit, rather than as an individual. They ate, slept, and learned together. Rising early, strenuous exercise, drills, skills in various types of weaponry including rifles, bayonets, grenades and explosives, how to prepare your pack, how to pitch a tent, kitchen police, and even the proper way to salute, were all a part of the training process. Soldiers learned early that orders were to be followed to the letter or repercussions would be swift. Inspections were conducted at random times, some every day. Soldiers had to make sure guns were cleaned properly and everything was in good order. Disobeying an order could cost the life of a comrade. There was no room for slacking. Guns were to be meticulously cleaned, beds made, uniforms tidy, shoes shined, and examinations passed.[4]

In a World War II memoir, housed in the Archives of Appalachia, Edward R. Feagins states that beds had to be made "every morning so tight you could bounce a quarter on it. We had to mop the floors and hang our clothes on the rack. We had to place everything in our foot locker just exactly like the army wanted you to. Someone would inspect the area and if they thought we had not done a good job we would have to do it over."[5]

Feagins also shares how scary some of the trainings were, especially with live ammunition. "The infiltration course was scary ... you climb over a bank and crawl about 200 yards on your belly with your rifle in your arms. While you are crawling they are shooting 30 caliber machine gun bullets over head and blowing up explosives all around you. The explosives were in holes and you knew not to crawl over or in one of those holes."[6] Feagins goes on to explain that soldiers were wounded in these exercises.

Goodin expresses how tired he is, making jokes about being too tired to write letters saying, "maybe next year."

Goodin struggled with dental issues throughout his military career. It is possible he had a wisdom tooth extracted in July, as he mentions an appointment to have work done in an undated letter below. Then on July 23 an order was issued that he was to be hospitalized. In a letter dated July 27, he tells his parents he has been in the hospital for several days with an abscessed jaw.

Appalachia to Dessau

```
WAR DEPARTMENT DENTAL CLINIC CAMP WHEELER, GA
REC. OFFICE STATION HOSPITAL

Dental Clinic

  Camp Wheeler, Georgia July 23 1941
  Request that Pvt Goodin, J. D. be admitted to Hospital
Temp: 99.6
  Information furnished Form 258 Attached.

                      H. M. Schroeder
                      1st Lt. D. C.
```

Goodin mentions kitchen police in this letter. He does not go into details about K.P. In Edward R. Feagins' memoir, he describes how exacting and meticulous the duty was: "After each meal, we would scrub the tables down with soap and water and then move them around so we could mop the floor. After we would dry the floor, we lined the tables up using a string. We also lined up the salt and pepper shakers and the sugar bowls with a string. This mess hall was about twice the size of a basketball court. Being in the mess hall was easier than being on pots and pans because washing pots and pans all day was back-breaking work. The garbage detail was the easiest of the three jobs."[7]

```
No date No Envelope (Camp Wheeler Stationery)
Probably End of July

Monday a.m. 9:30
Dear Folks,
```

   Have 10 minutes off & will write a couple of lines. Wanted to write yesterday but caught K. P. (washing dishes, mopping, etc.) and had to get up at 5:15. I had planned on getting off yesterday & catching up on my sleep and correspondence, but I didn't make it!!
   The 5:30 a.m. business is getting me down. I got "sick call" this morning & went over & had some work done on my teeth. He took my false one out & won't put it in till Friday. & me going to an invitation dance tomorrow nite. I won't dance much - I'm too <u>out of sleep</u>. But, well, that's the army.
   Reg is crazy as h---, talking about only working 4 hrs. We are on duty from 5:45 [a.m.] till 6:30 at nite. Drill, lecture, details (all kinds of work - I'm even a cement mixer now, & we do all kinds of work). We never have more than 10 minutes off at any one time. Saturday, we're supposed to be through at 12:00. But most of the kids worked till 3:00 & then a bunch worked till 5:00. I finished my cement job at 2:00 & quit.

One. Basic Training

Our 13 weeks of "basic training" starts today. I'm missing part of it. I worked too d--- hard last week, & I'm coasting this week all I can. If only I could get about 18 hours sleep <u>once</u>.

When are you all coming down? I had a nice letter from Jean. I thought you all would be down yesterday, but glad you didn't, since I had to work all day. I took a 1/2 hour nap yesterday a.m., & a short one yesterday afternoon, but I could still sleep about 14 hours!! I haven't been able to even write <u>cards</u> for the last week.

I sure appreciated Sis's letter - but I'm going to need <u>one</u> of my <u>2 checks</u> (I should have a retail credit) pretty soon. My expenses have run about $1 a day since I've been here - I left home with $21, & I have about 6.25 left. I've bought a few odds & ends, necessary to army life which aren't furnished. I'm going to buy some shoes, a shirt or two yet.

I got my fill of milk & drinks yesterday. I had about 6 or 7 1/2 pints, a quart of grapefruit juice, a couple of gallons of grape juice, and so on. I really went to the toilet yesterday. Usually, all I go is about 2 or maybe 3 times a day - it just <u>sweats</u> out of you. It sure gets <u>hot</u> here, & I don't mean maybe.

If I had time to think & were awake enough, I could write an interesting letter, but I can't quite make it today. So maybe sometime next year I'll be able to make it for you.

If you all should happen to come down, & Jean can't come, why couldn't you bring Kat or Lou? I haven't had a date in about <u>3</u> weeks now, and I'd love to have one!!

I'm supposed to meet a girl from Randolph-Macon Tuesday nite, if I make it to the dance. But I may <u>sleep</u> instead. Thursday nite, the Macon lawyers are giving all the camp lawyers here a barbecue - and I'm hoping to make <u>that</u>, too. 1/2 of this "intelligence" is lawyers, 1/3 teachers, & the rest a duke's mixture. But they're nice kids - they're from Pa., N. Y. Tenn., La., & all Southern states. Some brilliant, and others medium, & rest of us <u>dumb</u> like me.

Well, my outfit is not back yet, and I got to finish this. Best of luck, & write when you can.

Love, Johnny

John's father, T.E. Goodin, is always straightforward with John about the good, the bad, and the ugly. He minces no words about his disgust for Goodin's maternal Uncle Pyott, whom his mother appears to adore. He also exudes condescension when speaking of the antics of John's

Appalachia to Dessau

mother, Glenna. This sometimes places John in the role of marriage counselor. He uses his father's candor, and his mother's wit, to chastise his dad about his mother. John's advice is often sought by his parents. The closeness and respect shared among them all is evident in the wording of the letters.

```
JUL 27, 1941 Stamped Macon, GA Marked "Personal"
Camp Wheeler Stationery
```

Saturday Camp Wheeler (as usual!!)

Dear Dad,

    Was glad to get your letters and want you to know I appreciate them. And you asking me for advice about trading is sort of ironic, isn't it? You're the teacher, not <u>me</u>. But my advice would be to buy you a new car, jack it up, & run the <u>jitterbug</u>!! Seriously, George <u>is right</u> in his cars, & I haven't caught him wrong yet. And you know he's pretty <u>solid</u>. Also - get you a set of new tires and <u>store</u> them.

    <u>Don't</u> plan on waiting till <u>I</u> get out before getting one, cause [sic] unless I'm discharged for something unusual, I won't be out of here for two and maybe 3 years at least. It's not official, but our officers tell us that, and they certainly <u>aren't playing</u>. This is serious and they're trying to get volunteers for Puerto Rico & Panama now.

    Now, Dad, another thing on my chest to get off. When you write, skip all this patriotic feeling, and don't try to cheer me up.

    I <u>don't need it</u>. I pride myself on the fact that I've got enough of <u>you</u> in me to face and tackle anything, big or little, one year or <u>10</u>. And I realize that you've been all any boy could ever ask for for a Dad. I've criticized you and even you'll admit you've your faults, and you've spoiled me some (ha?) - but still I wouldn't want any other Dad than you. I know you so well, I can about tell what's in your letters before I open them. I know what you're thinking now. But, don't worry about me - I've got enough of Mother in me to make the best of <u>everything</u>, good or bad. Even getting in the "intelligence" - where 90% are casualties, which is the highest percentage of loss in any department. Cause, well - I'm in a good bunch of boys, good officers, and <u>hard work</u>, mentally and physically.

    But, as I say, <u>don't worry</u>.

    And now, Dad, a few words about Mother. Sometimes, I know, you could turn her across your knee, and probably be right in doing it. But, Dad, she's always stuck to you,

One. Basic Training

even when she could have (and maybe should have) turned <u>you</u> across her knee. She's having a tough time, now - the <u>worst in her whole life</u>, and please, for my sake, if not hers, do what you can to make her remaining years a <u>little</u> happy. Because you've never had close contact with your family, you couldn't understand what I'm talking about, and I couldn't explain it - but I know. She's had a couple of close calls to a nervous breakdown already, and if she gets through the summer - it will be a <u>miracle</u>. Dad, you are a <u>man</u>, and even the collapsing of your financial empire didn't unnerve you - but with Mother, it's different. Remember <u>that</u>, and regardless of what happens, please don't ever tell her "I told you so." Spare her that much. I know this is vague and doesn't make sense to you, but then again - you may know. I know that you know tens of thousands of things you aren't supposed to know. At any rate, regardless of what comes up, try and help her. It may hurt you, too, but being the man I think and know you are, you'll swallow your thoughts and <u>grin</u>.

   I hope you and Mother <u>can</u> come down. Why don't you come to Chattanooga on the Streamliner, and then come on down? Of course, for her, it would be better to come to Spartanburg, spend the nite, & come on over the next day. As for that <u>Streamliner</u> trip, which you & J. R. would come down on <u>that</u> <u>trip</u>!! I'd like to see him. And Pop - you have a little saved up now, you could relax just a little and enjoy yourself out once in a while - and I'd <u>love</u> to see you. Macon is a nice place - but it's Georgia, & that's enough said.

   I've been in the hospital since Wednesday with an infected, abscessed jaw - where my wisdom tooth was. I'm O.K. now, and leaving in the morning. Don't tell Mother, as she would only worry. And incidentally, when you get through reading this letter, maybe you'd better tear it up, & burn it.

   It seems a funny sort of letter for a kid to write to his Dad, but well, if anything should happen to me - you'll know how & what I feel about you, and everything. I'm afraid there have been times when I've been an awfully bad boy, especially to you, but being like you are, you've overlooked them in me when you wouldn't have anyone else.

   Don't know whether you can work out anything for Reg or not, but for Sis's sake, hope you can - and don't <u>say</u> <u>anything</u> to anybody that would kill any chance. Like what you said to J. R. - that made <u>me</u> mad!! You might be taking a chance, but that's what we all are doing, so - try & give him a break.

Appalachia to Dessau

Since I've got to write to the rest of the family, I'll be closing now. Pop, try to understand what I've said - and <u>don't think</u> about it.

                With all my love, as always, Your son,
                Johnny

Goodin learned to type in 1937 while in college for easier reading of his law cases. While an excellent speller, Goodin's letters often have typos that he makes no attempt to correct. As he is learning, he teases his parents about his bad typing, saying, "I guess you all will suffer."

Saturday Afternoon
Camp Wheeler, Georgia Stationery
Probably Early to Mid-August

Dear Folks,

I've resurrected this portable typewriter and now maybe I can get a letter or two written. My fountain pen is on the blink and until I find time to get it fixed, I guess you all will suffer.

Well, I won't be able to go to Spartanburg next weekend, as no one is going—we are all hoping for a pass over the weekend of Labor Day, and no one is going to Spartanburg this weekend.

I don't know if I'll be able to come home or not, but if I do get a chance, I'll be there. Incidentally, we won't get paid until after we get back, so I may have to have some financial assistance to get home on.

Sis tells me that you are looking at a Pontiac and an Oldsmobile. Oh well--you better get a car of some kind quick.

Last weekend I visited up in Newman, Ga.--where I wanted to go when we were down there a couple of years back. I almost thought that I was in Va.--I was treated so nice. Mrs. Owens told me that she wanted to treat me like I'd be treated if I got home for a weekend, and they sure did. And eat - I really did enjoy myself. They got a negro cook and boy can she cook.

There wasn't much to do - Sunday and hot as h--- in Ga., too. So we just had a good time talking, and riding around some. It sure is a pleasure to mingle and be with nice people. The girl herself isn't too pretty, but as I've always said looks aren't everything.

Last night I met a big real estate man here - his niece [sic] graduated from Randolph-Macon with Va. [Virginia] Campbell, and knows Ann Carter. I had a date with her. They have a nice mansion in the suburbs, and a Steinway grand piano in the living room. So you see that when I

One. Basic Training

do have the time to do anything, I can have a good time. But between grass detail and Kitchen Police, I never know what I'm going to do.

Well, write when you can and let me know what's going on. I see that Ferdie Powell is going in on the 20th. I feel sorry for him - but it'll do him a lot of good.

Love to all

Postcard dated SEP 8 1941 Sunday p.m.

Dear Folks,

I've been over to Columbia & Cheraw S. C. this weekend. Had a good time and met some very nice people while there - even went to Presbyterian church. Got back without mishap. Had a blowout coming from home, though. Guess I'm getting along O.K. but don't know. Only 4 more weeks definitely here.

Love, Johnny

1941 SEP 9
WESTERN UNION

To: T. E Goodin

Sorry I haven't written. But may get to see you this weekend. Just hoping you have fifty more birthdays. Love from a grateful son.

Johnny

SEP 24 1941 Stamped Macon, GA

Addressed to Capt. Thos. E. Goodin
c/o Hotel Morgan, Spartanburg, SC
"Special Delivery"
America First Stationery

Wednesday p.m.

Dear Pop,

Just got your letter and boy - guess you know how I appreciate that!!

I did get to Knoxville, but couldn't call Sat. nite & I slept till 11:30 Sunday, & I thought you would be gone by then.

However, I think I'll be home soon. If for just a while. Don't know when.

I'm going back to Knoxville this weekend - I can have more fun there for less money than any place I've been so far.

Appalachia to Dessau

    The only trouble is it's about a 6-hr. drive up there. I spent the nite with H. Tipton. Saw Joe Goforth - & heard for the first time that Mother had hit him. Somebody probably thought somebody else had told me and no one told me. He's looking O.K.

    Mrs. Bailey & Mrs. Sweetser (Charles Brown's aunt) both said to give you their best regards. Mrs. Bailey is sending me a cake soon!!

    Well - gotta go eat. Will finish after supper.

    I expect I'll be home the weekend after this, & maybe the one after it - Doc Yelton's nephew is driving to J. City & I'm coming in if he does. If he doesn't, we have a ride to Asheville, & I'll call & get Mother to get Jean or Kat & drive over. Keith might come after me - over & back in one day is a little too much for Mother. But I'll have to wait.

    It got down to 44 here yesterday & Yankee & Rebel suffered alike. Brrrrr - We are getting more winter clothes soon, though.

    Sorry about things - but I know they can't help now. It's just one of those things that it's too late to do anything about - & like this army - we just must make the best of it.

    Well, I want to get this mailed, so until a little later, so long.

                          Love you, Johnny

T.E. Goodin mentioned the attack on Pearl Harbor in a letter to John saying, "It looks like we are at war with Japan." In response, John tells him that all Christmas leaves have been cancelled. Before December 7, 1941, soldiers were given numerous passes and were allowed to attend dances and wear civilian clothing.[8] After the attack on Pearl Harbor, restrictions were tightened. Passes and furloughs were cancelled. Uniforms were to be worn at all times.[9] Combat commands were formed and training intensified, with rumors of a move coming soon.[10]

Monday night [Probably Dec 1941]
See Dec. 13, 1941 Letter from T. E. Goodin to John

Dear Dad and Mother,

    Got your letter last night, and glad to hear from you again. It was the first time I've heard from you since I've been back, and I rather expected to hear a comment one way or another on Jean. But, since things are like they are -- your comments would be of little or no effect only perhaps in that I could file them for future reference in case I get back in a year or two.

One. Basic Training

   Was in Louisville over the weekend, and had a good time despite the fact that our peaceful Sunday quiet was disturbed by a sudden burst of news bulletins relating to Japanese attacks.
   Surprisingly enough, everyone is cool, calm and collected, things are going on as smoothly as ever, perhaps with a bit more deliberation than otherwise. At any rate, the apples hadn't come in yet, and are probably down there today. I'm hoping to get back in this weekend, although it is possible that we will be restricted to the Post area until further orders come through.
   Christmas vacations are also definitely a problem as well as only a possibility. The War Department says that they are all cancelled, and our Captain says that they will probably go through as was expected. I hope so, as I'd like to get home again. One of my very good lady friends is expecting to be home, and I dearly would love to see her -- as well as being home with you all. Don't know how much time I'll have there, but I intend to get all that I can.
   Sorry to hear about your rheumatism, but am glad that you can throw it off like that. My side gives me a good bit of trouble, but I can wear it off without too much trouble. As long as we don't do any more than we are doing now, I won't be bothered.
   And so far, I've had it very easy.
   Well, there is not a great bit to say about things. I would like for you to send my cards up here to me, as I won't get a chance to send them from home. I told sis to send them here, but with her usual knack for getting things messed up, why I suppose they landed at home.
   Thanks for all the apples, and I'll be down to get them as soon as I get a chance. I'll let you know as soon as I find out whether I will get home or not for Xmas, and approximately when I'll get there.

                       Love, as ever, Johnny

Postmarked December 17, 1941 Fort Knox, KY

Sunday afternoon. Dear Folks,

   Well, it looks like at last we may have something to work for instead of wondering just what we are doing in this army. For some time, around next summer, perhaps, we will be out of here on our way to South America, Africa, the Coast, the Phillipines, or even China.
   Not too much has been going on lately. I was on the range last week most of the time during which it was cold as heck, and you really should have seen me: Long

underwear, and extra undershirt, a pair of wool trousers, our combat suit, wool lined and water proof, and over that a pair of coveralls. Plus two pair of socks and a pair of arctic overshoes.

Xmas is approaching very fast, and as usual -- I'm not ready for it. All the Xmas furloughs have been given out, so I know now that I won't be home for Xmas, and probably not at all. The 1st sergeant told me yesterday afternoon that if I were lucky, I might get a three day pass from the 28th of December to the 1st. So I may go home on that, if I'm lucky enough to get it.

Well, as a Xmas present from one of you -- or join it together, as far as that goes, I will owe $12.70 on my insurance with Bryan Woodruff, and if someone will pay that up for me, I will not only appreciate the cash involved, but also the trouble that I would save by having it done for me. As you know, there is nothing that I need here, so that you won't have to worry about getting me anything -- and that will be something that I can use of some _real_ value. If anyone asks what to send me -- tell them nothing -- or stationary or stamps.

Liz and Paul aren't going to get home either, it looks like, at least not for Xmas day, so we may spend Xmas here at their house. Marcia Wood has asked me down to Lexington to spend Xmas day with her if I get off, and if Liz and Paul do get to go home, why I may run down there.

Well, I gotta be closing. Write when you can -- and don't worry about me any Xmas -- only my insurance, and I will be very happy indeed. Sorry that I can't make it home, but I just can't, so you'll have to wait until perhaps I get a chance to get in.

                Love to all, Johnny

P.S. Sure am enjoying the apples. In fact all of us are. J.G.

Page Two

Tuesday nite Dear Folks,

  Got your letter this afternoon and enjoyed it as usual.

  Well - am at last going on the range to shoot for a change. We've pulled targets for a week and today began our preliminary firing.

  Well, Dad - if you can I'd like to have about $15 or $20 before Xmas, and I'll pay you back after Xmas. If you can't why it'll be all right - but I could use it.

  I'm sending a box home for Tom, Betty & Jean which you all can deliver. Sis is sending my presents for Carolyn, and you can take them all down at the same time. Don't

One. Basic Training

know when I'll get it <u>sent</u>, but at least I can start. I hardly think it will be necessary to explain that $30 a month doesn't go far.

Well - write when you can. And if you send me any money - send is as soon as you can!!

                      Love, Johnny

Envelope dated DEC 28 1941 (Sunday) Postmarked Louisville KY

Friday night [December 26] Dear Folks,

Thought I'd drop you a line (although I guess by now Liz and Paul have seen you too) and tell you that despite the fact that I didn't get home, I had a most enjoyable Christmas anyhow.

Came down to the Duncans and boy oh boy -- we stayed up till practically all night and opened up presents and had a good time generally.

Saturday afternoon -- will try to finish this now, since I didn't get to last night. I got too tired and went back to camp and to bed, and do feel much better today.

I'm still getting packages and things -- I've never had quite so much attention from people that I hardly expected a card from -- much less presents. I got a very nice clock (which folds up for carrying) from my little secretary in J. City, a little zipper bag from Jeanie for carrying my toilet articles in, a box of stationary [sic] from Eliz. and Paul, a box from a girl friend in Atlanta, a swell pair of pigskin gloves from Libby (Guinn), a big box of candy from the Carters, shaving mug and equipment from Love and Kat, and today I got a box of candy and a shaving outfit from Eloise Fullen. So -- that with everything else that you know of, I really had a big Xmas, and a very practical one. All that I needed to make it complete was to get home and see everyone -- but of course that was impossible, and so I had the best time I could here.

Got Dad's letter today, and glad to get the ten dollars -- It will get me home in case that I get a chance to come anytime soon.

No news about the "war" -- but it will be a long time (at least 5 or 6 months) before the army gets in. Strangely enough - we are itching to get into it -- prepared or not.

Well, some of these days soon, I hope to get into Tennessee again. I'd like to come home now, but it looks as though it will be a good while before they let up on the strictness.

With best wishes as always, and hoping that you all are

Appalachia to Dessau

all well and happy. Write when you can. And once again -- thanks for the fruit cake -- we <u>all</u> enjoyed it <u>tremendously</u>. Love from your

                Johnny.

U.S. Army Stationery
Wednesday nite [Probably late January 1942 or February 1942]
Mother's Birthday January 15th

Dear Mom,

   Your son is a low down----… I've been reminding myself for 2 weeks you had a birthday & then when it gets here, I forgot all about it. Anyhow - hope you have <u>60</u> more birthdays!!

   Art is getting married at the end of the month & wants me to be the best man. If I am, I'll have to <u>fly</u> to Washington, & I'll have to "borrow" some money from somebody. There is a chance I'll be on my way to California though, so I don't know. We are leaving around Feb. 4 I think.

   Had an awfully sweet (and <u>encouraging</u>!!) letter from Ann Carter when I got back. Also one from Margaret - crazy, but nice.

   Well, I gotta close. Write me once in a while & give me the "gossip" of Erwin. Margaret covers Johnson City!!

                Best wishes again - and may Santa
                bring you that Mink Coat!!
                Love Johnny

Envelope dated MAR 1 1942 Postmarked Louisville KY

Sunday afternoon Dear Folks,

   Got into town yesterday to find your most welcome letter -- news as well as financial column being greatly of interest, and my many thanks and gratitude for the latter.

   I've been getting along swell -- I've gained another five pounds or so. We haven't done anything since I came back, but loaf -- waiting for the school. I don't get up for reveille, breakfast half the time, and usually go back to sleep. I was A.W.O.L. for one whole day and never was missed. My sergeant of course knew I wasn't there, but being a good Tennesseean [sic], he didn't say anything, and everything was all right. As a matter of fact, our whole detachment is technically A.W.O.L. as there are no special orders leaving us here. I'm going to try and get home again before school starts.

   As to my "Girls" -- I'm tickled. If I get back -- then I'll worry about them. In the meantime - they are all

One. Basic Training

drifting as far as I'm concerned. I haven't heard from Jean since I got back, and I can't marry the girl I love -- so maybe some time or some day -- I will talk things over with Marg. In the meantime
 -- I treat them all like sisters. Well......
 Well, write when you can, and let me hear from you. Hoping to get home some time soon, your prodigal son,
No signature

Postcard dated March 19, 1942 Postmarked Fort Knox, KY
From:
Candidate J. D. Goodin 6th Candidate Co.
O. C. S.
Ft. Knox, KY 3-18-42
Dear Folks,
 Please see if you can find my <u>glasses somewhere</u> at home. Don't know where to tell you to look - but probably in your writing desk. They won't be in mine & you can't get into it, anyhow - I don't think.
 Everything is O.K. - so "have no worries." Love & kisses to everybody!!
Johnny

MAR 25 1942 Stamped Fort Knox, KY From Candidate J. D. Goodin March 25, 1942 Tuesday p.m.
Dear Dad,
 Just got your letter - and <u>some</u> day I'm going to lose my <u>disposition!!</u> I told you <u>specifically</u> to <u>please</u> stay out of my desk, as I <u>knew</u> my glasses weren't in there. If I get home again, I'm going to get me 14 boxes at the bank for <u>personal</u> <u>stuff</u> that <u>no</u> <u>one</u> can get into. It's not what's in it, but the principle of the thing. Among your few faults - curiosity and too great an interest in some things are your biggest.
 I'm sending back your check - as you probably have my card by now that I found them here (It still makes me mad that you do the very thing I ask you not to.), and won't need the money for glasses. I have a lot of incidental expense here, but until I need it - I won't ask for it. My cleaning (just one week) was $1.25.
 I spent this morning blowing up trees, and <u>rails</u> with dynamite & TNT - more fun than when we used to blow up <u>stumps</u>. I'm also learning how to tell how much weight a bridge will stand, and the functions, parts, and nomenclature of rifles. The days sure fly here - and I hope June comes quick.

27

Appalachia to Dessau

   I knew about the shooting Wednesday (it was in the Louisville paper). Sorry to hear about John Miller. Good nite, but things happen down there.
   Tell Bill Simpson I'm sorry I didn't get to see him - but I had girls on the brain!! By the way - remember that Sat. nite trouble?? Both boys got fined very heavily - and the little girl wasn't mixed up in it - which was all I was worried about.
   Gotta close - thanks for the check - but don't need it right now.

Love, Johnny

Having achieved a status change from Private to Candidate in early March, this official letter declares John is now Corporal and enrolled in Officer Candidate School.

April 1, 1942
The Army of the United States

   To all who shall see these presents, greeting: Know ye, that reposing special trust and confidence in the fidelity and abilities of **Private 1c1 John D. Goodin, 34142319**, I do hereby appoint him **Corporal, 6th Co., O.C.S. [Officer Candidate School], Armored Force School, ARMY OF THE UNITED STATES**, to rank as such from the First day of April one thousand nine hundred and Forty-two. He is therefore carefully and diligently to discharge the duty of Corporal by doing and performing all manner of things thereunto belonging. And I do strictly charge and require all Noncommissioned Officers and Soldiers under his command to be obedient to his orders as Corporal. And he is to observe and follow such orders and directions from time to time, as he shall receive from his Superior Officers and Noncommissioned Officers set over him, according to the rules and discipline of War.
   Given under my hand at **Headquarters Armored Force School, Fort Knox, Kentucky**, this First day of April in the year of our Lord one thousand nine hundred and Forty-two.

S. G. Henry
Brigadier General, U.S.A., Commandant

April 6, 1942
USO Letterhead Stationery Sunday afternoon
Dear Folks,
   Another weekend gone by and time really is flying for me -- three weeks have gone by already, and it seems only

One. Basic Training

a few days since I've been over here. I came into town this weekend, and went to church this morning. Although I worked on my maps and "homework" for tomorrow from 9 last night till 1 this morning. Eliz. and Paul had gone to party, so I had everything nice and quiet and got it done. Its get kind of rough at times, but I think I'll make it o.k.

In the meantime -- I'm having difficulties -- there is a heck of this army that I know nothing of and am having to start from scratch on. Mainly - tanks, and heavy artillery and mortars -- also the engineering department, which I'm very weak only as my exam so aptly showed. On the stuff I've had though -- I've no time. And I have no time any more -- whatsoever.

As it is, I must be closing and getting back to camp. We bought Liz a box of candy for Easter, and she and I went to church this morning. Take care of yourselves and write when you can.

      Love, Johnny

MAY 21 1942
Stamped Fort Knox, KY
Addressed to Capt. Thos. E. Goodin
c/o Hotel Morgan, Spartanburg, SC
Wed. nite.

Dear Dad,

Guess I've kinda neglected you lately - but I have enjoyed your letters and hope you realize I'm busy. I could write on the weekends, but I'm usually trying to get my mind off of my work and relaxing, so that about 6 weeks ago I quit writing on the weekends even. I only have 3 1/2 weeks or so more to go & then I hope to be home for a while before leaving for God knows where!!

Sis sent me some pictures today of you & Glenna & Jean & her & Mother. She sure had a good time while she was there, I guess.

By the way, mother intimates you are raising sand about her "Unaka" camp or whatever it is. Gee, Pop - can't you or won't you <u>ever</u> understand that she'd go crazy if she didn't have something to do?? Don't we all know that when <u>you</u> - the sanest of people - lay off for 4 days that you're pacing the floor like a caged lion on the <u>3rd</u> day?? As long as she's interested in <u>anything</u>, for Heavens sake <u>encourage</u> her, and don't <u>discourage</u> her - if she even wants to fly to England. It's hard enough on her losing everything she has without adding on to it. With all the freedom you've always had - you can't realize what living

Appalachia to Dessau

in one place week in & week out means. If I had to stay here over the weekend - with the same people (which is ten times better than no people at all) - I'd be ready for the nut house. So - ease up a bit on her & let her do what she wants to do as long as she's not hurting you.

I took Virginia Woodward on a boat trip up the Ohio River Saturday afternoon - $1.05 for the both of us - me being in uniform. Had a good time. It's kinda funny talking to her now that she's growing up like she is. Reminds me a lot of Anne Carter. Well, I gotta get to work. I hope to have a few days off & be home in about 3 weeks (around the 15th of June). So - if the gas ain't rationed - hope the Oldsmobile is rearing to go - for it might be my last fling of home for a long time.

      Love, as always, Johnny

MAY 21 1942
Candidate Goodin Fort Knox, KY

Dear Mom,

 Sure enjoyed your letter - I still say when you do write, you make it worth while.

 I've gotten 2 letters from Sis - the first of which bubbled over about 6 pages about how nice the house looked, how well you had things going, and things in general pleasing her through & through. And what those girls had to say & did. She's worried about getting home now. Confound it - I told her to leave the car there while she was there. But that "I'll get by" of hers.

 I'm still plugging. Have flunked 2 exams, still have more demerits than merits, and time is growing short. 3 1/2 weeks, & I hope to be home. I may meet Sis in Virginia (I can meet her & drive on home in the time it would take me to get home) if she decided on coming on in. She's worried sick that there's not much way for her to come but to drive. Sent me some pictures - Glenna sure looks skinny to what she did - but she's growing.

 Go ahead finish your Unaka plans. I may live through this mess & want some place to keep my mistress!! Seriously, go ahead.

 It'll always come in handy.

 Took Virginia on a boat trip Sunday afternoon up the Ohio River - she really is growing up. We had a good time, lost our glamour and self-restraint - got ice cream all over us, & I blistered my feet dancing. Came back, ate a quart of ice cream & talked for 2 1/2 hours before I had to leave.

 Had a date with my "Kitten" on Sat. nite, [sic] took her

One. Basic Training

Officer candidates outside the battalion barracks, Fort Knox, Kentucky, April 1942.

   to dinner, and made her wait while I spent $95 on a uniform. Still gotta buy some shoes, & odds & ends. And - with my usual aptness for getting involved, I'm falling in love with Ann Carter's roommate. Fortunately - most of my loves are purely platonic and no serious difficulties arise. Besides - it's fun getting out of scrapes, altho [sic] I don't realize it!!
   Well - write when you can & hope I see you before another month is up.

                      Love, Johnny

P. S. - Tell all our neighbors hello for me!!

Postcard Postmarked Fort Knox, KY 5/25/42
Dear Folks,

   3 weeks to go and I'm still here. Am O.K., still going strong, and weight staying about the same. (Had another physical exam this weekend - and no unfavorable reports as yet.) Was on ground last night - my last nite - my last one here I hope. Didn't get to stay in town but about 6 hours Sat. nite and went to a show with Kelly - first one I've been to in months. Haven't heard from Sis so don't know what she's planning. But I'll be home anyhow - I

Appalachia to Dessau

hope. Some of the boys from 5th Div. are back in school and say Anderson may be back in 3 weeks. Sure hope so. Best wishes & love as always.

<u>Johnny</u>

After graduating from the Armored Force Officer Candidate School in Fort Knox, Kentucky, Goodin received the following letter confirming his appointment as a Second Lieutenant of the United States Army. The next stop would be Camp Polk, Louisiana.

This photograph is labeled "Shavetail John Goodin" referring to his new status as a second lieutenant upon graduation from Officers Candidate School, June 1942.

HEADQUARTERS
THE ARMORED FORCE SCHOOL
 Fort Knox, Kentucky
 IN REPLY REFER TO 201
Goodin, John David
 Subject: Temporary Appointment

To: 2nd Lt. John David Goodin, A 0-1010821 Army of the United States.

The Secretary of War has directed me to inform you that the President has appointed and commissioned you a temporary Second Lieutenant, Army of the United States, effective this date, in the grade shown in the address above. Your serial number is shown after A above.

 This commission is to continue in force during the pleasure of the President of the United States for the time being, and for the duration of the present emergency and six months thereafter unless sooner terminated.

 There is inclosed

32

One. Basic Training

```
herewith a form for oath of office which you are requested
to execute and return. The execution and return of the
required oath of office constitute an acceptance of
your appointment. No other evidence of acceptance is
required. This letter should be retained by you as evi-
dence of your appointment.
            By command of Brigadier General Henry:
            W. E. Watters
            Lt. Col. (F.A.), Armored Force Secretary.
            Inclosure:
            Form for oath of office.
```

On Tuesday, June 16, 1942, the *Johnson City Chronicle* printed the following article, titled "Erwin Youth Graduates from Fort Knox School."

> Lieutenant John David Goodin, son of Thomas E. Goodin, Sr., of Erwin was graduated from the Armored Force Officer Candidate School at Fort Knox, KY., as a second lieutenant in the Army of the United States. He will be assigned to duty with an armored division or tank battalion, officials announced this week.
>
> Lieut. Goodin has been in the service 12 months and was a member of the sixth class to be graduated in this special department and the fifth since the Pearl Harbor disaster. Under the new expansion program, the school graduates 5,000 officers annually instead of 700, the original quota.[11]

Chapter Two

Dog Biscuits and Dust Devils
July 1, 1942–September 14, 1943

An article in the *Johnson City Chronicle* printed Sunday, July 26, 1942, titled "Goodin Assigned to Armored Group" stated the following:

> A former local attorney, Second Lieut. John D. Goodin has been assigned to the 32^d armored regiment at Camp Polk, La., Major General Walton H. Walker, commanding the division, has announced.
>
> Lieut. Goodin, son of Mr. and Mrs. Thomas E. Goodin Jr., of Erwin and a former State Teachers College student is a recent graduate of the Armored Force Officer Candidate School at Fort Knox, KY. He was awarded his LL.B. degree at the University of Tennessee, Knoxville, in 1941 and also attended Washington and Lee University at Lexington, Va., where he captained the rifle team in 1939–40. He practiced law in Johnson City before joining the armed forces.[1]

```
Envelope dated JUL 1 1942 Postmarked Camp Polk, LA From:
Lt. J. D. Goodon July 1, 1942
Inside address:
Rcn. Co., 32nd Arm'd Reg't. 3rd Arm'd Div'n.
Camp Polk, La.
Tuesday night.
Dear Folks,
  Well, I at last feel like I'm earning my money -- and
all that I must not have earned when I was on furlough,
pass, and when I wasn't doing anything just then. I've
really put in some time the last couple of days, and
have done things that I used to think that I wouldn't
have done for love, money, or government pension. For
instance, supply officer, range officer, and so forth. But
I'm doing, and not disliking them too much. I'm still
dying from this cockeyed heat down here, and nothing I
seem to do cools me off so very much.
  Went into Shreveport (116 miles north of here) over the
weekend, and lived the proverbial life of Riley -- should
```

Two. Dog Biscuits and Dust Devils

have seen me on Sunday: stretched out on a Beautyrest mattress, in my birthday suit, a radio playing, and a lovely fan cooling me off with the assistance of a big pitcher of ice water within easy reach. All I needed was some lovely maiden to scratch my back and whisper sweet nothings to me. Ahhhhhhhhhhhm-m-m-m-m-m-m-m-m-.

Don't know what the story is for this weekend -- I'm sure glad that I got a raise in pay before I came to Louisiana, otherwise it would break me up to live -- along with Pop's income and Mom's and the help I might get from any other friends or neighbors, intend to get out of this place though if at all possible, and if no one happens to tell me or change me, I think I'll either [go] to New Orleans, or back to Shreveport. Met an engineers [sic] daughter who is right cute -- plays a piano, sings, and her father is a Mason who disapproves of drinking and smoking. Lididi.

Still have a couple of weeks here and am slowly getting on my feet, learning the ropes, and finding out things I never knew.

Got a letter today from Frank Headley, my roommate at

Shortly after graduation from Officers Candidate School in Fort Knox, Kentucky, John D. Goodin is photographed with his parents, T.E. and Glenna Goodin, at home in Erwin, Tennessee, June 1942.

Appalachia to Dessau

John D. Goodin poses in front of an airstrip in July 1942, before heading out to Mojave Desert in Rice, California.

U.T. [University of Tennessee], and he is in the Air Corp over in Mississippi. Was drafted in May and tried to go to Ft. Knox, and of course, wasn't, and even put into the Air Corp. Missing his wife a little bit, and even more -- missing Knoxville.

Guess that his defence [sic] job wasn't much help to him when the time come for the draft to catch up with him.

Well, got to go to Officers School in another few minutes, so gotta close. Write when you can, and tell me what is going on around in those lovely mountains besides making love, moonshine, buttermilk, and trouble.

       Love, Johnny

July 13th, 1942 from Camp Polk, LA
Dear Dad,

Sorry that I missed you yesterday, but it was Anne's birthday and I had not had time to get her anything, I decided I would call her, and then while I had Johnson City, it was no trouble to call Erwin, so that is what I did.

I'm enclosing you my check, which I want you to deposit for me--you can make it a joint checking account--with you, so that we can both draw on it if necessary, or I will authorize you to draw checks on me, as for taxes, or

Two. Dog Biscuits and Dust Devils

something that may come up. You can add the $15 bank dividend to it, and after that, I want you to buy me a $25 bond out of it - that will leave me some over $50, for a checking account. (I think you can still have one over $50 and if it doesn't cost anything—-let me know and in the meantime put it in your name.)

It is hot as H--- down here, but I may get used to the desert better, at least you don't stay soaking wet there and all fagged out like you had a steam bath going on all the time. I'm getting used to this down here a little better, although last week I had to do about an hours physical work and it almost killed me—I was winded, and unable to hardly breathe for quite some little time. But I did what I started to, and ended up with a couple of blisters on my hands, which you would laugh at if you could see, I suppose. Anyhow, I think I'm going to have to start doing something to get back into shape. I can walk all day or anything like that, but if I have to use some of the rest of me, I don't have any strength — lack of use I suppose.

I suppose I've spent my last weekend in Shreveport for some time. This last time cost me some $15, but I had the best time I've ever had down here. Ran into a little German girl from the middle west originally, and talk about a supper — we really ate one out at her house last night. I had fried chicken — all that I could eat, good ice tea, and some ice cream that you would have thought you made— they have a 3 gallon freezer. She's not so pretty, but wow—with all those eats, I could do without the looks. She's one of the few girls that I've met that didn't drink, or smoke, and she hasn't missed church but three times in her life. --She is a Catholic, but doesn't mean much—-everyone down here is.

Well, gotta be closing. Take care of this check for me — I've gotta build up a little bit to pay off my income tax next year, and I might as well start now. Besides, I might have a tendency to spend it if I kept it.

Take care of yourself—and cut out this foolish worrying that you must be doing. As to other things—let 'em ride.

Love to all, as always, Johnny

Orders were received in mid-July for a transfer to the Mojave Desert. The trip to Rice, California, took four days by train.[2] The Rice Army Desert Training Center in Rice, California (formerly Blythe Junction) is located on the southern tip of the Mojave Desert, and is the largest military reservation in U.S. History. The Desert Training Center encompassed three states: California, Arizona, and Nevada. The area was strategically chosen due to an existing railroad, which brought in most of the soldiers, and also the proximity of the Colorado River Aqueduct, which would supply all of the water for the troops. General George S. Patton chose the area because of the heat and harshness of the surroundings. Here, soldiers would experience the closest thing to real battle, training with real munitions which would prepare the soldiers to attack and defend.[3]

Upon arrival, the troops stepped out into 130-degree heat.[4] John Steinbeck describes the Mojave in the book, *Travels with Charley*. "The Mojave, a burned and burning desert ... its hills like piles of black cinders ... the rutted floor sucked dry by the hungry sun ... a terrestrial hell ... a big desert and a frightening one. It's as though nature tested a man for endurance and constancy to prove whether he was good enough to get to California."[5] Day and night the heat persisted with sudden wind, sand and dust storms that could yank a tent up by the stakes and send it sailing away. There was no camp, only 18,000 square miles of sand. The entire camp had to be set up from scratch. Bulldozers formed "company" streets where tents, latrines, kitchens, rigged showers, etc., were built.[6]

Training in the Mojave toughened the 3rd Armored for combat. Fighting "enemy forces" (other U.S. soldiers) with little water and few rations that consisted of sardines or "desert trout," and rusk, also known as hardtack, was a replacement for bread, and would later be referred to as "dog biscuits" during the western campaign. While nearly unpalatable, and a test of the teeth, these rock-hard biscuits were inexpensive, long-lasting, and traveled well. Soldiers learned about camouflage, coordination, and dispersed formations. All divisions had to be coordinated to work together: tanks, planes, and artillery.[7]

A YouTube video titled "Freedom's Desert—Rice Army Airfield and the Desert Training Center," features soldiers who trained at Rice. The following are quotes from these soldiers:

- Major General John Henry, the former Commanding Officer of Rice Army Airfield, said of the Rice Desert Training Center: "To say we were isolated is putting it mildly. In our war, we knew what the stakes were, we just had to stay with it and do—and we did."
- Captain George B. Edwards, 92nd Infantry, described some of his experience: "They gave you two hours to dig a foxhole, and they brought the tanks in and run over it. It was a hell of an experience. They would tell you, the tank is gonna be here and it is going to run right over you. Marches could be anywhere from 8 to 24 to 100 miles and you had

Two. Dog Biscuits and Dust Devils

to be disciplined with water. You had only a small amount from 8 in the morning till 11:00 at night for drinking and bathing."

• Sgt. Horace Barrett, 709 Tank Battalion described it this way: "We didn't have any sleep from Sunday night to Wednesday night. We were on the road with the tanks all that time. It was hell."[8]

Goodin tells his family in one of his letters that he is learning to stand in his tank for 10 hours at a time. He spent the next three months on maneuvers in the Mojave Desert.[9]

The harshness of the training paid off in the end. The men who trained at Rice were some of the most highly decorated of the war.[10]

```
Somewhere deep in the heart of Texas.
Tuesday night July 1942
Dear Folks,
   Well, after all of these years, I have finally arrived
at another one of my desires which was to see the state
of Texas, and if it is as hot as this part right here, I'd
just as soon go back to Tennessee for a spell. Anyhow,
things aren't going too bad, and I'm enjoying my trip
immensely--I'm train mess officer, officer of the day,
custodian of the funds for the rations, duty officer, and
just any thing that comes along that happens to have to
be done. However, I'm getting them done, and I think I'm
even--even on my accounting. So far, I've spent about
$660 of the government's money on food for the men, and
the Major said that he was pleased with the way I was
handling things.
   So--if I don't go off somewhere else, I may put a small
feather in my helmet--which could look funnier than [word
marked out] but I look that way anyhow. (You should see
my crew hair cut which I now have--about ½ inch or less
in places.)
   I have never felt quite so wonderful as I have all day
-- I'm working, getting things done -- the railroad has
cooperated, not 100%, but 1000% with me, and everything
so far has gone in good shape. Everyone in Houston Texas
cheered and yelped at us as we went by, waved bye bye -
and the soldiers in the air corps yelled "suckers" --
probably thinking that they would be there before we
do. Incidentally, I've never enjoyed responsibility so
much in my life as I have now. I feel like I could lick
the world with one hand -- and take unto myself a wife
with the other -- which is certainly a wild burst of
confidence.
   I'll be going through Kingman Arizona in a short time,
and although I know I won't get to top off on the way, I
```

Appalachia to Dessau

expect to go up there some weekend and see the McIntyres and their friends the Crawfords. All in all -- I'm not unhappy, and I think the whole darned train is happy to be away from Louzyana, which you may have gathered none of us loved too well. Of course, it may be from the frying pan into the fire, but no one seems to give the well known Norris Lake - youknowwhatI'mtalkingaboutdon'tyou?

I'd love to tell you about our train, but can't do it at present. Will confine myself to saying that most of my time is spent in the kitchen car, where I down quarts of juice, choice fruits, and lots of ice water and other cooling things. I haven't slept for a week, but guess that I'll catch up on it tomorrow, since, being duty officer tonight, I can take a break tomorrow.

As I said, I'm actually happy -- curious to know what new adventures I'm going to have next, and frankly I'm afraid that I'm a little over confident, or else I may just be finding myself after all of these years. Still wish that I had gotten married, and guess that if Anne had been in a receptive mood, I might have -- but anyhow that is past, and when I get back -- well, I may talk Margaret into it by that time.

Gotta go up and check my guard now, so for the present good night, and so long. Will try and write you when I can, but don't worry if I miss a few days -- the government will let you know if I get my feet wet and catch a cold!!! With acres and acres of love to all of you, and love to all my girls -- may God bless each and all of them for the happiness that all of you have given me.

Your wayward boy.

No date [between July and September 1942] Rice, California
Dear Folks,

Sure was a pleasure to get to talk to all of you last night and I suppose if I could have talked to the Carters that would have made it complete. However, the lines were still none too good last night apparently.

I had one of the most exciting days of my army life yesterday: Captain Cunningham (from Roanoke--his father was a conductor on the N&W for about 36 years) took me out "fishing" with him -- and we caught these little sun perch that aren't much bigger than a half dollar -- we must have caught 50 or 60. Besides we had a couple of automatics, and a couple of hundred rounds of ammunition, and went over to Texas for the fishing. Came back and my Shreveport blonde had come down to say goodbye. Well -- I hadn't eaten dinner yet and neither had she, so we

Two. Dog Biscuits and Dust Devils

Reconnaissance Company 32nd Armored Regiment, 3rd Armored Division headed by train to Rice, California, summer 1942.

decided to blow -- and Capt. Cunningham had told me about a good place to eat -- and he sure wasn't lieing [sic] -- that was the best steak that I've eaten in years. She couldn't stay very long, but anyhow -- we had a good time -- although I couldn't get hold of you when I tried to.

Now -- I want you to send me a check book - with how much I have in the bank, and how I stand -- I may need to cash a check this month in as much as I am having to buy a lot of stuff -- and I have a good time in this place -- too much so -- but I don't guess I'll have so much fun from now on -- and I've been working like the well known son of a --------------. There are only two of us on the train, and we have 14 jobs to hold down, and try to get them all done -- loading 317 men, getting 6 days supply of food (my job) making arrangements for feeding them along the way. It's been work -- night and day, but now that we're ready to leave -- well, I'm almost sorry it's over. If I could just get everything done and know that it would be all right, then everything would be all right.

I'm looking forward to getting to California again -- heard from Andy yesterday and it looks like they are going to be our "enemies" on maneuvers. Kelley and I were laughing if they "captured" us or vice versa -- that it would be some fun, and no kidding about that.

Appalachia to Dessau

Goodin labeled this photograph "enroute via train to Rice, California, somewhere in New Mexico some of the good country." Goodin wrote "where I slept" on the front of the photograph to indicate his position on the train.

>   I'll drop you a line as soon as I get there, and maybe along the way, if I get the time and can do it. But I can't promise anything, and don't even know how things are going to turn out there or anything else. I still think it's going to be fun, and with a little bit of luck, I may be able to get a promotion out of it. Due to transfers and new divisions, I already jumped from 5th ranking man in the company to second -- without doing a darned thing. This last 3 weeks has made a veteran out of me too--.
>   Well, gotta go and get my train lined up. Luck to you -- and write me when you can.
>   Did Sis get her package I sent her????? Love,
>   Johnny

Photographs in the Goodin collection show before-and-after pictures of wide areas of open space in Rice, California, with long rows of equipment lined up. The photo labeled "after" depicts a camp full of tents.

Two. Dog Biscuits and Dust Devils

When the 32nd Armored Regiment, 3rd Armored Division disembarked from the train in Rice, California, they encountered barren, wide-open spaces, and a temperature of 130 degrees.

Once the equipment was unloaded, they began to lay out their camp and get their tents set up.

Appalachia to Dessau

Evidence that their teamwork training was successful is evident here in this photograph labeled "After Setting Up."

```
1942
Recon. Co. - 32nd A.R.
3rd A.D.
A.P.O. #253
Rice, Cal.
```

Saturday night.

Dear Folks,

   Well, believe it or not, here I am at last in good old California, and what's good about it must be around the other side of the mountain -- it ain't here. However, it ain't too bad -- and finally have the company and things lined up. I'm learning pretty fast just what to do with the heat out here, and we quit work around 9:30 in the morning and don't get back until late in the afternoon and then work rather late into the night.

   The last part of the trip was rather uneventful, and I didn't have too much excitement, since there wasn't enough civilization for anything to happen. You'd be surprised at what has been done out here in just a short time: for instance, we have showers for 250 men at a time, and they are running 24 hours a day. Water comes from the Los Angeles viaduct, is pumped into a tank, and then comes out. We officers have a separate section, and it is not near as crowded as the rest of them, also -- we can use them almost any time we want them. It is about the only time in the day that it is cool, and you really

Two. Dog Biscuits and Dust Devils

Men sitting at a table under a roof enjoy a reprieve from the hot desert sun as they have a meal featuring fresh, cool water.

can get cooled off there. It gets very chilly early in the morning, although when you wake up feeling chilly, it isn't but a little bit later until the whistle blows -- and out here the officers get up at the same time as the men do. Helps morale.

Some of the boys are having trouble with the heat -- nose bleed -- of which I had a little bit, and heat exhaustion. However, there is a lot of ice, and if they are too bad we send them over to the hospital, and if they aren't we just keep them in the company and feed iced drinks, and keep wet towels on them. It is fun being father confessor, doctor, brother, sister, mother, and sweetheart to a bunch of dopes from the 48 states. One Tenn. boy said that he didn't know whether he'd ever get back or not, but "reckoned that if these Indians and Mexicans can take it -- he's dam-d sure that" he can.

Well, no news -- so will close. Hope you have my checkbook on the way out -- I may have to make a little tap to get by this month -- I bought a lot of juices on the way out and stuff -- so may have to tap "lightly."

By the way -- there is plenty of sunshine and vitamins here!!! Love,

Johnny

Appalachia to Dessau

JULY 28 1942 Stamped CALIF.
From Lt. J.D. Goodin
Sunday night from Rice, Cal.

Dear Dad,

Got your letter today—and don't get it. What do you mean you sent my "check back to La.?" Didn't you deposit it? I guess it will clear up later, but for the present—well, I got your letter, and that was what I wanted most.

It still is hot here (as it probably will be until we get out of here and for a couple of centuries to come) and still having trouble with the heat, since so many of the boys don't have sense enough to try and take care of themselves properly, and won't give into the heat when it hits them.

I'm just waiting until the time that I can get up to Needles, to L.A., or to somewhere around here. Right now, we are sort of parked along the highway with nothing in view. A few cars pass by and an occasional Greyhound bus drops through. I haven't shaved in three days and I think I'll have to shave or get court martialed.

Just one of the many uses a steel helmet may be put to—here is a sergeant in an unposed shot doing a little "home laundry." It was too hot to stand up and work.

Got a letter from Marg. Carter today, too. Did I tell you she sent me a picture and said that I was too bashful to ask her for one, so that is why she sent it anyhow?? She is quite a character—wish her sister Anne had a little more of her instability.

Also got a letter from the La. girl today—darned fool wants to come out here—must think I'm nuts about her, when I told her very frankly I wasn't. But then—these

Two. Dog Biscuits and Dust Devils

John Goodin takes a break from tank maneuvers to test his prowess on another form of transportation.

girls now a days have their own ideas--and I'm not one to change 'em.

One of my buddies at W&L [Washington & Lee University] (the boy who came down to get us the time we wrecked at Christianburg at 3 a.m.) is down here with us -- got married just before he left, and now is out here, with his wife at home. However, he's taking it very philosophically, and since he is able financially to support her, guess it is all right. Incidentally, haven't heard from G. Vance except through the Sherrill boy. Art Meyer has been promoted up the ladder a grade, and is very much pleased with himself--sends his best regards to you, and says that if the war is over and he can get off--he's coming to Tennessee for a "vacation"--as we all are.

Well, this may be the last letter I'll be able to write to you for a while—so as I said before, don't worry about the chicke [sic] 'cause you don't hear from me. Hope that you are all right and doing fine. Tell Sis to write to me as soon as she can and let me know what she is doing and where she is going to be. And let me know about Love's and Bill's "wedding." Keep your chins up!!!!!

                        Johnny.

Appalachia to Dessau

Always one to quickly acclimate, Goodin labeled this photograph "Home."

```
July 30th, 1942  Inside address:
Recon. Co., 32nd A.R. 3rd A.D.
A.P.O. #253
Rice, Cal.
```

Dear Folks,

Sorry that I haven't had a chance to write any sooner, but have been busy as the dickens. This desert out here is really beautiful, and the nights have been really beautiful with the moon, the stars, and faint glows of light here and there. And the mountains give us cool breezes at night, although in the day time we do get a little warm. Luckily, so far, I've been getting along fine, what with change of altitude, temperatures, and all that stuff. One of our Lieutenants got sick and went to the hospital the other day, and some of the boys have wilted up for a little while but most of them have come through in pretty good shape. They were all so happy to get out of La., that I guess even Stan would have looked fairly good to some of them.

We are having a convoy over to Los Angeles on this weekend, but I think I'll be taking a convoy up to Needles -- more of our boys want to go there than to Los Angeles, and someone has to go with them, and I'm not quite ready to go over [to] the Angels.

Got a short note from Sis that she was on her way North, and that Reg was about to be assigned or something or other. You all know how she writes. She apparently hated

Two. Dog Biscuits and Dust Devils

John Goodin, center, "JIVE" and Thiesan on Desert Maneuvers 12 miles from the Desert Center, 1942

   to leave home, as we all do, but it was one of those things that has us scattered all over the U.S. from coast to coast.
   Well, gotta close and get some more work done. This is the first time I've had any time to get any writing done in a week.
   Hold down the forts, and don't do anything drastic!!
Love, as ever to the best Pap and Mam in the whole world.
                Johnny

No date [between July and September 1942] Rice, California
Friday night.
Dear Folks,
   Haven't heard from you in several days, but suppose that you are all right, else I would have heard. Got a

Appalachia to Dessau

letter from Sis, and she is all up in the air not knowing what to do or anything. Guess she is having fun.

Well, we start on maneuevers [sic] around Monday, and it looks like it's going to be fun. Hope so, anyhow, although it may be rough, too. But as usual, I'm enjoying it -- I get something new out of life every day out here. It seems this desert is inexhaustible in its treasures and things of interest.

Saturday -- some time later as you may well know.

In the meantime, I have been on a company beer party -- and found out that the boys hated to see me leave, and have been around checking up on various things. I had hoped to go into Los Angeles this weekend in order to see my little girl, but don't guess I'll go anywhere now. Still - there's nothing out on what we are going to do or definitely just when we are going to do it. So I'm in just a bit of a muddle.

I had a very nice letter from Ruth Moseley in which she sends you both, Mom particularly though, her best wishes and regards.

Also had a letter from Sis in which she sent me some pictures of Reg in his uniform and he is really a honey!! She's very proud of him for one time in his life going out and getting something on his very own. So, along with the prospect of going to Fla., and getting away from up there, I suppose that she is very happy. I'm sure glad for her -- as Lord knows she needs a break after all these years with those '   ' yankees.

Johnny Sherrill, a boy from W&L [Washington and Lee University] got married on his leave, and I saw him this morning, and he's rather hurting -- going out on maneuvers away from his little chickadee, and though he's taking it very calmly, still - and all, I can tell, that it's a pity. I rather admire his courage in taking the fatal step, and if there comes a break in my life, I'll probably jump off the weekend. In fact - if certain parties were on the West coast, I think I would have already gone overboard. It is not good to go along for such a long time -- I was almost ready to get married last weekend and that definitely would have been a <u>big</u> mistake. But then -- you all know more about such things than I do!!

Well, I gotta close and get this mailed. Write when you can, and I'll do the same.

      Love, as always,
      Johnny

Goodin describes his training for commanding a tank.

Two. Dog Biscuits and Dust Devils

14th of Aug. [1942] Friday night
Rice, California

Dear Folks,

I haven't had as happy a day as far as the mail goes since I've been in the army. Somehow, I think it sure would be wonderful if you all could come out here, and I want you to come. This desert, with all its beauty, still ain't them good old mountains and all the trimmins [sic]. It is a lot of fun, it is beautiful, but there are times when I wish that I were back home for a little while. After all, I only lived there!!
You ask me what I'm doing here. Well, military secrets--but we are getting in a little training. I, personally, am learning how to handle a group of men, and be able to control them in good shape a[t] distances up to a couple of miles. So that is what I'm doing. I'm also having lots of fun. I wish you could see these dumb jackrabbits--they are messes. They remind me of our donkeys--there [sic] big long ears flip in the wind when they run, and they are slow sometimes and faster than the breeze at other times. In the cours[e] of a morning, I have seen the vultures (perched on the cross arm of a power line), a turtle, snakes, lizards, quail, all kinds of funny looking bugs, and even foxes. Then there are some funny looking birds with really long neck[s] which are also very funny looking.
I sure would like for you all to come out, and anytime --I should think right now, the sooner, the better--that you can make, you'll find your Johnny with wide open arms. We, of course, don't know when we'll be moved or where, but, hope that it will be about a couple of months or so. You may be surprised at me. I haven't lost weight (which I thought I would, I've tanned up like an Indian, and perhaps you would almost call me rugged - er sumpin [sic]. I can stand in a vehicle for ten hours a day directing my men, and do it for two or t[h]ree days and don't seem to mind it. So, you can see I'm not having too much trouble. Kelley has gained about 5 pounds out here.
Sis wrote me about Reg, and I guess she'll be home or somewhere. She sure is happy to be leaving Mass. though. Like a bird let out of a cage--that's my sis. And I'm darned happy too.
Jean sent me a write up of me in the J. City paper which was on the same page as her picture!! She is a good little girl--but I'm afraid not for me. I still want a long lean lanky gal, like Margie or Margaret.
How about some more nice interesting letters like I've

Appalachia to Dessau

been getting. You sure can carry me home in a couple of seconds.

    P.S. The 10th of Sept. is good a time as any to come out. Will be looking for you.

          Your hoofed and horned, (but not tailed yet--)
          Johnny

Envelope dated AUG 28 1942
Barstow CA

    In this letter, Goodin's address changes to Barstow, California. Fort Irwin, formerly known as the Mojave Anti-Aircraft range, was a remote location 37 miles from Barstow, with over one thousand "desolate" acres and temperatures that could reach 120 degrees. This area was used for anti-air gunnery training, and was located between Los Angeles, California, and Las Vegas, Nevada.[11] Tank and artillery training included mock battles against "enemy forces." These maneuvers, which were conducted in as close to real battle conditions as possible, including rationing of food and water, toughened the 3rd Armored, and they excelled and "never failed to turn in a creditable performance."[12]

Hq. Co., 32nd A.R.
A.P.O. #253
Rice, Cal.
Aug. 28th 1942

Dear Folks,

  Well, I've thought it all over, and I've decided to ask you to revise your plans. I'm now working in headquarters, and I think from what I know now, that it will be all right if you do come on out. I've spoken around, and I know that if you hit here or close here on a weekend, that I'll be able to see you for a while anyhow. So -- well, I'll be looking for you around the 10th of the month. In the meantime if anything turns up that I think would warrant your not attempting the trip, why of course I'll wire you or call you in time to prevent your making a useless trip.

  The desert itself is wonderful now. The days don't get over 120, and the night[s] drop down to 70 and 80, and are actually cool enough to use a couple of blankets. It sure is a wonderful feeling to wake up in the morning, and go out and feel full of pep and energy. This morning, I got up, shaved in ice cold water (evaporation on water bags cools the water sometimes down to freezing temperatures)

Two. Dog Biscuits and Dust Devils

went down, had a quart of ice cold milk for breakfast, along with cereal, eggs, toast, peaches and orange juice. Then took a brisk half hours calisthenics, and then after that <u>ran</u> about a quarter of a mile for the heck of it.

Marg. Carter is writing me regularly, now, and says that Jean and Charley Sherrod are engaged. Also hear from Margie quite regularly, and there is a smart well read intelligent girl -- I sometimes wonder if maybe too much that way -- but hers are the most interesting letters I've ever gotten from anyone, though they may lack the love interest that most of them have. Haven't heard from Sis in ages, and don't know where she is or what she is doing.

Am taking a convoy to Los Angeles Tuesday probably -- 2000 men. Hope to go in myself tomorrow morning although Gen. Devers from Ft. Knox is due down here this afternoon and may prevent that. Don Houghtons sister and father are in Los Angeles, and S. M. Anderson's brother runs a store down there. So I guess I'll try and see all of them, as well as go up and see Ruth Moseley.

Heard from Posey -- nice letter, and will write Charley Moss as soon as I get some pictures back. If one of them turns out any good, I want to send him one (not of me -- but one he'll like).

Love to all of you, Johnny

In this letter, Goodin describes one of the infamous Mojave Desert sandstorms, but in typical character, counters it with one of the benefits of being so close to cities in California.

Goodin also mentions rumors of a move to the West Coast, but does not know for sure where the next move will land them. Some thought it might be Northern Africa. The uncertainty of location is par for the course in the U.S. Army. Soldiers are trained to be ready to move at a moment's notice without question.

```
No date (probably September 1, 1942)
Tuesday afternoon.
```

Dear Folks,

Well, I really had an enjoyable weekend in Los Angeles -- you must think that I sure am being extravagant, and maybe I am, but after 6 days out here (which I must admit aren't too bad at all, though) It sure is a pleasure to go to town and get cooled off, filled with food and cool drinks and see pleasant company.

Last night I saw my first sand storm. It was peculiar looking, and --- well, actually beautiful. Tents were

Appalachia to Dessau

blowing down, papers were floating here there and yon (our tent managed to stay up some how or other), there was some thunder, and the lightning was really odd to me: instead of the long vertical streaks to which we are accustomed, these streaks stretched themselves out horizontally over these mountains around here.

What was even more funny -- altho the storm was blowing <u>all</u> around us, one little patch right over us was filled with the <u>stars</u>. Once we got our tent fixed, as usual, nothing interfered with my sleeping, and I dropped right off. But sand was everywhere and in everything this morning, and most of the office boys were in an uproar due to their papers being blown high wide and handsome.

Wednesday morning.

Went over and saw Andy and the boys last night and so didn't get to finish this when I thought I would. Andy is o.k. -- weighs about 200 pounds and is fine as a fiddle. All the other boys are o.k. too.

Well, it looks this morning like the boys are actually getting that second front started over there, and we are all up in the air over it. Haven't heard much reports on it yet, but it seems that they are getting something done finally over there.

We got our freezing orders yesterday - it seems that after about a month or two of maneuvers we may be sent somewhere or put on the West Coast as a sort of guard out there. This latter possibility seems to be the best rumor at the present, although the rumors are flying fast and thick. I, incidentally, think that it isn't advisable for you all to plan to come out until the maneuvers are over, and as I don't know when they start or end, I can't give you any information on them. But as soon as I find out, I'll let you know by telegraph or telephone. Or if time enough, will write. No one seems to know anything definite, as usual with such things.

Well, got to work on a property check so will close for the now. Find out what is the matter with Marg. Carter that she has quit writing to me.

Well, hope you are all o.k., well and happy. I like this place more every day, despite the fact that I don't like it - or at least, that I'm not <u>supposed</u> to. Got a card from Eliz. Woodward yesterday showing the Toe river near the N.C. Tenn. line, and it sure looked good!! But there is something about this desert that gets you. Particularly since I'm getting used to the heat, it is really o.k.

                      Love to all of you, Johnny.

Two. Dog Biscuits and Dust Devils

John Goodin took the opportunity to visit friends of the family, the Moseleys, while in California. He took every opportunity to go into Los Angeles when time permitted, as he was able to sleep in a comfortable bed and take a good shower or bath—luxuries not afforded at camp.

Goodin mentions several women throughout his army career and is never without a female friend no matter where he goes.

```
Sept. 10th, 1942
3 P.M.
```

Dear Dad,

Well, it hardly seems that another year has gone by since I last saw you around a birthday—a good meal in Spartanburg, lots of beer and whiskey and meats and good food (well—most of it's true, Mom!!) but the way time is flying, I guess you'll be 66 before I know it. I sort of think that you've been looking forward to 65 for a long time, and actually, bet you worked just the same, and if you hadn't told someone they'd never know that difference. Anyhow, sorry that I can't be with you, sorry that I'm not some place I could call you, or wire you, or get you something you would like. But I do think I have a surprise for you (a mild one in a way) when I do get away from camp next time, but I'll let you wait for it.

I'm still getting along, not too many complaints, and my diorrhea [sic] hemmhoroids [sic] are gone. I've just had a quart of sweet milk (celebrating your birthday) a few fig newtons, a 15-minute nap (get them occasionally) and am waiting on my two sidekicks to come back to work. We are fixing to leave on a three-day problem over the weekend which means that I won't get to Los Angeles, probably. But I can stand one weekend with-out going in, I suppose, altho I had a darned good time last weekend - met a girl from Honolulu with the greenest eyes I ever saw, and Sunday I took two baths about an hour each.

Getting worried about Sis-- haven't heard from her in weeks. The Carter girls have been writing me lately (Marg is staying on the job), and I'm getting most of the news-particularly the gossip end of it. But I've gotta get to work, now, so I'll write again when I can find time. Take care of yourselves-- and maybe I'll be home for keeps before you hit 75 years an hour!!

All my love to you all,

Johnny.

Appalachia to Dessau

```
Postcard dated September 25, 1942
Postmarked Blythe California
```

(Rice, California, was formerly named Blythe Junction)

```
Hi Folks,
    On maneuvers - got a break. Got my mail today - first
time in a week, & in town tonite. Gets better - I even
got to fly some.
    More Tenn. & Va. people floating around on this desert.
It's O.K. tho! Will write sometime soon!!
                Johnny
```

John Goodin's family and friends would become very familiar with the location of "somewhere." Soldiers were not allowed to divulge their location.

```
Letter dated Oct. 1, 1942
Somewhere on maneuvers.
Dear Folks,
```

Got a break this morning & will write while I have the time. We are still "maneuvering" (for a cool place, ice water, and a beautiful gal - blonde, brunette, redhead, sheep, cow, goat, jackrabbit or what not) and having a fairly good time. I'm getting almost fat - have gained 4 pounds & am getting a little bigger in sports - no giant, of course, but still - hardening up. Getting so I can't sleep on a darned cot anymore. Altho last nite the ants kept me awake for a while. The nites are getting beautifully cool and this morning I reached for my 3rd blanket. So, life once again is livable.

Actually there ain't a hell of a lot to write about. No news, not even any good rumors out. Looks like we may go back to Camp Polk tho - I won't mind too much. But - nothing is definite.

NOTHING.

NOTE TO SIS: IT'S ALL OFF.

Got a nice letter from Charley Moss, and heard from Beulah. Got a long letter from Helen Hall, and Aunt Julia lives about 15 miles from here. But don't know when I'll ever get a chance to look her up. Haven't had a chance to get back to see Ruth Mosely - she may be gone back East by now.

Marg Carter has poison ivy and is living a painful existence. See if you can get Love's & Bill's Washington address for me. And - count me in on a family present, & how much do you need??

Sis, get my cards - about 100 and I'll send you a

Two. Dog Biscuits and Dust Devils

"mailing" list. Or if I'm here - which looks like I will be, you can send them to me, O.K.??

We are to have 15 straight days away from camp - we get breaks, but we bivouac wherever we happen to be - possibly Needles, or the other end Blythe - 175-200 miles away.

This county is still so big - I don't "get it."

Pop, sometimes when you are in Johnson City, see if you can get a case of 16 ga. shotgun shells, and you'd better buy all the bullets for that 38 you can get. Now don't do like you did on the tires - but get them & send me the bill. That's an order (you may not be able to get them, but try.

Well, gotta be closing. Write when you can. Love to all,

Johnny

John Goodin trusted his dad to take care of his finances while he was in the Army. Numerous letters throughout the collection address banking business, as well as life insurance and Goodin's will.

Oct. 9th, 1942
Rice, California

Dear Dad,

I got your letter this morning and while I have the chance to answer it, will try and get it done..never know when I'll have to move out and not get a chance to answer it. I got a little time off yesterday and got about 6 business letters off for a change. (Went back into base camp with a kid on an emergency furlough and took him up to Needles last night - saw the Crawfords, ate a bite and got back in by reveille this morning, in time to go back to work again - but had a good time in camp, catching up on my sleep and on my correspondence).

I never have gotten my will straightened out quite like I want it, but as it stands, it won't hurt you too much or differ very far from what you wanted. The only difference is, right now I have it set up as a combining income from the Yellow Cab Co and the bank stock as a trust fund for Jean and Glenna in case anything happens. I still think Jean should go to college, and I want her to have all the advantages that I can give her.

Betty will be taken care of somehow, and I am not going to worry about her. The Rock Creek property is to go to Mother as it is now set up, and outside of my "estate" that's about all there is to it. Some of these other white elephants I have on my hands I have acquired since I wrote the will, and so they will fall in my estate if it happens.

I sent you a couple of $50 bonds from last months pay check. You can put them in the bank for me and by the way, I'd like to know just how much bonds (what amount) I have. I got paid in cash like last time, and being unable to send it home, I thought I'd put in war bonds (more than half of it, and then it would be as good as gold.

Sent you all an enlargement of a picture I had made of me yesterday. Hope you like it, and some of these days maybe I'll get some more of them. It's hard to get those things out here very easily, and it's just once in a while that we manage it.

I thought I was going to get into L.A. this weekend but an order just came out that we won't get passes, so don't guess I'll get to go. I have an awfully lonesome war widow down there who needs comforting and besides she is a swell cook.

HEADQUARTERS 32ND ARMORED REGIMENT
Office of the Regiment Commander APO 253, Rice, Calif.
October 22, 1942 SPECIAL ORDER

28. A leave of absence for a period of three (3) days, effective on or about October 26, 1942, is granted to 2nd Lt. <u>JOHN D. GOODIN</u> O-1010821, 32ND Armored Regiment.

Camp Pickett, Virginia

In typical army style, the order to move out was swift and without warning. Once again, the 3rd Armored were boarded on trains and shipped to Camp Pickett, Virginia. This move would prove to be a drastic change. After months of training in the vast, open landscape, and hot winds of the 130-degree desert, the barracks of Camp Pickett were claustrophobic and cramped. There was no lapse in training, and the extreme change in temperatures accompanied by cold winds, caused many of the men to catch colds. Uncertainty would prevail here, as soldiers knew it could not be long before they were sent overseas.[13]

Goodin's hometown newspaper, *The Erwin Record,* reported on Thursday, December 3, 1942, the following: Headline: With the Boys in the Service. Lt. John D. Goodin, son of Mr. and Mrs. Tom Goodin, Sr., is now stationed at Camp Pickett, Va., after a long period of training at Rice, Calif.[14]

Two. Dog Biscuits and Dust Devils

Postmarked Camp Pickett, VA November 6, 1942

Inside Address:
Hqs. [Headquarters] Co., 32nd A. R.
A. P. O. 253
Camp Pickett, Va. Wednesday

My dearest Sis and all,

I can't write with this pen - so <u>please</u> send me my pen, my 2 overseas caps (1 Khaki & 1 wool) & whatever else I may have left behind.

Had a grand time - decided I wanted to marry Marj Carter, but after spending 6 hours with Va last night - am afraid she'll be my love light for a long time. Funny thing - but that's the way I feel. <u>BUT</u>, I'm going up to see Mary this weekend!! Oh, me.

It sure is nice here - hot water, steam heat, steel cots, electric lights, movies, bus service, - even women working on the post. H'm. Sure is wonderful!!

I could have had more time at home - 2/3 of the regiment (including my company) is not here yet. Had a train wreck (no one hurt) and delayed them. But - another nite at home would have <u>about</u> wrecked me. I guess I'm in fine shape now. A little sleep. ah...

Let me hear from you all. And let me know if, and <u>when</u>, you are planning on coming up!!

How much of the money I borrowed do I pay back & to whom?? Love to all

<u>Johnny</u>

P. S. - How's teaching???
P. P. S. - Got here with $1.48 how'm [sic] I doing?

Postcard dated November 12, 1942 Postmarked Lynchburg, VA 11/11/42

Dear Folks,

At Lynchburg again. Having a wonderful, peaceful, quiet time. Don't know when I'll get home, tho may make it this weekend for a few hours. Am weighing the advisability of such action. When are you coming up, or planning on it?? Would like to see you all.

Love to all, <u>Johnny</u>

Postmarked Camp Pickett, VA
November 23, 1942 Friday night

Dear Mom and Pop,

Just a few minutes to drop you a line or two from this end of the line.

Appalachia to Dessau

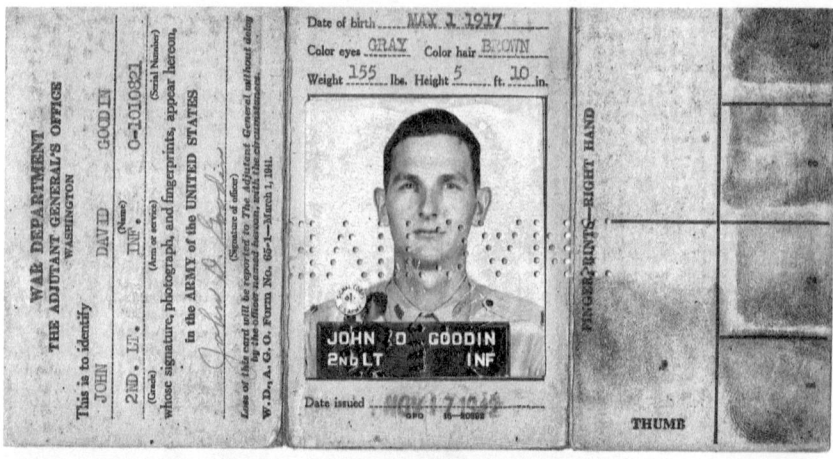

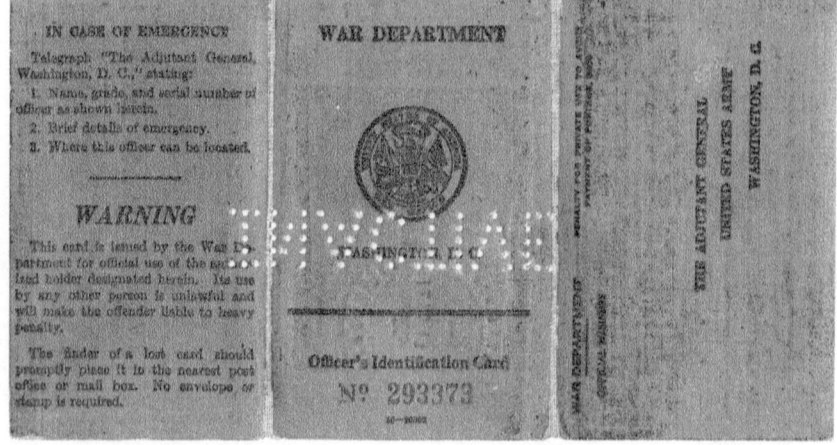

Top: John D. Goodin was issued an officer's identification card on November 17, 1942. *Bottom:* John D. Goodin officer's identification card cover.

```
    Have had comparatively little sleep this past couple of
nights, due to poor railway accommodations and one Miss
Margaret Carter. We went to the VMI-VPI football game in
Roanoke yesterday and had one swell time there. We rooted
for the winning team, and had heart failure, and all
that silly stuff, as well as peanuts, Cocacolas, popcorn,
candy bars, and even flowers for her delicate shoulder. As
I say we had one swell time, but there seems to be a sort
of heaviness today in some portions of my body -- lead
I believe it is sometimes called -- in the seat of ones
trousers!!
```

Two. Dog Biscuits and Dust Devils

So -- 41 years with each other. How could either of you stood it??? I guess you couldn't, if it had been all of the other one. But when you have three others to bother and be aggravated with and worry over, I suppose it takes a little bit of time away from thinking about the other one. Right??? And aren't you lucky to have three such charming brats to answer to your name?? Ah me -- it must be a wonderful feeling to look back over the years, and say -- well, now if I'd married soandso, or whatchamaycallit, I wonder how things would have turned out!!

And I can see the little gleam in your eyes as you both of you (I don't imagine either of you will admit it) are sorta well pleased with the things as they are. And you wouldn't change more than 99 and 44/100% of your married life, now would you?? And stubborn?? -- hasn't it been fun to try and read the next move?? Beats me -- I can't fathom either one of you yet, and I've lived almost 26 years with the two of you!! Wish I could be home for this party of yours, but guess I'll just think about it, and maybe if I get the chance I'll call you!!

Received the package also. Also a wonderful package from the Woodwards -- the most delicious cookies you ever tasted and am I eating them??? Wow. Gotta close an get to bed now. Write when you can and see you soon.

John

Postcard dated December 29, 1942 Postmarked Camp Pickett, VA
Mon nite.

Dear Folks,

Arrived O.K. - tho had to stand up to Roanoke. Got in Lynchburg, ate supper with Bertha (she had sent me a bracelet for Xmas) and caught a special bus (had to stand up) into Blackstone & got here at 11:30.

If you find my cap - send it up along with my address book which is in with my cards, also the typed list of names & addresses.

Santa Claus stopped here: shaving materials, 2 identification bracelets, a duffle kit, a book, and <u>23</u> Christmas cards & letter P. S. <u>some bills</u>!! also sent me Eloise's picture. Saw Jean in Bristol - another Santa Claus. Had a swell time coming up. By the way - can't deny that I had the <u>bestest</u> Christmas ever while at home. Will write you all more later!!

Love, Johnny

Appalachia to Dessau

Once again, in mid–January, the move to Indiantown Gap, Pennsylvania, was swift and unexpected.

```
Undated - Sometime between January and March 1943
[Indiantown Gap, PA]
```

Dear Folks,

I guess you think I'm forgetting everything in not writing to you - but I'm finding out once again what a pain and patience tests the army can be at times.

It still is cold here - about 10-20 above with occasional splurges each way. The Army certainly has given me a beautiful experience education. I've now seen sand and "nothing" as far as the eye can see - and, as well - last Sunday, for the first time in my life, I saw a large river completely frozen as far as the eye could see - a beautiful sight glistening in meager sunlight and to me almost unreal in its beauty. I still think I've been a fortunate soul - for I've seen so many of God's wonders of nature that certainly not everyone has seen.

Atlantic, Pacific, Great Lakes, Gulf of Mexico, Grand Canyon, deserts, frozen North, and my prospects for future sights are practically unlimited - unless those birds quit before we get a chance to "get over." Guess maybe I'm getting a little more anxious each day to be moving anywhere, but here.

Well, we certainly do admire our Commander-in-Chief these days. He certainly is doing more than any other President before him, excepting of course, Washington, who was Commander-in-Chief before he became President. Frankly, I'd rather see him put these stinkers in the Army, tho, or hang them to a scaffold as high as Haman, than getting ready for invasion. We're not over- confident, but we are GRIM and determined. And when we get back - there'll be some changes.

Mommy dear - did you deliver that picture??

I heard last night that Art "unexpectedly" married some girl from Norfolk. No confirmation as yet. I wouldn't be surprised, but neither do I believe it.

For your benefit, I am now located about 30 miles from Harrisburg, and 12 miles from Lebanon. The country here is very similar to E. Tenn. Except for the bitter cold winds that drive and blow. We took a hike the other day - up one of the mountains, and cracked rib or no - I was the first one in my company up the mountain. If I'd had Charley Brown, a dog, and a rifle, and didn't have 300 soldiers, I would have sworn I was on one of our hills.

People, of course, are quite different than our own.

Two. Dog Biscuits and Dust Devils

They recognize their lack, tho, and also our problems. I haven't been out much - tied down fairly close, but the few I have met are pretty nice. Confidentially, I've found a nice little kid who cooks wonderfully and has <u>plenty</u> of sweet milk. ½ Pa. Dutch, and ½ Austrian - plus a little bit of Italian. I think - don't know. Anyhow she breaks the monotony of life, and is something to look forward to. P. S. The Mama + <u>2</u> kid sisters are <u>excellent</u> chaperones.

Incidentally - FOR THE LAST TIME - I'LL MARRY WHO I PLEASE, <u>WHEN</u>, PLEASE, AND <u>WHAT</u> I PLEASE. Also - people who live in glass houses shouldn't throw rocks - more specifically - but I hardly think I <u>need</u> to be. Some people should know that the quickest way to get a Goodin to <u>do</u> something is tell them not to, or they can't, and VICE VERSA, as well. So - relax on my love life - will you??

I've been made assistant Defense Counsel - some of my "friends" (grrrrrrrr) had my better interests at heart I suppose. A title means darned little.

Received glasses subscription in beautiful time.

Mom - heard from Rosa Charlton - and have answered her. She tho't I was still at Pickett, and wanted me to come up. By the way, call Mrs. Hatton and get me Anne Adams address - right now - while you are thinking about it. I'm practically sure she lives somewhere closely.

Well - I'm gonna close for tonight. Write when you can, come up when you can.

       Love, Johnny

During the two-month gap in the exchange of letters between January and March 1943, Goodin appears to be doing some sight-seeing and visiting friends as he is sending home postcards to his family. He mentions that his leave has not come through, and he hopes to get home before they send him overseas.

March 14, 1943
Postcard Marked Lynchburg, VA

To: Mr. & Mrs. T. E. Goodin, Sr. Hill

Well - sugar-puss is as sweet as ever and just as independent. May be crazy - but I'm getting to see her for 6 hours!! Slept at Bertha's last nite - what a palace. She sends her love to you. Mary does, too!!
      John

March 20, 1943
Postcard Marked Philadelphia, PA

Think Dad brought me here [Betsy Ross House] about 16

```
yrs ago - but it seems a long time. Meeting a buddy here
tonite.
                    Love, as ever, Johnny
```

Letters apparently crossed in the mail as Goodin's dad wrote on Tuesday, March 22, that they were expecting him on Saturday night (March 20). Goodin, in a letter dated "Saturday Night" tells his parents that no one is getting leave, and no one knows what is going on. The letter is posted from Indiantown Gap, Pennsylvania, and was posted four days after it was written.

Training intensified with even colder temperatures and deep snow. "New infiltration courses necessitated crawling through an area deep in mud and barbed wire, sown with small charges of dynamite, and covered with machine-gun fire, was required of each officer and enlisted man."[15] The twenty-five-mile road marches, slogging through the frigid temperatures and snow, while carrying full equipment that weighed 45 pounds, was a critical exercise for building stamina and endurance. Tank crews slogged over the "pine-clad slopes" learning the tactics and techniques of indirect fire.[16] The conditions and training in Indiantown Gap would prove invaluable to the 3rd Armored as preparation for the brutal winter they would face in the Ardennes.

```
Envelope dated March 24 1943
Indiantown Gap, PA
Saturday Night [Probably March 20]

Dear Folks:
  This will be a telephone call which I would probably
reverse, so actually you are saving money. It will also
keep me from getting completely out of practice in
dictating letters. (Rom's sister took the letter down &
wrote it out for me!) Such a golden opportunity has not
presented itself since I left civilian life.
  First of all, I might explain that I am at R. P.
Legnini's home, where I have been since about 6:30
tonight. I have been dined at all the sweet milk I could
drink and with as lovely company as one could ever hope
to have. They have a baby grand piano, which, needless to
say, I have had a grand time playing on and driving
the neighbors crazy. Yolanda has been playing with me,
and with about two more rehearsals we will be read to
take the air. (Secretary's notes -- to be interpreted
in any suitable way!) "Rom" is expected in tonight or
tomorrow, and for me, it will be a happy reunion, since
I haven't seen him since I was on the desert. I am also
```

Two. Dog Biscuits and Dust Devils

looking forward to the prospect of a good Italian dinner tomorrow.

Tonight I called Art Porter, with whom I stayed in W & L [Washington and Lee University]. He gave me some late dope on different ones of the boys back there. Quite a few of my friends have been lost in action, and some of the rest of them have distinguished themselves on the battlefield. Nice talking to him, of course.

My leave has not come through as yet, but I am still hoping to get home once again before taking off overseas (or wherever the H--- we are going!)

More

My sister hasn't written me this week, but I got an "elegant" box of candy from her which has been enjoyed extremely much. I was a little selfish with it, but the company officers got a good share of it. Anything you could do to promote the continuance of these shipments will be greatly appreciated. (I do realize that there is a war and sugar rationing on.) Please call up my big brother and tell him I would appreciate a card from him, telling me what happened to the knife I was supposed to get from him some time ago. P.S. -- he knows all about this, and should have some dope by now.

I wrote to J. R. and explained to him about the income tax and expenses. Please keep me posted as to his condition and progress. If there is anything I can do along any lines, please tell me and I'll do my best.

I have gotten over my cold, feeling wonderful -- even have my platoon on the ball. As usual I refuse to worry about anything and still take off on weekends as I have been. If for any reason you want to call me,

-- And more -

I can be reached any night after 8:30, with the possible exception of Saturday and Sunday nights.

I sent Mother a small package today; if you do not receive it within the next week or so, let me know and I will check up on it and see what has happened to it. Have been spending money foolishly again on records, but at least I will have something when I come back, to enjoy. Please write when you have a chance and let me hear all the local gossip (and I understand there is plenty).

Yours as always, Johnny

Another two-month gap in correspondence between March and May could be explained by the intense training schedule and ongoing testing. By this point, the men had been exposed to every element and

Appalachia to Dessau

tactical combat situation including live fire, booby traps, land mines, explosives, aerial bombardment, tank traps, flame-throwers, dynamite and grenades. Every skill was tested until mastery was accomplished. Firing qualification, tank battalion tests, armored infantry tests, reconnaissance, combined arms problems, and physical fitness tests were all conducted during the month of May. Physical fitness tests required the officers and men to complete "33 push ups, a 300 yard dash, and a five mile hike with full equipment, to be completed in 60 minutes. Obstacle courses included scaling walls, rope climbs and tunnels."[17]

Goodin mentions that it seems like it has been longer since he received a letter. He loves his mother's crazy, lengthy letters, and apparently reads them to everyone, as he says they were "received well by all."

```
May 28th 1943
Indiantown Gap, PA
```

Well, it was good to hear a little bit of news from home -- it seems longer than it really is come to think of it -- but when you put in from daylight to dark (and I ain't kid[d]ing one bit -- from 5:30 till 8:30 with 20 to 30 minutes off to eat in), it doesn't take long for the days and then the weeks to go rolling by.

Letter and contents from "me Mudder" well received by all - particularly one JDG. Gossip was a bit light (gets that way when Sis isn't around I suppose), but then nothing new for "Me Mudder." I had some filfthy [sic] jokes and stuff and things I was going to send you, but I guess you are worried enough about my "morals" without endangering myself more.

Except for the details (I actually promised no news of this to anyone -- so it is strictly a military secret) I will tell you that you came awfully close to an unwanted, daughter-in-law a couple of weeks back -- where the idea came from I don't know, but even diamonds (and there were some beautiful ones), money, everything didn't interest me somehow or other -- not counting the baby grand piano. That's the trouble of being too nice though -- guess maybe I wouldn't make a bad $10,000 catch!! (Note to Pop - don't worry - there wasn't any trouble - thank Heaven!!)

I don't know any news -- don't even know when I'll get home, if I do. Things are so sloppy, screwed up, and generally messed up around here that no one knows anything. The men are not getting furloughs when they have qualified all their guns (7 days). I'd have to get married to get a leave of any length, and I don't know whether it would be worth it or not. All my prospects somehow don't suit

Two. Dog Biscuits and Dust Devils

me when I think of the lifelong proposition involved with it. But then, I may be different, or maybe over cautious!!

Sorry that I don't get to write more often -- I often have good intentions, but they usually end up with me in bed sound asleep. And don't think I don't sleep when I get the chance at it!! Whoof!!!!!!! I could sleep about a week now, and not miss too much of it anyhow.

Write when you get a chance to and if you don't -- why I'll call. If you want to call me, you can call "Indiantown 9604", and if you don't get me on a person-to-person call, it won't cost you anything.

Take care of yourselves, and don't work too hard.

                Love to all, as always JDG

P. S. Got Pop's letter this a.m. Thanks for everything - including the clipping!!

Thursday, 24 June 1943
Indiantown Gap, PA

On July 16, 1943, Headquarters issued the Third Armored Division a Packing guide of Individual Equipment to be carried on the individual (28 items), carried in a field bag (21 items), carried in "A" bag [general purpose bag] (20 items), and carried in "B" bag (9 items).

On the list to be carried on the individual were the following: Belt, drawers—cotton shorts, handkerchief—cotton white, helmet, steel, M-1, complete with helmet liner, band head and band neck, necktie—cotton, mohair, khaki, Shirt—wool, socks—cotton, tan, undershirt—summer—cotton, blanket—wool, necklace—Identification tag, with extension, canteen—M1910, Cup—M1910, Mask—gas, pins—tent, pole—tent, pouch—first aid, packet, M1941, tags—identification, tent—shelter half with rope, trousers—wool, shoes—service, bag—field, belt—rifle, carbine, pistol, individual weapon, cover—canteen, suspenders—belt (if issued), leggings—pair, pocket magazine (if armed with carbine), pocket magazine (if armed with pistol).

The field bag and general-purpose bags contained toiletries and extra clothing including suits, caps, gloves and an overcoat.

Determined to see John before he was shipped overseas, his parents paid him a visit in Indiantown Gap. John expresses his pleasure at seeing his parents. The Goodins talk about their dogs throughout their letters. In this letter, John says he has named his dog "Stinky." Stinky will become a faithful companion to John and serve right along with him through thick and thin.

Even though the official letter above regarding packing equipment

Appalachia to Dessau

HEADQUARTERS THIRD ARMORED DIVISION
Office of the Division Commander   R:ECO/jms

A. P. O. #253,
Indiantown Gap Mil. Res., Pa.,
16 July 1943.

PACKING GUIDE OF INDIVIDUAL EQUIPMENT.

CARRIED ON INDIVIDUAL

ITEM	QUANTITY	ITEM	QUANTITY
Belt, web waist, M1937	1	Pins, tent, (Inside shelter half)	5
Drawers, cotton shorts	1	Pole, tent, (Inside shelter half)	1
Handkerchief, cotton white	1	Pouch, first aid, packet, M1941	1
Helmet, steel, M-1, complete with helmet liner, band head and band neck.	1	Tags, Identification	2
		Tent, shelter half (with rope)	1
Necktie, cotton, mohair, khaki	1	Trousers, wool, OD	1
Shirt, wool, OD*	1	Shoes, service	1
Socks, cotton, tan	1	Bag, field	1
Undershirt, summer, cotton	1	Belt, (rifle, carbine, pistol)	1
Blanket, wool, OD (rolled in shelter half)	2	Individual weapon	1
		Cover, canteen	1
		Suspenders, belt (if issued)	1
Necklace, Identification Tag, with extension	1	Leggings (pair)	1
Canteen, M1910	1	Pocket Magazine (if armed with carbine)	3
Cup, M1910	1	Pocket Magazine (if armed with pistol)	1
Mask, gas	1		

CARRIED IN FIELD BAG

ITEM	QUANTITY	ITEM	QUANTITY
Drawers, cotton, shorts	2	Soap, shaving	1
Handkerchief, cotton, white	1	Razor, safety	1
Socks, cotton, tan	2	Blades, razor	5
Undershirts, summer cotton	2	Brush, tooth	1
Socks, wool, light	1	Powder, tooth	1
Can, meat	1	Soap	1
Fork, M1926	1	Comb	1
Knife, M1926	1	Towel, bath	1
Spoon, M1926	1	Towel, huck	1
Brush, shaving	1	Suit, 1 piece, Herringbone Twill	1
Raincoat, dismounted	1		

CARRIED IN "A" BAG

ITEM	QUANTITY	ITEM	QUANTITY
Cap, garrison, cotton, khaki	1	Undershirt, wool	2
Cap, garrison, OD	1	Gloves, heavy leather	1
Drawers, woolen	2	Shoes, service	1
Gloves, wool, OD, leather palm	1	Towel, huck	1
Handkerchiefs, cotton, white	2	Leggins, canvas dismounted	1
Jacket, field, OD	1	Trousers, cotton khaki*	1
Necktie, cotton, mohair, khaki	1	Trousers, wool, OD	1
Shirt, cotton khaki*	1	Cap, herringbone twill	1
Shirt, wool, OD	1	Overcoat, wool, rolled collar or Mackinaw	1
Socks, wool, light	2		
Mattress, cover	1		

* - If khaki uniform is worn when leaving this post the woolen uniform will be placed in the "A" Barrack Bag.

Above: This packing guide of individual equipment to be carried on the individual was issued on July 16, 1943, in Indiantown Gap, Pennsylvania. This document is typed into the manuscript. *Opposite:* Packing guide page two.

Two. Dog Biscuits and Dust Devils

```
                        CARRIED IN "B" BAG
ITEM                    QUANTITY    ITEM                             QUANTITY
Cap, wool knit, M1941      1        Gloves, horsehide, riding, lined
Coat, wool, serge, OD      1          (if issued)                       1
Cap, winter                1        Trousers, combat (If issued)        1
Suit, 1 pc. herringbone twill  1    Coat, combat (If issued)            1
Gloves, horsehide, riding           Helmet, combat (If issued)          1
  unlined (If issued)      1

            By command of Brigadier General HICKEY:

                                            RAYMOND A KNOX,
                                            Captain, A. G. D.,
                                            Asst. Adjutant General

DISTRIBUTION "A"
     plus 25 copies to G-4
```

is issued on July 16, it is obvious that Goodin has no idea they are about to be shipped out as he asks when his sister will visit, and also mentions visiting other friends.

```
July 27, 1943 (Visit from parents) Monday night
Indiantown Gap, PA
```

Dear Folks,

Well, sure was fun seeing you all again -- nothing like it frankly, and having you here at the same time Andy came up was like having cake and then find ice cream with it. I forgot to tell you that he said to tell you that he sure appreciated being with you and everything -- seemed he was just a bit flustered when he started to leave you all.

As for Ellene, want her to let me know when she is coming up, and what she is going to do, and when and all.

Got back home o.k. last night - rained some more, but it cooled things off and made it very enjoyable. No one was around much, and they all started to drift in about the same time that I did. All of them felt much better having had a letdown for the weekend that sorta relaxed them for a while. I personally will take my own letdown that I had -- it was much more fun, and I didn't have any hangover or anything this morning. Have named my pooch "Stinky" -- not a very romanitc [sic] name and not a courageous one -- but I'd rather he had a name like that -- then no one will expect too much of him, and if he isn't housebroken -- then no one will kick him around till he learns better.

Appalachia to Dessau

    The breezes have definitely cooled off, and I'll have a good time for sometime to come yet. If I can just see the people I want to see, everything will be o.k. -- the only thing being getting off to see them. Lots of fun.
    If Miss Carter wants to come up - bring her on up - I'd rather she had someone with her to sorta look after her - not that I don't know that she can take care of herself - but it's just that I'd feel better about her.

                  Gotta close and get some more things done.
                    Love, as always - and more than you think.
                    Johnny

August 23rd 1943
War Department Post Card Notice of Change of Address
APO 253 New York, NY

Only one month after the visit with his parents, on August 25, 1943, Goodin was issued a 58-person passenger list for train No. 7, Car #6, on which Goodin was listed first as the commander.

    The much-anticipated day of departure finally arrived for the 3rd Armored Division, 32nd Armored Regiment on August 26–27, 1943, when they headed to Camp Kilmer, New Jersey.[18]

Chapter Three

England "Somewhere"

September 15, 1943–December 30, 1943

Upon arrival at Camp Kilmer, New Jersey, on August 26–27, the next eight days were spent at this processing center. Troops were given physicals, injections, briefed on censorship and security, and shown the mandatory battle indoctrination films. On September 4, they moved out by train to New York Harbor for overseas embarkation. As the Capetown Castle moved away from the American shoreline on September 5, Goodin and members of the 3rd Armored Division watched as the Statue of Liberty slowly faded from sight.[1] Suddenly, the reality of being a soldier during wartime, leaving family, friends, and country with the possibility of never returning, loomed starkly.

Goodin wrote a letter to his parents on this same day but did not mention his departure.

> I am quite happy, and even thrilled. And by the way, Pop, Happy Birthday to you. Wish I could greet you from here as I did 5 years ago. But know you understand. And don't bawl out the poor censor if sometime I cause him to cut some of my letter - he's got a very important job, and any deletions cannot be charged to him, but from us who write.
> Must tell you about the wonderful dinner I had - I can't elaborate as much as is deserved, but I had clams on 1/2 shell, and then the most luscious sirloin steak with French Fried Potatoes & shoe-string onions - a delicacy I haven't enjoyed before. Anyhow with iced tea & dessert - well right then $4.00 seemed a small amount.
> Must close for now. Hello & love & stuff to all. You will hear from us!!
>
> Johnny

On September 8, the 3rd Armored learned that Italy had unconditionally surrendered, and while this was cause for celebration, they

Appalachia to Dessau

John D. Goodin poses outside the gates still stateside.

understood all too well that Hitler and the Nazis were still to be defeated.[2] Goodin commented about this news in a letter written September 9, aboard ship, and posted after landing. Upon arrival in Europe, Goodin is unable to disclose his location.

```
SEP 17 1943
Postmarked U.S. Army Postal Service
A.P.O. 507
From: John D. Goodin
Co. "B", 32 A. R. A. P. O. 253
c/o Postmaster, N.Y.C. NY "Somewhere"

9 Sept., 1943.

Dear Folks,
    (I love you, Stanley loves you - what a hell of a way
to start a letter, but with two unofficial advisers &
quasi-censors, it is a start.)
    Left last week, excellent ship, nice accommodations,
excellent food and fair weather - surprisingly enough.
Everything was fine till one morning Stinky got sick &
lost his breakfast, ate no supper, & we have been doing
well since. I got involved in a friendly game of chance,
it became unfriendly, I got hold of Stinky, & immediately
my luck turned for the better.
    Hoping by now you have received my last communications
```

Three. England "Somewhere"

tho frankly I don't remember when it was written. Days have ceased to have meaning. We do hear the news flashes and it was really sweet to hear about Italy. We shall finish up the other 2 so & so's shortly.

By the way, saw a kid named Walker (who lives on Maple St in J.C. [Johnson City] - a block from Bill's) just before I left. What a small world. And one of the Tapp boys that used to be in my S. S. [Sunday School] class is on board, too. I think I told you of seeing Mr. Meyer. I probably didn't tell you I saw G. Vanta's sister for a couple of hours - too, but this was sometime before I left.

Precious little I can tell you, as there is little I know, and nothing of importance has happened. I've read a couple of books, caught up on my sleep, met a couple of VMI [Virginia Military Institute] boys (one from Richmond), renewed a W & L [Washington and Lee University] acquaintance, & generally enjoyed myself. We eat twice a day - and I've never been fed quite so much in two meals ever. Really works out nice. Our regular diet is varied but little, and except for milk, I'm still getting all the tea I want.

The Red Cross has been very, very nice to us, and it's almost unbelievable what they've done. In fact, when I get back, one of them has promised me my "3-phases" of happiness in reverse and is she cute!!

For Sis's information Bullenger was broke when he came on board but I lent him $5 & he now has more than I!! A shrewd man no doubt.

I'm wondering if our ex-girl has woke up yet. The last couple of letters I had, she apparently hadn't, so I suggest to my sister that she tell her sometime that I definitely have a mind of my own - and when it comes to females - regardless of my own vices, they either don't have them, give them up - or I move on to greener pastures.

And as long as she has known about that particular hate of mine [smoking], and thinks still she can get by - well, maybe the shark won't bend her - but it _is_ too late for her to do anything about it. The set-up was perfect - but I'm still the one who has to live with me.

Well, didn't get to celebrate Pop's birthday, but
sometime tomorrow I'll drink a ginger ale, or ginger beer (no worry - there ain't no alcoholics on board) to it. "We're" getting old, ain't we?? I only hope by the time I'm around sixty, I've got more than three brats to show - but I'll settle for the 4 grandchildren if there are 3 _boys_ & _1_ gal!!

Appalachia to Dessau

If you're doing any worrying, you might as well quit. I've never felt quite so safe in my life. And my somewhat involuntary prayers go up to Him in thanks for the marvelous protection we have, as well as the other million things a day. And even if He does see fit - I can hardly complain as it's not everyone who is blessed as I have been in so many things. Particularly my family.

       Must be closing.
       Hello to everybody & my love to you all.
       Johnny

For eleven days a convoy of two dozen ships traversed the Atlantic. Arriving September 15, in Liverpool, Goodin and his comrades got their first glimpse of the war-scarred landscape of England, greeted by barrage balloons and Spitfires. Soldiers were billeted and taken by trolley to their assigned locations, some in English villages, some to Division Headquarters in Bruton, Somerset, others to various locations in the English countryside. The 32nd was assigned to the southwest at Codford in Wiltshire, England.[3]

WAR AND NAVY DEPARTMENTS V-MAIL SERVICE
New York NY
23 SEPT 1943

Dear Mom,

Have a little time so will dash you a line. First of all, your letters which I brought with me are still a source of pleasure, which I not only enjoyed coming over, but since as well. I wish you were along with me - you would enjoy seeing the cathedrals, the homes, the people - even tho they don't love the Irish but I'll be back before long to tell you, and sit by an open fire with a quart of Jersey milk in one hand and just someone's "container" in the other, and blab away. I think I made a mistake in Sis's letter - packages may be sent until <u>October 15th</u> without special request. Packages are not to exceed fifteen inches long and thirty-six inches around. I asked her to send me a couple of fountain pens and a cheap watch. I've gotten some educational letters since I've been here and - well, I've not found any one who can reach the top shelf of your cabinets as yet.

And I still think you and Jean might get along. Hello and love to all. How is my Jeanie? Write when you can.

       <u>NO HOOFS AND ALL HORNS</u>

Three. England "Somewhere"

John D. Goodin with a tank in England, 1943.

```
Envelope WAR & NAVY DEPARTMENTS OCT 4 1943
Vmail dated 26 Sept., 1943
```
Dear Folks,

  Wish you would look in the trunk I sent home and see if there is a cotton khaki shirt therein underneath the flap of the left breast pocket you should find a small gold cross. If you find it notify me immediately (by mail) as I evidently mixed up my shirts somewhere and misplaced it. Am liking it more and more everyday over here. Quite a few of the boys are buying bicycles over here and I may do the same after next pay-day.

  Don't worry about us as we will get along! Would like to hear from you - as I haven't yet. Better get hold of some V-Mail or Air mail. With all my love as always,

               Johnny

Top: John Goodin on maneuvers in England, 1943. *Bottom:* Walter H. Coons and Meyer L. Levy, comrades of Goodin, take a meal break while on maneuvers in England.

Three. England "Somewhere"

Goodin's tank driver Roy L. Pearson and his comrades Ben Feldman and Herman A. Pearson grab a bite to eat while on maneuvers in England. The supply truck is camouflaged in the trees in the background.

Within three weeks of arriving in England, units were issued equipment and tanks. According to a description provided in the book "Spearhead in the West," the landscape was quaint and beautiful with "thatched cottages, abbeys and ancient castles," which soldiers would be allowed to visit in six weeks when they received a pass.[4] Once settled, training began in earnest. Familiarizing themselves with the landscape on marches and obstacle courses, the troops learned the advantages and disadvantages of the terrain. They soon became familiar with English weather, blackouts, ack-ack, air raids, and the ever-present Spitfires.[5]

Exercises in range firing, and field and arms problems, were common throughout November, with no regard for the chilling rain or frosts.[6]

```
OCT 10 1943
New York, N. Y.
WAR & NAVY DEPARTMENTS V-MAIL SERVICE
Dear Mom,
   Have a little time off this beautiful Sunday afternoon
and will try and get you one of the many letters that
```

Appalachia to Dessau

After intense training, soldiers enjoy some much-needed downtime and camaraderie. Goodin labeled the back of the photo without indicating directionality: Wilburn A. Stuart, David (Pencil) Shoopla, Al "Snuffy" Smith, Zack Crisp, Theron Tomasello, George W. Dixon, Gene Fisz, George M. Krisle, Jr., Chester Mathew, Larry S. "1/2" Kafrewaz, Robert L. Melton Esq., John A. Ford, Ron P. Legnini, George B. Shields, Park C. Keirick, Stephen Swantko, Frederick J. Wade, Jr., Shep Anderson. Goodin is pictured on the left, second row back, writing a letter.

> I try to write and never quite get around to. To begin with, last night I got on my little bike and pedalled [sic] down the road to see what kind of condition I'm in, and found that I'm not quite so good as I used to be. However, I'm not very sore today, which is some consolation. This afternoon later I'm going to try and make it down to see my Tenn. Gal friend and spend the evening with her. Tomorrow I go on leave for a few hours and have to have more little treasures to store away in my memories to tell you about once I get back home. I can see you chuckling over me about to ride some ten or fifteen miles to see a girl on a bike when you used to have trouble getting me to ride into town on my bike at home. Well, conditions are some different at this place, and that is

Three. England "Somewhere"

the only way I shall be able to get there without walking and well***&"()*!!! I've done enough of that since I've been in the Army to last me for quite some time. I still haven't heard from you to know whether you know where I'm at now or not. I should have heard at least that you received my cable, but guess that eventually I will...I still enjoy myself thoroughly around here, with the exception of the weather, and I usually freeze real early in the morning. Another thing that is affecting us all, is the water or the damp weather or something...really is hard on the kidneys, and frequent rising in the wee wee hours of the morning is the general rule. With the latrines some distances away, we have resorted to the use of buckets that are very similar to the ones that my sister's boyfriends used to be serenaded with. And at the time of my return, I will tell you of an incident in which a young lady and myself were treated to a serenade ..and there was nothing to camouflage the racket with. Fortunately, she is a very understanding soul, and nothing was said about it. But I can at least now sympathize fully with my poor sister in her younger days.

What a life. Since coming over here, I think I have reached a greater appreciation of the life we led and the happiness and little things than I ever had at home, and many things that were without humor then, are bubbling over with humor now, and I think of your little word that you picked up in South Carolina frequently-- "Sneak!!" and wish that sometimes we could have done more "sneaking" than we did..but then on the other hand any more and father dear might have taken drastic action against his "children"....

I have written to Uncle Pyott, but due to censorship measures I couldn't elaborate on the things that I know he would enjoy quite like I'd like to, so will store them up, too until we get back. If anyone in the world could appreciate the English people I think you two could. Only last night we ran into a group of them, of the Air Force, and despite the Irish situation over here, they were singing Irish songs, English songs, and we countered with our own American songs. Sis would enjoy their version of "Coming Around the Mountains"--They add a western "Ki yi tippe Ki Yi Yo" all of their own, which we never would quite associate with that hill billy song. Also, their version of Dina being in the kitchen - tacked on to the end of "I've Been Working on the Railroad" is slightly suggestive if not plainly put of a study of the finer things of life. And speaking of the finer things of life, the moon over here the last couple of nights has been

Appalachia to Dessau

very nice, but as some one has said, it is only one half as good as a North Carolina moon and one tenth as romantic as some other moons we have seen.

Our whiskey is rationed over here, and being the sot I am, I gave away my ration, and will try and stick to my cider...it is pretty good, but can't compare to the twenty cents a gall [sic] stuff that we used to buy on top of the mountain coming back from North Carolina. Some of it is good, but some of it has a taste very similar to vinegar.

Well, I'm almost out of space here, so will have to be signing off for this time. Hope that you now have a magnifying glass to read these things with. With all my love, and everything that goes with it.

                  As always, Your Johnny

Many of the soldiers suffered motion sickness on the voyage from America to England, as Goodin describes in this letter to his mother.

Vmail 18 Oct., 1943 Somewhere in England

Dear Mom,

Thank Heavens you write big as your V-Mail came through perfectly and wondrously legible, which is more than I can frequently say of mine own. No, my Mother Mary, no gangplankitis or jitters, no storm, no lightning, no thunder, no excitement. I got sick the 3rd day out, lost only breakfast, and felt good the rest of the way. Nope, no kodak or films, but indelible prints on my mind. Censorship on films is stronger than that on mail. Besides, with a few exceptions, you would only get pictures which you could get at home.

And my dear old one and only, there's nothing over here that looks as sweet and pretty as Jean B., nothing so genuine and motherly as that Jersey Cow that I'll never stop grieving over, no kids as sweet and mean as Jean Goodin, or as loving as our little Glenna! War has had a terrible effect, but even in peacetime - there still wouldn't have been any of them. Me with Queen's daughters? Ha. My Juliet was a kid who didn't know for sure where her next meal was coming from, yet knew Shakespeare, more about London than Churchill, and above all, had a big picture of what a country boy and his first visit to town would like to see and do. We see all the cathedrals, the State Houses, the Parliament, Waterloo Bridge and so on in daylight. At night, we ate well, and went into out of the way places where lights were low, where soft music was playing, when other kids away from home were forgetting

Three. England "Somewhere"

loneliness, or the buddy who didn't come back from a raid, or the gal back home who had just married a 4-F, or the quarts of sweet milk and peach ice cream. Stinky whined once in a while and howled at the full moon and was contented that no bombers flew over. At 3 & 4 in the morning, even tea and toast, and what not, calmly discussing her problems, wishing I could help her and inwardly cursing those who brought the catastrophe that humanity in war areas know so well. And relieved that my own were safe and secure, even tho some of the pleasures and privileges of life are gone for a while. Somehow, blissfully unaware of life as such for one of the longest periods of my life, as I drank deeply of the finer and realer things of life - architecture, history, art, music, literature, while experiencing the actual drama of life in love, companionship, understanding, sorrow, pathos, and even eating. And still not sure that Mother Mary wasn't sneaking around behind me nudging and egging me on!! - Because she, as no other, could know everything, and maybe not with a blessing or approval in toto, but still could understand and ponder them in her heart. And even tho our second meeting will probably be a terrific disappointment, I'm still looking forward to it, and those devilish blue eyes, those feet twinkling faster than my eye could follow, tho my ears did, and a general makeup that my own Mom might have had when she was in her twenties.

And the muse from Tennessee - we keep each other out of trouble. the nite before I left for London she kissed me and said "Just to keep you out of serious trouble while you're gone." I was sort amazed, and yet, I can't say it didn't work. I was reminded of the card I got from you the time I kissed Ruth L. goodbye at the station and Pappy nearly exploded, and I could see you sniggering behind his back, and I knew despite our little human faults, God had chosen me to have the best parents a kid could have, and I felt kinda glowish because I felt they know and knew I felt that way, and it <u>didn't take</u> <u>a war</u> to show me as it has so many kids.

And now, my dear old Witch of Endor, I'll grab my serenading can, bury myself in the covers, and drift off to sleep until Stinky wakes me up, either for a serenade, or for breakfast.

I'll be waiting for those volumes, and <u>send</u> them air mail if there's not enough room on V-Sheets. "Hoofs & one bent horn."

Appalachia to Dessau

VMail
October 23, 1943

Dear Dad,

   I got a letter from Marg today and she said that Joe Summers had been killed in a plane crash. Not having anymore particulars than that, I did write to Mr. and Mrs. Summers, and tried to tell them how I felt. Doubt if I could have succeeded very well, but anyhow I did. Wish you would find out some more and let me know. Although I saw very little of him in the last few years, he was still one of my best buddies as a kid, and my liking of him never really diminished much during the years. He is the first close friend I have lost in this mess.

   I am going to get a check cashed tomorrow or sometime soon, so watch for it at the bank. I finally convinced them that this is an emergency, and got it through. So if you haven't sent that requested second money order, skip it, as I won't need it, I don't think.

   Got a letter from Paul Duncan and he thinks that maybe he will be over here soon somewhere or other. If he does, sure hope that I'll get to see him...that would be an awful get together...I might even have a couple of glasses of cider.

   My trip to London was very successful, and I hope I can tell you all about it some day. Hardly think it would do to do so now, and besides, if I tell you everything now you won't have anything to listen to when I get back home again.

   Marg says she has quit smoking really this time, and I could believe her, but I won't. She told me I did lots of things that maybe she didn't approve of...but damn her, she at least knows practically my every move..or did up until I left. Since then, it wouldn't do for her to know very much, although I feel very much the same, and in fact a little better.

   Got my first *Erwin Record* today. Sept 2. Really enjoyed it thoroughly. Gotta close.

                      With all my love to all of you.
                        Johnny

Vmail
1 Nov. 1943

Dear Folks,

   Got Dad's letter this afternoon and it sure seems funny to hear of snow back there, when it is still warm here, and fruit is still on the trees and while it is not warm

Three. England "Somewhere"

enough to run around in shirtsleeves, well, it still beats snow again, I suppose. Wish I were there to enjoy some of that snow you are having, at any rate, I am still getting along again. Went to London again this week and while I didn't have near as good a time as I did the last time, well I had a good time, went by myself and ran into couple of Tennessee boys and a couple of captains from my own outfit. We had a good time running around, found a gold bracelet I liked - it was old and antiquish [sic] looking, but when I found out the price I realized there was a war on. They only wanted about fifteen pounds for it and a pound is four dollars in our money which is twice as much as I'm getting a month these days, anyhow, we did have fun looking around and found that most anything that you can't get in the U.S. can be gotten for a price over here. There were even Westclox Clocks for sale and Elgins and what nots. Also a few radios and odds and ends that people told us we wouldn't be able to buy when we got over here. What they meant was that we wouldn't pay the price for them, I suppose, for they sure are high.

George Pierce says hello for you all. By the way, once again, you can write all you want to airmail and I'll get it rather soon. It's not too slow, and usually reaches here in good shape. Once in a while it comes over by boat, but even so, it is O.K., and you have all the space you want to write in. Have gotten some very nice letters lately. Got a long one from W. J. Carter and Co., Jean writes rather often, and a couple of the Penn. [Pennsylvania] girls write regularly, in fact one of them I hear from at least twice a week, as regularly as the week rolls around. Right now, I got to close and leave. I'm going over and see my Tenn. [Tennessee] nurse.

We went to a party last night and had a swell time, and are getting along quite well, thank you. She is keeping me out of trouble.

                    Love to all, JDG

The 3rd Armored were participating in Command Post Exercises in which battle readiness is tested through communication between the commander, staff, and headquarters. Soldiers were being acclimated to accomplish their mission while ignoring the elements, which at this time of year in Salisbury Plains, located in Wiltshire County, in central Southern England, were brutal with "maneuvers over the chill downs, in frost and raw, driving rain."[7] In this letter Goodin describes how he tries to keep warm.

Appalachia to Dessau

Vmail
NOV 15 1943

Dear Mom,

[Pal?] are you on strike again, or is the ink out, or didn't the yellow house pay enough to buy a few air mail stamps? If it didn't I'll try and get hold of some and send them over to you. O.K.? I'm only making a few thousand a month now, so it won't be any trouble.

Seriously, wish that you would drop a few lines, by way of Uncle Sam's airmail some of these days and let me know what you and all the pets (including Pop of course) are doing, and who is doing what and how, and how often, and so forth and so on.

Am not doing a lot of things these days, more or less routine--and trying to stay warm and keep healthy and all that. Believe it or not, I'm taking our old exercises at night and getting back into good condition. Plus the fact that it helps me keep a little warmer after I get to bed. We have a nice place to live in--one other officer and myself have a section of a hut with a heater in it, and we keep it fairly warm and dry in there by means of said heater. I, unfortunately, have to move my bed when it rains, since the huts were rather hastily constructed and I get a slight shower right on my head (remember the summer morning when you dumped a big dishpan full of water on my head while I slept out on the back porch???) when it starts raining. If I'm asleep, I just bury down in the bed, and if I'm awake enough I get up and move my bed out of the line of fire.

It's fun--and we are getting hardened to this darn weather. I'll really appreciate home when I get back. I'm sorta glad in one way you aren't over here, and you'll wonder why--but it is because of the fact that you would literally freeze and couldn't enjoy your trip like I'd want you to. Of course, now if we were in France or Italy, or somewhere like that--that might be different.

Well, guess you know your angel, halo, wings and all, got herself engaged to Charlie Sherrod--which I suppose is well and good. She [Jean] was one swell kid...but I'm used to having the swell ones get away anymore, so I'm not to [sic] disillusioned. I am reminded somewhat of the story you used to tell me in a careful Mother Mary manner about the man who went out in the woods looking for a straight stick, found a fairly good one, thought he'd find a better one, didn't, and then when he came back for that one, someone else had walked off with it. Am beginning to wonder if that will be my fate. I'm really not worried,

Three. England "Somewhere"

though, because I think I'm better off single over here that I would be if I were married..because I see what the others are going through with while I'm having one whale of a good time and not worrying about anything or anybody. Well, maybe my sister gets a little of my worries but she is old enough to take care of herself by now, surely. Right??

As told to you before, I haven't found any English girls that appeal to me so much that I might take off with one of them over here..as yet. They tell me that the Scotch girls are really nice, and of course, my Irish (Hi Grandma) might feel a native strain and a little urging if I met one of them. After all, there [sic] musci [sic] is rather good, isn't it? How is your Irish these days, anyhow?? Keeping yourself under control, or are you raising H--- in general when your righteous indignation about something boils over?? Ah me--to hear some of your choice expressions and spells would be sweet music right now. Like the hasty, angry, turbulent stormy whispers I used to get on occasion, as the night I mentioned mistress in the presence of above mentioned angel.

Well, looks like I'm going to have to close. Stinky is being a good pup, well fed, and even gaining weight over here--the shiftless skonk [sic]--no "poop" though.

      Love and kisses, Johnny

Vmail
November 16, 1943
Dearest Pop,

Got your letter this afternoon with Lloyd's address, and I got one from Paul Duncan and Eliz. also. Think that Paul is over here now and have written to him and also to Lloyd tonight and hope that within the next few days that I will have located the two of them enough to find out where they are and get hold of them. I think that Paul may even be in our outfit though I won't know until I hear from him, which I hope will be darned soon.

Nope, I don't think I overloaded myself on the insurance deal. If I were a civilian, I think you are exactly right, but what I intend doing is building up a surplus while I am in the Army—you might call it a savings account, and if I can't carry it when I convert it into a paid up policy, and still have it. I'll admit that it is stiffer than what I thought it would be, but I'm getting along o.k., and even if I don't get much time off now and then, I have enough to carry me through when I do get off. Once we hit battle, it won't make any difference

Appalachia to Dessau

about the money that I get anyhow, since we won't be able to spend it, and I can even save that up until the end comes.

Then when I have enough to start housekeeping or a family, or whatever the hell happens to me then. O.K.??? In the meantime, all donations are appreciated, and if I get overloaded with money over here, I can always send it back home. I hope.

I'm going out on a few problems now, nothing serious, just continuous training, and hope how soon the training ends and the real things start happening. All the training in the world can't take the place of the real thing, and just hope that things will work out for us when that day comes along. I'm getting my platoon into fair shape and with a few more rough edges knocked out of it, it will be getting along all right. In the meantime I'm trying to build them up from all the angles that I think that they will need. Myself I'm gradually getting back into the condition physically that I need.

There has never been anything the matter with me mentally, unless it was lack of mentality, as my own morale is always fairly good.

Wish I had time to continue a long letter to you, but I have to be leaving in the morning around 6 or so; will close for now.

Appreciate your airmail letter very much, as I not only can read all of it, but believe that when you write one of them you aren't worried about running out at the end of the page.

Tell all the folks hello and that I appreciate the news that I get from them and the kind words and well-wishings that I receive from them. Goodnight for now and will get you a few more words off towards the end of the week. With best of everything and love

    Always, Johnny

Vmail
NOV 19 1943

Dear Mom,

Well, today I have seen what I know you would want me to see, and what you would see if you were over here with me. To begin with I left rather early this morning, and it being cold as (uhuh!!) I almost froze in the Peep, and so we stopped off in some Inn in -------- England, and had a cup of tea, and dinner, before continuing our trip. (Someday I'll tell you how I happened to be making this trip) Anyway, it was a dream. There were old guns, old

Three. England "Somewhere"

candlesticks (no sis, there weren't any cockeyed toothpick holders, or I would have swiped them at least), bed warmers, and everything that an antique collector would go crazy over. As I relaxed comfortably in front of the biggest fireplace I ever saw--I got in and stood in the darned thing for a few minutes, bumped my head on the thing that holds the big kettle coming out, and there was room for at least a dozen more. It was so big, that in the place which they had obviously cut down for modern fires, the fireplace part was as big as any of ours which would include all but the mantel piece itself. That, my dear was a good deal, and I'm not kidding you. Anyway, the gal came dragging in a big glog [log - sic] which in true Southern chivalrous manner I carried the rest of the way in, and put it on the fire, and then I relaxed--so beautifully. There were a couple of seats about half a foot off the floor and you relaxed in them, and drank tea with me, and we chatted about the guns, the quaintness, the hand-carved [sic] fire board (it was naughty in a way--or maybe it was art--anyhow there was a woman on it, with one ---- exposed and the other held gracefully in her hand...she was a nice big girl too--or had been a couple of hundred years ago..the wood was all eaten, it was so old and I could hear you say "Isn't that the prettiest thing you ever saw?"..And you gave the kid your piece of chocalate [sic] (I kept mine and gave him some chewing gum, which he gave to his Mom, since he wasn't old enough to know that it was made to chew) Well, that my dear was a deal I shall not soon forget. In the meantime, the tall hard blonde was telling us about the collections of guns that she had gotten along with her husband, and another lady came out who looked like Mrs. Woodwa[r]d, and was fully as gracious, and she helped us out also. In another letter I shall tell you about coming back, as there is more that I want to tell you in this and I won't have room for all of it.

I visited the ruins of Corfe Castle...a fortress which stood for years and years and years against all kind of opposition until 1646 when by order of Parliament (the damned fools) it was destroyed. It had been a stronghold of Kings from around 1200 and earlier until its destruction. There is a lot of interesting history concering [sic] it, and I'm sending you a folder on it sometime soon. In the meantime, hope that you get the postcards that I am going to send to you cost a dime to enter it, and it was well worth it. What nice old gruesome dreary Thad Cox place it must have been in the old days.

Appalachia to Dessau

Still think that I was born ages and ages too late, or too soon--but I'm really enjoying life as it is. There is still so much to see. A young lady in London wants me to come up and visit her interesting sights of London. Well, be as it may, that will depend on what the little English gal and I met today does and so on. She's the cutest thing I've seen over here..her eyes, naturally, are brown, and dark hair, and cute upturned nose. No Pop--step pop is a Col. in the British army, and they seem like nice people. How I met her will also be contained in my next letter to you.

Got a letter from my big brother yesterday..almost fell over from the surprise. He does get around to writing once in a while, doesn't he?? Well, some of these days, I'll have to write him. In the meantime, tell him not to worry about me--I ain't so old yet that I need any help... at least along my love life...if they all do get married or engaged or something to someone else. Hope to hear from you soon. Don't worry about me..I'll get along O.K.!!!!!!!

Love from you know who!!

Mail was a great morale booster for soldiers during World War II, a tangible connection from home. The armed forces deemed it so important that when the volume of mail was causing delivery delays and taking up valuable cargo space, VMail or Victory Mail was invented to keep the lines of communication open between soldiers and their loved ones. Letters were photographed and reprinted in labs.[8] Goodin was a case in point as he always mentions in his letters if he hasn't received mail in a while.

Vmail
NOV 23 1943, Tuesday night.

"Dear Mom",

Just a few lines tonight while I have the time...I'm planning on going up to London town tomorrow and don't know what is going on there--but I must go!! Our passes are now limited to only 2 1/2 hours, so will have to take it easy from now on on my leaves. May result in my having more money to spend at the time I do leave.

It's rainy and muddy here again, it seems its [sic] always damp here. (I know--I'll get a letter telling me about not getting my feet wet, and to stay warm and dry, and all that baloney that I've been getting for years and there's nothing that can be done about it. But, we make the most of it, and I'm almost a coffee drinker--have to

Three. England "Somewhere"

drink something hot and warming up these cool mornings. What a life...I'm certainly filling it up with experiences over here...and quite some interesting ones which I'm afraid that I'll have to wait till I get back before I can reveal all concerning them. "Sneak"...you'd laugh your head off, and I'm laughing at you right now for all the curiosity that I've succeeded in arousing in you by now. Even Dad might not approve of everything, but I'm not really worried about any of it from a moral standpoint, and you needn't either--it's just that it would be funny to anyone who knows me. No mail today...but the boys really got packages last night, and in my hut. We ate pickeled [sic] herring, cookies, candy, cake, dates, figs, more cookies, and washed it all down with water, and anything else that we could get. As a matter of fact, someone, bless them, sent a pound of coffee...evidently thinking that we were short of coffee when we aren't at all. Oh well, bless their hearts, and I'll bless anyone who sends me some of that stuff. Surely did enjoy eating stuff like that. It was nearly 12:00 before we got to bed, and then we got up all night long! But that was that. Sure did enjoy it all right.

No mail has come in lately for me, and that hasn't helped either. Have heard rather regularly from Lou lately, and don't hear much from the Carters at all...and since you know about Jeanie, well, I don't expect to hear from her. Hear from my Lucie gal every once in a while, even though she is still supposedly engaged to that guy.

Don't know what the situation is around that place, but would like to know some of these days. Anyhow, I'm going to keep in contact there...Lou might not come through after this darned war is over.

Think I told you I met a British general and had dinner with the British colonel the other night, at which time I had a most enjoyable evening and afternoon. Took the walk in the afternoon that we used to take together, and thought of you as we ambled along over the English countryside, even to the she-dog that went along with us, and got lost when she strayed over after a rabbit, and we had to chase her down. She is very good at coming when she [is] called, so we didn't have too much trouble!!

Our party for this Thanksgiving is definitely on--for Saturday night, and it looks like a good time will be had for all. I'll try and let you know the details, if I'm still sober enough by the time Sunday rolls around to get to writing you a letter. Don't get excited...you can worry over Stinky, too much.

Love, Johnny

Appalachia to Dessau

Vmail
NOV 27 1943

Dear Mom,

  Got your letter last night, and frankly I don't give a darn whether you write about a lot of stinking gossip and things of that nature..you just write in your own style and to heck with what happens when I get it. I really enjoyed your letter, and got it out in the field when I was cold as the dickens and wished that I could be back where I could sit in front of the fire, and so on and so forth.

  Also got a letter from Sis, typed and intended for V-mail. But she went over the margins with her typing and they don't accept those kind, so you can tell her that she will have to watch what she is doing and stay on the paper. Also the "one" on a typewriter is only an "1" or to be plaigner [sic] a small "L". So much for that.

  Really enjoyed both of your letters, and got a couple of others, but of course yours took preference over all of them. Got a package from Lou, and think that it must be a cake, and also got a copy of "Esquire" which I am also enjoying very much and haven't finished reading as yet. May get to it some of these days, you know, even with my opening about every other package, I'm still getting quite a bunch of them, and am storing them up until the time that Christmas actually comes. Just ho[p]e that I'm still here to open them leisurely and in my own time. One never knows really, though. I ate some of the candy bars in your package this morning, and they tasted good out in the field. The nuts,,well...I'm saving them for a little while yet, too. But everythi[n]g is darned good, and I appreciated it all. Amazingly enough, all of your packages have come through in darned good shape, and so far, I haven't received any that have been in a damaged condition. Which is very unusual.

  Well, got to go to an officers [sic] call, and then go out on the range, so must be closing for now. Keep up the good work, and write when you can. With all my love to all of you as always, still your

                Hoofs and horns.

Training intensified in December with tank battalions participating in an exercise of coordinated attacks led by General Hickey. This was a complex exercise involving tanks, infantry, artillery, and an engineer platoon. The mission was to "demonstrate the employment of a covering force in lieu of an advance guard when contact is imminent, the

Three. England "Somewhere"

occupation of attack positions, and the detailed fire plan necessary for a coordinated attack, and the employment of battalion supporting weapons in the initial stages of the attack and as security against counter attacks during organization."[9]

```
4 Dec. 1943
Dear Mom,
```
   Haven't heard from you lately, but must tell you that I've been out again..on duty, and had the most relaxation imaginable..stayed in a hotel, had hot and cold running water in my room...a real honest to goodness bath tub with plenty of hot water..Meals nearby and while no chambermaids (men either), no lobby, no radio, no ice water delivered to the room...had one swell time. Even honest mattresses which I sunk so delightfully and blissfully into each night. But today I'm back, and back into the swing of things. Am not going over to see Kay tonight..too many letters to write, too tired, and I didn't have a way over, as well as the fact that I've got to get to bed and get some sleep. Maybe I'll go over tomoroow [sic]...Don't know.
   Got a package of nuts from Jeanie today--just wondering if she is literally saying "Nuts to you, Johnny"??? [sic] Maybe not..but I sure will enjoy them..they are just what I love and engaged or not..I'll still love her that much more for sending me those. What a gal..well, you know what I think about that anyhow.
   Wish that you could have been along. Got something for you that will arrive sometime in the next six months..you and Sis can fight it out over them. No history, no long tales, no sentimentality...but I can hear you saying "Johnny sent me this from England" or words to that effect, and I can even see the gleam and pride on your face when you say it. If you and Sis don't fight too much over them. In the meantime, I'm still looking out for all sorts of things. Frankly, they just don't have them anymore..particularly after 4 yrs. of war. A string of pearls was 40 pounds--or $160.00. Which ain't hay, little girl, and I don't make that by a long sight..Am hoping to get off on a pass some of these days and may go up to Scotland if I have the chance...may get something there. Did I tell you Shep Anderson is over here?? Got a letter from him the other day. Trying to meet him, but no details as yet. Gotta close and go to be. Best of everything, merry Christmas, and a Happy New Year with me in it.

```
              Love to all, Johnny.
```

Appalachia to Dessau

Vmail
13 Dec. 1943
Sunday night in the ETO [Eastern Theater of Operations]

Dear Dad and folks,

Hope that this reaches you by Christmas or thereabouts and conveys to you my best wishes love and hope that I will be with you all again on next Christmas. Frankly, I may be too optimistic in wishing that, but at any rate, it can always be a goal to drive to.

Has been rather warm for a change over here..the weather has been nice, the nights cool, of course, but clear and rather beautiful. The most beautiful thing about the weather lately has been the cold..without dampness. Seems wonderful to be just cold...and you can get warm, whereas the damp air just penetrates without seeming to be cold at all--more like South Carolina weather.

We are having our usual routine of problems, of days and nights in the field, and our usual garrison details. Tomorrow night we are pulling a formal guard mount for the first time in my army career and the first for most of us. To go into the difference suffice it to say that the informal does not have all the frills and fatness of the regular formal guard mount. Something new and something interesting to try out.

Took something I haven't had since I've been in the army Saturday night, a big dose of oil chased down by some Algerian (actually Italian sour) wine. The taste was just the same, the wine sour, but much more pleasant to taste than the good oily goo of the oil.

Results were obtained, and in fact, if I had gotten up 30 seconds later, the results would have been disastrous to me..as you well know the possibilities of "oil." I hope that is my Mom that I hear sympathizing with me..can't imagine the rest of you bothering!!!!!! So far, though, it hasn't succeeded in breaking up my cold, as I had hoped. Anyhow...there is always tomorrow.

How have you all been? I wrote Sis an airmail yesterday, so it should be over anytime. As for myself..well, no mail in quite a while..two or three days except for Sis's airmail...no one is getting any mail at present though so we assume that things are either 1. kind of quiet or 2. that the Christmas rush has tied up things for a spell. Rather imagine the latter of the two has blocked things at home..what with everything being in a bustle for the last minute rush and what not.

Wrote to Reg the other night after so long a time..

Three. England "Somewhere"

probably thinks I am slightly unappreciative of his watch. But on the contrary, I was very pleased, and hope he realizes that. Missed seeing Lloyd Tapp, Cecil apparently didn't get off to see him either. Haven't heard any more from Andy, but if I locate him, will try to arrange my furlough so that I can see him when I'm off on it. Missed my leave for this period, but at any rate, may make up for it next month or so.

Had any company this Christmas, and who were they if any? I sort of will miss the wild wooly, happy go lucky Christmas that we had last year...it was one of the best I think I ever had. Don't think Paul Duncan landed over here after all, as I haven't heard from him and don't have any idea of where he is. Had hoped he would get here so we could get together somewhere or other. But in the army, we aren't surprised at anything. Think I told you where someone had written into our paper over here looking for Buddy Woodwards [sic] APO number. Also saw that Bob had gone to Mississippi some place or other.

Well, must be closing..going to be[d] early tonight for a change and see if I can't sleep part of this miserable cold and cough off of me. Got to get in shape for this week end in the field.

Tell all the folks hello for me and give my regards to Ike Tapp and the Clyde Browns for their Christmas cards which I appreciated very much. Will try and write them if I get the time. In the meantime..have an extra piece of chicken for me, and an extra quart of milk--I'll steal them from you on next Christmas!!

      Love to all, Johnny

Envelope WAR & NAVY DEPARTMENTS DEC 24 1943
Vmail dated 22 Dec., 1943

Dear Pops, Momma and Sis and all,

Got your swell letter while I was out in the field this week and this is the first time I've had a chance to write to all of you except for a short V-Mail to Sis last night since we got back. Came back in last night for a while (got dried out good) and then went out again today for another short session..Had quite a time, but nothing that you would be interested in. I thought once that I'd shoot a few rabbits, but the umpire on the problem said that it would be dangerous for other troops, so didn't get to fire.

Think I told you that I'm rooming with the Chaplain now..and he sends his regards to all of you. He is o.k. - but confound him, he never stays at home, never has

Appalachia to Dessau

a fire, and generally stays down in the chapel where he spends most of his time..in fact, I'm not so sure that [he] doesn't sleep part of the time down there!!!

Nothing cooking particularly for Christmas...still have a few packages to open. I buried into some of them already, and there are a scant few that I have left. I'm itching to get into them though. Naturally...well, the candy is almost gone but was darned good while it lasted. Wish that you could arrange to send more of that over. One bar a week hardly suffices, though I could get by on it easily enough if I had to. I'm sure tired tonight, but will finish this anyhow.

I guess that by the time this reaches home, Sis will have been up to see her husband, and probably one of my future wives. Don't know--- am just waiting on the report to come in on that girl...sis doesn't like Jersey cows... but I'm going to have me two varieties when I get home, and I sure am going to eat and drink the rest of my days. May have to teach her how to make cornbread, and to do lots of things that she don't know how, but she may make it o.k. I don't know--I don't care...I just know that I ain't ever going to spend any more cold nights sleeping by myself anymore!!! Such talk...from your youngun [sic] to......I'm ashamed of all of us....Really I am.

Got a letter or rather a Christmas card from Mr. Charles and W. C. Morrow today. Dad--wish you'd find out what ever happened to his son, W. C. Jr., and his daughter, Virginia-- shve [I've] often wondered about her, and never thought to ask you about her to see what actually did happen to her. Have gotten quite a few cards lately, but haven't had a chance to acknowledge them. Found quite a few in my trunk tonight that I bought and intended to send. But haven't got them sent as yet. Well.....that is me..put off things till I get back, and then don't send them when I do get back.

Have had a few laughs the last couple of days...to see us all warmed up, wrapped up, trying to keep up with the English over here..is something else. I still think that if a girl of mine ever sees me in these long-handled drawers that we wear here...she'll never write again... they are glamor [sic] <u>plus</u>. But then, I might not be so favorably impressed with some of them if I saw them in a bathing suit either...so don't guess it makes much difference, does it???

I'm still so darned tired that I sure will love getting to bed, and think that is just what I'm going to do. Sure enjoyed all your letters, and hope to hear from you again soon. Am still trying to see Andy with no luck as yet. Love,

Johnny

Three. England "Somewhere"

Christmas arrived in England, and the 3rd Armored celebrated with beer and scotch, parties for British children, visiting friends in the hospital, and dancing with WAAFs (Women's Auxiliary Air Force) or Land Army Girls. Soldiers even experienced home traditions with turkey and cranberry sauce.[10] In the dark landscape, with blackout curtains on the cottages, children could be heard singing Christmas carols. Many of these children had only ever experienced war. The tankers came up with a plan to make this Christmas special for the children by combining the treats they had been sent from America and giving out treats of gum, chocolate and Christmas candy.[11]

Goodin is away from home at Christmas for the first time in his life and is missing his family. In this Christmas Eve letter, he waxes eloquent as he longingly reminisces about Christmases past, and all the traditions he holds dear. He also explains in detail how he and "his boys" are spending their Christmas in England. Goodin had been "hoarding" candy bars since September to share with them at Christmas.

```
ETO-Christmas Even.

Dear Mom, Dad and all the folks,

    Tonight is the first time that I've been so far away
from home at Christmas that I couldn't at least think of
being home some time or other near or during Christmas,
and while I realize that there are bigger things to be
done, I at the same time realize what a happy home we
have always had and how fortunate we have all been to
have been together at times in the lovely home that I
love so well. Just realize that all the time in the few
years that there have been a gang at home shooting fire-
crackers, eating, necking, and having a swell time---
even the night we were all curled up so comfortably in
everybody's arms, and Lovey told Willy the story of the
Christmas Carol—things like that burn deeper than one
realizes I guess…anyhow, it was part of the home that I
know—fires in the fireplace, apples, popcorn, and all that
goes with it. Tonight, I can't help but miss all that,
and know that it will probably be another Christmas gone
before I get back to it…if at all. Frankly, on the latter
part—I'm not even worried—cause I still think that if I
don't—well, all the fun I've had, the pleasant memories
that I've built up…are enough for any average person to
have, and it sure is not everyone who can boast about
their home like I can, and -----back it up.
    In about two hours from now I'm taking up my boys some
cider, orange drinks, and other junk...cookies and cakes,
```

Appalachia to Dessau

which I've managed to get...as well as candy bars that I've hoarded since I got off the boat (got them on the boat) and chewing gum and such stuff that I've saved here and there. As well as my cigarette rations which I've acquired. Also going to give one of my sergeants who has a very tough beard a few blades to keep up on the beam. May all be in bed— if so it will be that much better. Wish you all could see me carrying on around here. Had intended going over to see Kay tonight— she's in bed with a temp. of 102, so I guess I'll be lucky to see her tomorrow night even. They are having a dance tomorrow night, but I told her we wouldn't go...just have a good time as best we can.

Tomorrow we are having another big feed like we did have at Thanksgiving time over here. Steak and turkey so I hear, with cake and pineapple for dessert. Don't make much difference...we still get fed darned well, even if we don't have buttermilk. Although I hear that it won't be long before we start getting such stuff. Don't know. We now have a Red Cross open right here in the Camp and it should improve morale around here. There is a Red Cross girl from Lynchburg who brings us doughnuts and coffee..redheaded and the sweetest Southern Drawl you ever heard...just like Lou Baker's, and it sure is music to our ears. She knows Art from school days as she used to go to his frat dances. We have quite a time, but I only see her when she comes around. Going to find out where she lives and maybe drop in for a real chat some of these days.

Have had several good days in the field lately...am completely thawed out and dried out, and none the worse for it. Valuable experience which we couldn't get if it weren't for the help of the British, who have proven very cooperative since we've been here. They may pass for us yet!!

Got a lovely letter from Mr. Charles on Clinchfield R. R. stationary with the road on the back of it. Sure is good to go over it...but where is this station called Frisco on the road just above Kingsport??? Never heard of it...maybe I'm getting old. As a kid, I used to know all the stations on the road..times change—even the Clinchfield I guess. He also says that Pop sure can deal the spades without any signals at all. Of course, I've seen that happen before and it didn't surprise me any.

Think I told you that I'm living with the Chaplain..he keeps later hours than I do, but maybe I'll get to church more now...he wakes me up. Got an awfully sweet letter from Jeanie......guess maybe I did mess up that deal...

Three. England "Somewhere"

```
but guess God knows what I'm doing...I'm quite sure I
don't.....gotta be closing. Love to all.
                    Johnny.
```

Goodin writes yet another long letter to his parents on Christmas Day, imagining a fresh apple pie topped with "real Jersey butter, and milk skimmed off a big crock out of the icebox," as opposed to "dehydrated apples, condensed milk, and whatever the heck we get for butter." His detailed description of activities and meals is his way of sharing a connection with his parents across the thousands of miles of separation. Goodin excitedly informs his parents that he has received "gobs" of mail.

    Goodin mentions he is going to have dinner with Kay, and they are supposed to go to a dance, but he says "my feet don't feel too good from the hike that I had yesterday morning." Road marches were a continual exercise in order to strengthen muscles, and acclimate soldiers to various terrains regardless of weather, while carrying heavy loads of weapons and equipment.

```
Christmas Day in the ETO Same Envelope
Dear Folks again,
   Well, after writing to you last night, took the stuff I
had up to the boys, came back and went into the kitchen
where they were just taking some lovely pies out of the
stove. I let my imagination run with me, imagined I was
home, eating a fresh apple pie out of the oven and not
dehydrated apples, that I was putting real Jersey butter
on the pie instead of whatever the heck we get for butter,
and then when I poured the condensed milk on it, I just
thought that I had just skimmed the milk off a big crock
out of the icebox, and sneaked in with it. Then after
eating it, I just could hear someone raising sand (who
could that be in our happy home???) about John taking all
the cream off the milk and not leaving any for the
coffee!!! Welll, [sic] anyhow, I thoroughly enjoyed it!!
   Got up this morning the band was playing Christmas
Carols and along with it every so often such tunes as
Beer Barrel Polka, and the like (they are broadcasting
this evening—Chuck Bills Armored Force Band— they won a
contest from all the other ground units in the ETO, and
won the right to broadcast back home), and the Chaplain
finally got me out of bed. We had for dinner: Potatoes,
turkey, dressing, candy, peas, usual bread, and the
apple pie for dessert (only after eating a whole one last
night, I wasn't particularly hungry for just that!! After
```

Appalachia to Dessau

eating, went back to my little hut, and opened up the remainder of my packages..and joy oh joy. Jeanie had sent me a big box of nuts; Libby (though I've not corresponded with her all year nearly) sent me two boxes: 1. a big box of nuts - luscious, and 2. one of Sis's Christmas packages....chewing gum, stationary, [sic] soap, razor blades, chocolate bars, etc...I was really hurt by all that from her. Don't' know why...but she just does those things. The Chaplain and I ate fruit cake, and after he left, we (the others of us) ate more fruit cake, with a little wine and a bigger batch of cider. At 4:00 I'm going over to --------------and have dinner with Kay, and then they are supposed to have a dance tonight..don't know whether I'll go to that or not, inasmuch as my feet don't feel too good from the hike that I had yesterday morning. Mail--in gobs lately: heard from Liz, and Scotty—the girl that Kelley and I dated together in Louisville..and today I heard from Kelley..he is out in Texas..had a scrap with is C.O., and said C.O. tried to ship him cross, and ended up by being sent himself. Has a seven pound girl...not bad, is he. Has no sympathy for me in regard to Jeanie, but does resent her taking up with the Navy.

So...well, until something bigger or better breaks loose, I'll have to be closing for the present. As I stated, there is not a lot going on around here, and we make the most of our lot. I'm perfectly happy, don't miss home too much under the conditions, while some of the Mama's boys are having a tough time today. Others are going so far as to work right on. Of course, there are always the usual details to be taken care of!!

Must be closing, as I have several letters yet to write, and I must get ready to go over to Kay's. So long for now, and hope everything is all right with you and our's [sic]. Best of love, thanks for everything (the Hersheys were simply wonderful) and I even appreciated Carters gloves tha[t] she sent me. Should write her a letter, but haven't as yet. So long for now, and I'll be closing.

       Love to all from your ETO Johnny

Chapter Four

Somebody's Johnny
January 1944–June 1944

John inherited his talent for weaving a story from his mother, whose letters are infrequent, but very dramatic and very long. John derives great pleasure from her letters and loves them so much that he always shares them with his comrades. While always one for innocent gossip and a good joke or laugh, there are times in her letters, when her mother's heart wins out. She expresses to John that he is constantly in her thoughts and she, and all mothers, are "in this war and fightin'" and that he was "lifted right out from under her heart" and "part of me is in England." She tells him that every time she hears a plane she says, "O God, he's somebody's Johnny."

The year 1944 dawned and, though there were rumors that the war would end in 1944, the training of the 32nd Armored intensified with the din of weapons firing on the ground and air attacks overhead as weekly maneuvers were conducted. The troops were trained in "waterproofing vehicles, combat swimming, anti-aircraft spotting, and chemical warfare."[1] Combat swimming required successfully reaching your destination through water while wearing full combat clothing and gear.

```
Jan 3, 1944

Dear Folks,
```

Have just gotten back from London on a twenty four pass, and have I had a time...ummmmm. Thought I was home for a while last night for a change. Anyhow to give you the big picture, I'll have to go back a little bit further.

Some time ago I wrote you that I had met an English girl (actually she's Scotch originally I think), and was with her a very few times in London. Met her at the Red Cross Club, and from there, we went to a show, a movie and what not, and generally put her on the tram about 12:00, and that was that. Well, recently she asked me up to spend the holidays with her, or have dinner, or what

Appalachia to Dessau

have you, if I could get off, and to bring Andy with me--but I haven't been able to even see him yet. Anyhow, there was a regulation that we couldn't travel over the usual 25 miles during the holiday, so I couldn't go. In the meantime, I wrote to her that I might drop in on a 24 hour pass some of these fine days...to which she replied, come on. So I got off yesterday about noon (it was Sunday, and we had a heck of a big party on Saturday night for New Years celebration) and took off. Arrive in London with only an address, and a great lot of brass--well known in this family wherever I go these days..I guess. Anyhow, an American sailor with his girl friend who lived in the neighborhood volunteered to take me to where they thought it was, and sure enough the gal was right. To add to my troubles, though, her sister, whom I had never met answered the door. And she wasn't at home. Well, after the traditional cup of tea, we took off by street car and hoofs to find her, and did so after asking about three people in the block, and ending up by finding the fire warden who has everyone's names and he got us there. She was quite surprised, and so were the rest of them. To make a long story short, we went back to her home with her mom and sister, and ate supper (delicious turkey soup incidentally) and also fruit cake for dessert. We had a nice fire in the living room (which was incidentally messed up just like ours at home usually is), and about 12:00 Mom showed me my room (which was the son who is in Ceylon's pride and joy--and what a lovely bed it was too) and she and the sister took off.....we enjoyed the fire. Anyway I dropped into that bed, and don't think I turned over a single time even. This morning: when the Mrs. came up to wake me up she brought me a tray with a big glass of water, and a hot cup of tea. Wow---that was the final straw. I just groaned long and loud...and downed both!! Got up, and we went up town after breakfast of real cream in the tea, and French toast, and real bacon. What an enjoyable time I had. I sure hated to come back to this mud hole after that. Didn't see anyone I knew in London for a change, and just as well.....had one more good time to write home about. I am planning on going to Scotland around the 13th if I can get off at that time, and I'll probably have plenty to write about then.

My own New Year was rather quiet---we reminisced about the year from beginning to end and I was in bed by 12:00 sound asleep. Then Sat. night we had our party, and Kay came over (we were the only ones but the Chaplain who weren't drinking and celebrating--we parked in front of a fire and stayed there) and we had a rather swell time.

Four. Somebody's Johnny

It's nice to just sit and be quiet some times. And that is about all one has time for over here. The Colonel's daughter of the peep incident is home, but has gone to London to spend a few days of it, so, should have something to tell about her once she gets back.

My mail has piled up on me lately. I just haven't had the inspiration to write, or some thing. And if I hate to write, then I don't usually write worth a darn. This letter is an exception--I wanted to get it off while I could, otherwise, I would not be able to remember everything..like just now it came back to me that we had dinner today in an Indian restaurant--Lobster in the funniest fashion, but good nevertheless. These tall Indians, or Ceylonese, wait on you, and then give your order in their language, and it sounds like a bunch of old hens getting together for a gabfest. Really interesting. Right in the heart of London, too!!

Well, my dears, think I'll close and go to bed. I have had quite an exciting and strenuous weekend, and we are going to the field tomorrow, so shall have to be closing for the present. Hope to hear from you as soon as you get the chance.

                    All my love, as ever, Johnny

Goodin often shares with his sister, Ellene, and his friend Anne Carter, dangerous situations and events that he does not choose to share with his parents. In this letter he tells Ellene he experienced his first real air raid.

Monday Night—Jan 3 [1944]
Dear Sis,

Haven't heard how things were at Christmas at home yet, but by now you should know how my own turned out. Wonderful..and New Year's Day I was still drinking and eating candy. Ah me..it was wonderful.... anytime you want to send over Hersheys you do it, o.k.???/ Anywho, I have made the necessary contacts in London to pick up something that you might want, and it may take a time or two yet before I can get it, but I'm in good shape now. I left a couple of bars of chocolate up there, and that stuff is like gold over here. You'd never believe it, would you??

I was in my first air raid last night—the sirens started about 15 till 12...and then we heard planes and then the darned guns started off. In about less than 20 minutes it was all over with, and London was back asleep again almost as suddenly as it had been awakened..it was my first one, and I enjoyed it..read in the papers this morning about the number of planes shot down...but it was my first real experience around an area like that.

Got a swell letter from Jeanie..said she'd like to adopt me as a big brother. O.k. by me—only I don't trust those sorts of relationships. Do you????? Anyway, we are still writing (Mother probably won't appreciate that) and she thinks it may be several months now before she gets married. What a nice kid anyhow..have you been up to see Baker yet??? I rather expected you would while Reg was up there, but have heard nothing from either of you, so don't know what the score is there. I haven't written her very much in the past two weeks— haven't had the ambition to write anyone after I wrote to you all on Christmas Eve and the Day thereafter. As it is, I don't know---maybe I'm just getting lazy or something or other. By the way, Capt. Jack took off to Scotland with 94 pounds and four bottles of Scotch this morning. So he should have a big time in a big way. That's the only way that he could have one, I guess, at that.

Sorry that the note is so short, but I got to go to the field tomorrow and I can't be too dead on my feet. Like I am now. I haven't felt so wonderful in ages as I did this morning. Ah me—tea served in bed. And then hot water to shave in..towels and all. And an inside johnny that was not so cold to sit down on. These are things I love, or something!!

Take care of yourself and all the folks and write when you get a chance. You know, I always enjoy anything from you all - despite the subject...if you wouldn't ask me some things like you do occasionally and then I have to bawl you out over it.

> With love and kisses and all the things we know so well..........
> Johnny.

Various dignitaries visited and inspected the training areas in January 1944. Goodin commented on meeting the Duke of Gloucester, Prince Henry, brother of King George VI.[2]

Jan. 11, 1944

Dear Dad and all the folks,

Am writing to you tonight on the eve of my taking off to Southern, Northern, and generally just England and maybe Scotland and Wales. Tomorrow, I'm going down to see Lloyd Tapp, if I'm able to locate him, and the day after that, I hope to go back North and run into Andy. Haven't seen either of them yet, and may not get a chance to again.

Four. Somebody's Johnny

Naturally, if I get back here in time to -- my reports of the trip will more than likely be more interesting than this is.

Naturally, as you seem to think--I'm not all right unless I'm asking for money--and this time, I'd like about $75.00 (seventy-five dollars), as I've borrowed about that much to go on. I don't know what I'll see that I want, or anything, and that is the reason I'm taking so much. Just hope I don't lose it. You can send it by cable, or by usual money order--either way, just so I get it within a reasonable time. I thought I was going to get a check cashed, but we went to the field to put on a demonstration for the King's brother— the Duke of Gloucester, and are just now back, and I find that I'm possessor of a proud leave.

By the way, I'm writing a V-mail tonight with the same substance, so don't think I need 150 dollars--only this one. They are both dated the same, so you shouldn't have any trouble.

No mail for several days--though the mail service is excellent at the present time. I'm getting letters of the 30th--and I got your two airmails of the 27th in record time as I've already written and told you about.

Must be closing--I still have to bathe shave and so forth and go on duty officer until 8 in the morning before I'm off, and it is now 12:00. With all my love--and I won't add don't forget the $75.00!!! Everything is o.k. with me, and hope that it is with you. Goodnight and good luck.

      Love, as always,
      Johnny.

11 Jan 1944 Vmail
War and Navy Departments
Vmail dated 11 Jan. 1944
Tuesday night-ETO

Dear Folks,

Have written you an airmail tonight, and am writing this also--don't know which will get there first--but whichever one does--I want you to send me about seventy five dollars ($75.00) as I am on the verge of going on a six day leave--and I have accumulated a slight indebtedness which I must take care of along those lines. Since I know my bank account is in good shape, I don't feel too badly about this--for that is only what goes in every month--or at least I hope that Uncle Sam is depositing it every month to my account. Which ever letter gets to you first, disregard the other..as I hardly think I need $150.00.

Appalachia to Dessau

Have been out in the field for the last couple of days... and since the weather is beginning to warm up a bit, I have rather enjoyed it. Sunday I had dinner with my "Peep" girl friend..but she has taken up the habit since last I saw her, so don't expect to continue my acquaintance with her. At any rate, not more than socially anyhow. Other than that, my social life has been at a standstill due to existing conditions over here. Hope to make up for them this week though.

How is everything at home? Seems funny not to hear from you all once in a while---the mail has slowed up a bit again..probably a relapse from Christmas, at which time they really did a wonderful job. I myself must apologize for not writing to you since Christmas, especially, but we have been continually busy, and I haven't had the usual opportunity that I did have before Christmas. Haven't had but very little time..and most of it was occupied. Gotta be closing..hope to be hearing from you soon…either a cable or a money order---the latter would probably be the quickest. Hello to everyone. . .and some of these days I'll be able to write a lot.

Love to all,
Johnny

Letter dated 11 Feb. 44
Dear Folks,

Got 3 letters from you last nite - Pop's Mom's of Feb. 1 and Jan 29th, & Sis' V-mail of Jan. 24th. Glad to know you are all well, and able to run around. Ashamed my Pop can't play better set-back - a <u>good</u> player can beat the cards!!

Tell Mr. Charles I appreciate his sending me the Erwin paper, but I'm getting it anyhow - so - if he wants to send them - make it a Johnson City paper.

Not much news - the snow has finally melted, and now it's the wind that is rough. But - it's war - and I manage to keep my feet dry and most of the time warm - so don't worry.

Just leave my locker as is - did the customs office open it, or do you know.

Read another good railroad book - "The Boomer" by Harry Bedwell. Tell old Jess hello - got a letter from Bill Richardson. I should also mention MY MOM'S letter of Jan. 13th - but since I've already agreed with that letter about two weeks ago - I won't write anymore on it - I <u>wasn't asked</u>, but If I have to learn the hard way - it's better than not at all.

Love to all,
Johnny

Four. Somebody's Johnny

John makes a joke that shows his frustration of endless training and still waiting to join the war. Missing food from home, he asks his parents to send him a jar of sausage.

```
Vmail dated 5 Mar. 1944
Dear Folks,
```
   Just a short note (as these V-mails always are just that, it seems) to tell you hello, that there is a beautiful weather spell here for a change, and that I'm O.K...my reports to the contrary notwithstanding (someone seems to think that I might be dieing [sic] of a broken heart-- but you know me better that that, I think) Not much has been going on, more than routine stuff which is always present. The common report on the war around here seems to be: "the Russionas [sic] gained thirty five miles, the British stopped for tea, and the Americans had inspection." But enough cracks. Is the president going to give the soldier who struck John L. Lewis in the eye the Distinguished Service Cross??
   Have written to Bryan Woodruff requesting a package of candy from him. How am I supposed to know that he had it, until I was told???
   I still want a jar of sausage--you could pack it so it wouldn't break, I think. Apparently you didn't get the letter with that same request in it that I mailed over two months ago (it was right after you had been to Limestone, and had returned and the house was full of hog meat!!) Anyhow, if it is obtainable, or all right with you, I could still handle it o.k.
   Is everything o.k. with you all? I'm getting along o.k... am hoping to get off soon and maybe go to Scotland.. haven't made it yet..but may. Had a day off this week, first one since way back when--in January. But not altogether my own fault. Am sorta glad that don't have to worry about income tax this year...it seems to be a heck of a muddle, and I'll leave it that way till I get back, and then really have some fun. Cuess you are paying my local state and county taxes. Tell J. R. I'd like to know how we are coming along over there, too.

                    Love and kisses to all of you,
                    Johnny

```
Vmail 21 APR 1944
Dear Dad,
```
   Have just seen that I can make my mark in the coming elections - understand that you must make out some sort

Appalachia to Dessau

Goodin visited Bath in 1944 but could not escape the stark reality of war visible in the nearly decimated building in the background.

of certificate for me before I can vote. Hope you can get the necessary arrangements for me to get my vote in. I don't know who is going to be running - but am disappointed that Wilkie dropped out - think he might have been a help to Roosevelt by forcing the necessary issues which I think our folks back home would have to face sooner or later. And you and all the rest of the voters will <u>have</u> to force the issues. Will write you a long letter on that subject soon.

  Must be closing for now. Keep things under control and moving. I'll try to do the same for myself.

                     All my love as always,
                     Johnny

Sat. Apr. 15 - 1944.
My dear Folks!

  Rotten bunch of beloved heathen that all of us are!! Greetings from England - & a million thanks from your wayward, prodigal infidel for your letter - sorta slow indeed from the Witch of Endor (1st one in 3 months, 1 week), some letter from Solomon - the wise old owls (or

Four. Somebody's Johnny

Encouraged by his parents, John Goodin used precious leave time to travel while in Europe. He is pictured here, third from the left, with unidentified friends in England, 1944.

```
should we call him the Rock of Gibraltar?), and ever-
faithful Ellene - it would take all of us to figure out
a name for her - and then WE wouldn't agree on that, at
that.
   In answer to a few questions and observations - first:
Thanks for Peter Graybills address; to the W of E [Witch
of Endor] - Stinky stands guard and barks like a coyote
if anyone comes around where we are sitting. Incidentally,
he's lonesome since Kay has moved away - but I read Lou's
letters to him, and he ain't quite so lonesome. To Sis:
Thanks - on my oath - I'll tell her nothing about it!!
Don't worry about sending oranges - we are getting
Spanish, or Italian or some kind of them now. See nuts
are 45 & 50¢ a pound!! And apples - 11¢ a pound. Woof!!!
Got your package with candy, nuts, cookies & statuette in
it. Got 3 tins of candy from a gal in L'ville, Ky. Umm.
LISTEN - I GOT THE $75 - MONTHS AGO. Won't need anymore
for a while - in a couple of months I get a fogie [Fogey]
for 3 yrs. service - 5% of my base pay. Which reminds
me. I'm getting old in this ---- army. Better to get old,
tho!! Saw Cecil Tapp Tuesday - he's near me, real near me.
Last Sunday I saw my old outfit from Ft. Knox - quite some
changes. Legnini the boy from Philly that I visited last
```

summer when he got his commission came by to see me - looks good, tho aged - like all of us!!

By the way here's another monstrosity to add to your collection - whoops!! Sorta surprised. Date it Nov. 19th as I looked pretty good then - well fed, well loved, and happy!!

Well - everything is O.K. - still looking for that sausage.

                  Everybody - Love & kisses.
                  The Prodigal Son

The 3rd Armored was on tenterhooks and full alert by spring 1944. They could hear warplanes and gunfire in the distance. Goodin tells his family he is "in the field for now." The 3rd Armored were living in pup tents on the downs in order to make a quick exit once the orders came down for them to move out.[3]

Training was intense in England, and when possible, Goodin enjoyed leisure time with an unidentified friend.

3 May - 1944
Dear Folks,

Just a note - got your letters - money order $27, and the Birthday Greetings & got a couple of greetings, but none like yours, of course.

My birthday consisted of a fresh egg for breakfast (paid a shilling (20¢) for it; dinner - chicken, fried, and all the trimmings (no ice cream, tho). Have had my supper last nite; Col. Cabonias brought over a pkg. of grits - and with my sausage and jelly - it made a delicious meal. I invited Major Yarborough up - but he didn't make it. Capt. Carpenter really enjoyed it tho - along with the Col. & me.

Four. Somebody's Johnny

I'm in the field for a while now - am sitting on my front porch, looking around the tent-pole to the green pastures across the valley; listening to a beautiful radio program behind me. Contented (another good supper tonite), as can be under the circumstances. Hmm. Home is far away - and yet, not so far either in thought, faith and love. Got a swell letter from Mrs. Francis last night (she writes me regularly), pictures from Lou tonite, a swell letter from Lucie in Knoxville - it's a swell world to me - even here. Guess the love & respect people have for you means much more than anything else.

Goodin took every available opportunity to write letters home to his family.

Letter from Margaret telling me of Frank Hodges son - another tragedy in life's unending drama. But - takes everything!!

>With all my love. Just take care of yourselves!!
>Johnny

Vmail dated 3 May - 44

Dear Folks,

Wanting to thank both of you for your letters & the birthday present which arrived today - meaning the money order. Appreciate it very much and plan on going to get me a pair of boots with part of it. In today's mail, I also got a letter from sis, one from Mrs. Frances (S.M.'s aunt) and two letters from Lou. She sure is rather faithful in writing, if nothing else!!

Appalachia to Dessau

The rain is whispering over my head, my flashlight grows dim - but my "honey-bucket" alias - English modern conveniences, is right outside - but my heart - I got a letter from each of you in the same envelope!!

Guess my sister has gone to damn yank land - from your letters. Still don't know why, or who with.

Remind me when I come home, not to play Boy Scout any - altho the training was quite good and coming in quite handy!!

All my love - and don't worry!! Something else - the sausage was grand - the Col [Colonel] contributed grits- and three Southerners really enjoyed themselves!

        Johnny

Vmail dated 17 May - 44 Dear Mom,

Dear Mom,

Have returned from a range where I had a wonderful time along with a lot of hard work. I had lots of eggs - on toast, poached, scrambled, with ham, and invariably with tea. Met some lovely, friendly, lively and wonderfully <u>interesting</u> people. But will write more about that later. Got home last night to find several days mail piled up - two from you, one from Dad, one from sis - five from Lou.

Also got my package of <u>cheese</u> and cakes - <u>marvelous</u>!!

So - now, I've gotten the <u>sausage</u>, the candy - <u>peanut brittle</u>; and now the cheese and jello, and crackers. My family sure loves me - don't they?? Wish I could send you some nice things to let you know I appreciate all you are doing - but there's nothing I can get over here. Maybe I'll bring some memories home with me!! Well, Mom - gotta close for now. More, and <u>fuller</u> at a later time.

        Love to all, Johnny

Vmail dated 22 May - 44

Dear Folks,

Just a note to say Hello, I love you, and bye now. Am getting along O.K., weather has warmed up, and life ain't miserable by any means.

Had a nice letter from Lou - a big swell one from Sis - still in Mass., last nite. Hmm!!

Had a fresh egg for breakfast, and am going on a Red Cross detail tonite - so maybe will get some more fun and maybe eats.

Had a little excitement the other nite - an accidental fire at the ungodly hour of 2:00 a.m.

Four. Somebody's Johnny

John Goodin looks contemplatively out of his tent, saying in a letter to his parents, "am sitting on my front porch, looking around the tent-pole to the green pastures across the valley; listening to a beautiful radio program behind me." May 1944.

```
    I even slept thru it all. Leave it to me to miss
everything.
    Looks like I'm going to have more neices [sic] & nephews
when I get back - then I can locate adequately. Just keep
a list for me so I can get everything straightened out.
Still haven't heard from Keith or George David. Have from
Fred Whitton, tho.
                        All my love,
                        Johnny
```

```
Vmail dated 28 May - 44
28 May

Dear Folks,
    Am O.K., well & happy - sorry I haven't been able to
write to you often, but guess that from the papers you
know I have been busy. Not much to tell you - am getting
my mail - another box from you with vanilla wafers and
jam, and raisins. I think I'm getting everything I'm
supposed to these days.
```

Appalachia to Dessau

    Sure was sorry to hear about Sid Patton - Anne wrote me Bill was a pall-bearer. Guess I won't know the place when I get home.
    Haven't much news from this side of the pond - a couple in front of me (a mile away) are indulging in a little fun - will put glasses on them for better view!!
Love to all of you -
Johnny

Vmail dated 31 May - 44

Dear Folks,

    Just a note to tell you, Hello - I'm really feeling fine - and this summer weather has gotten us all lazy or homesick. Have absorbed a little sun, and some of the boys already have a beautiful tan on them. We continue as usual in our slightly impatient waiting. The weather eases our misery. Am having a beer party for my boys on Sat. nite I think.
    Had a very nice letter from Eddythe Hankins yesterday - she's in London; gave me quite a bit of news and remarks from home. Also had a letter from Sis, and one from my Scotland lassie. Haven't heard from Lou lately - two days now - but school closing, I guess she's busy.
    Gotta go now - take care of yourselves and write when you can.
Love, as always,
Johnny

Goodin sends his parents a brief note about a dinner provided by the Red Cross. The American Red Cross Mostyn Club was a service club that provided numerous amenities to the men and women serving in the European Theatre. Services varied depending on the venue but could include dinners, recreational activities, laundry services, and barber shops.[4]

Postcard dated 1 June 1944

Dear Folks,

    To-night is Tenn-Ky. State Nite at the American Red Cross Mostyn Club over here, and there are God knows how many of us present. We are having dinner together, and being entertained in Red Cross style. It is great to see the men from our State, and to talk about things back home. Not propaganda - as the ARC is doing swell.
Love, Johnny

    Missed seeing Eddythe - but may find her later.

Four. Somebody's Johnny

Goodin was introduced to battlefield "cuisine" of powdered eggs and powdered milk early on, but comments to his parents that he hopes the dried powdered milk doesn't cause him to lose his taste for the real thing.

Training continued through May and into early June with the sounds of war in earshot. On alert 24/7, the troops waited and trained expecting to be called out at any time. Goodin wrote his parents that he was on guard and "all was quiet, still rolling along as usual." After spending a restless night listening to planes passing over head, the radio broke the news of the Normandy Invasion on June 6. The men were on tenterhooks, but they were still ordered to wait. Camped in pup tents in the downs of Somerset and Wiltshire, they were soon given order to report to Southampton and Weymouth for embarkation. Their destination—Omaha Beach, France.[5]

```
3 June, 1944
Dear Folks,
    All quiet, nothing new, and still rolling along just as
usual. Haven't much time..am on guard and have a little
time right now...so thought I'd say "Hello." Was up in
London on a pass...you probably have the card saying I
was at a Tenn. KY state reunion, so you know the score
there. Had a fairly good time..spent most of it trying to
find Eddythe Hawkins, but never did quite locate her
definitely. Saw some boys who knew Bill and Cy Harison,
but, didn't see anyone I knew. Did run into a Holmes girl
from Greeneville who knew some people that I knew.
Anyway...London is still quite a town..still get some
awfully nice sensations of just walking in there, without
thinking of anything in particular. I sent Mom a check
for $25 yesterday when I came in from London..just to
show you that I didn't spend all my money there..although
I did spend $4.25 for three (3) Ga. Peaches—and they
were certainly lovely and juicy and tickled me palate
deliciously. It is my only extremely extravagant urge
I've had in a long time anyhow...and guess money really
doesn't make any difference anyhow...people are spending
20 and 25 dollards [sic] for whiskey…suppose I can blow
myself to that extent!!
    Got quite a letter last night from my Ga. Gal friend—
purely literary friendship I'm thinking..but she enclosed
me quite a blast from Drew Pearson's column on McKellar...
that guy must really have things under His control...
sorta makes me mad to see the condition of politics at
home, and so darned many little petty things, when there
```

Appalachia to Dessau

is a war going on to preserve what may be the carrying on of such wild and unfair and prejudiced conduct. Well maybe when we get back we can enforce some needed reforms and changes..our own generation has not seen fit to do that, and has tolerated it. I don't know how or why but guess we will some way or other.

I don't know where that sis of mine is...she seems to have vanished into thin air or something, or maybe she is just busy moving and getting to Greeneville..she seemed sorta anxious to get down there right away, and don't guess I blame her too much even at that. Just will be happy when I can get back and we can all go to Greeneville or somewhere or other and be together again.

By the way...don't know why or what to tell you to do with that money...suppose you could keep that $5...and give each of my nieces and nephew $5 each...in bonds or stamps or some thing or other that can't be spend [sic] right away (ain't I awful???????)

I got my tooth filled yesterday...I got the filling broken out while eating some English walnuts (breaking them with my teeth) and my teeth are naturally soft over here anyhow...something in the food the water, or maybe it is the atmosphere generally that makes you soften up a bit. Anyhow...will be glad to get some good old Tenn. water once again. Am also getting a slight little bit of a tan.. stealing the sunlight now and then when ever I can... which is not too often, as you may well know.

Hope everything is all right with you..how much gas are you getting, how are the berries this year, what is the price of milk, and a thousand other little things?? Just sorta wonder how things are back there..Mrs. Francis says that she never sees a herd of cows that she does not think of me...and that she promises me gallons of it when I get back…ummm...hope that this dried, powdered milk doesn't kill my taste for the real thing if and when I do get back. I've always said though that I'd not be too regretful because I always drank plenty of it while I could get it, and have no regrets there.

Say, I gotta be closing — got a letter from Lou last night and she hadn't heard from me in 9 days and she was almost worrying again...wrote and told her that she'd probably see the day that she wished it were only nine days that she had heard from me. We've been busy lately, and usually stay that way...always in spurts, and then it lets up, and we don't have too hard a time for a while.. and then I get caught up on my correspondence again.

Well, by for now and love to all of you. Write when you can, and please don't worry when you don't hear from me.

Four. Somebody's Johnny

```
From the papers, it looks as though you people are a lot
more excited about what is going on than we are. Sometimes
wonder if we are excitable, actually.
                    Love and kisses from your Johnny.
   P.S. 4 June - Just got a letter from Mom - will answer
when I get time. Johnny
```

John reassures his parents that all is well and that the 3rd Armored did not participate in D-Day. He expresses his relief that the waiting is over and it would only be a matter of time now that if he can "get started—the sooner I'll be on my way home." He informs them that his tank is stocked and ready, and named "Baker's Beau" after his fiancé, Lou Baker. He tells them not to worry if they don't hear from him.

```
   9 - June - 1944
   Dear Folks,
      Guess by now your nerves have calmed down and you are
   all settled down by now. Course, we haven't gotten
   excited yet - we are too much ready I guess to really get
   worried about anything. As it stands now, we are not
   directly in the D day but with a fair amount of luck I
   hope we can be used before too long. You know I've been
   waiting nearly 3 years for this & now it's here I'm ready
   to get started - the sooner I'll be on my way home. Righto??
      We're all relieved and happy to know it's started - even
   tho we know what we're going to face.
      Personally - I'm O.K. - well, bowels regular - feet
   sound - kidneys functioning, and sleeping every "waking
   opportunity." Not in the best of shape - but well rested
   and contented - feeling.
      Got my picture of Lou screwed in firmly right in front
   of me in my tank, have named & christened my tank "Bakers
   Beau" and have it well stocked with everything - food,
   gum, soap, lipstick and extras in various lines. Even
   an extra canteen (knowing my water capacity - you will
   understand).
      Had 2 letters from Keith Broce today, but too late to go
   see him now. Also got the record today - my name in it.
   Letter from Kay Morgan. Still haven't heard from K. King
   my nurse friend - she may be in the invasion for all I
   know. Oh me!!
      I don't know what goes from here on out - but just don't
   worry about me - for there'll be times when I won't have
   time to write. I'll try & get you a few V-mails now & then
   whenever possible, and will try to alternate between you
   & Lou - kinda believe the gal really loves me!! Hmm.
```

Appalachia to Dessau

   Just take care of <u>yourselves</u> and let me hear from you when possible.
   Tell Mrs. Swingle, once again - to keep up her hopes, as George will be back with any luck at all. And I believe he's got that much luck. Hello to everybody. And love to all.

Someday you'll receive my locker
with the enclosed items. Johnny

June 16–19, the 32nd Armored headed out to the ports of Southampton and Weymouth where they would set sail for Omaha Beach. Crossing the English Channel proved a challenge as storms caused delays. The 3rd Armored would first place their feet on French soil on June 23, 1944, at Omaha Beach on the coast of Normandy, France.[6]

16 June 1944
Dear Folks,
   Still wondering when you'll start getting our mail and not having any idea of "some." Guess when you do, or did - you got quite a batch of it.
   Wrote a V-mail yesterday in which I said I was sending you some money please don't worry about the odd number - pounds just turn out that way!!
   Am beginning - just beginning to get disgusted with waiting around for something to happen. Suppose when it comes I'll wish I were back in the comfort, peace, quiet, solitude and privacy of my own little tent. My eats from home - and my candle-light to read, study, and write by. My ever-present canteen. Still - I always wanted to tour in a trailer - so guess I'll get my fill of it!! On yesterday I had fresh strawberries as a gift from a NAAFI [Navy, Army & Air Force Institute] manager who also occasionally gives me tea on occasion! Something to break the monotony!! And also remind me of home. Oh me so far - and yet so near.
   I'm also enclosing you a part of my note-book. The addresses are of the U-T-Vandy Alumnae at the meeting I told you about. Also rather rough notes of my trip to Scotland. Save them please for me - someday I'll want them.
   Am just wondering if you are by any chance keeping a file of things I send home??
   I also forgot to tell you that some of these days my foot-locker will arrive - and <u>don't</u> break it open. (With the curiosity of my family - I can see you now - but don't anyhow.) Must close - so by [sic] for now!!

No signature

Four. Somebody's Johnny

Not knowing what was awaiting him in France, Goodin sent his parents a short Vmail telling them he loves them, and all is well. He asks them to contact Lou to tell her he loves her, too.

```
Vmail dated 22 JUN - 44 Somewhere in France
22 June 1944
Dear Folks,
   Just a note to say Hello, I love you and all's well and
feeling fine. 'Course can't tell you anything yet, and
don't expect to hear a lot from me. Just keep up your
prayers and Faith!!
   I'm writing to Lou, but wish you would call her if she
hasn't already called you. Call her at Ralph K. Baker,
1211 So. 2nd St., Roanoke - and you'll get her O. K. - I
guess. Don't forget to tell her I love her. Will write
again as soon as I get the time right now I'm just a
little busy!! In the meantime, love and kisses to all of
you and chins up!!
                      Johnny
```

Chapter Five

Normandy—Baptism by Fire, the Spearhead Is Born

June 23–September 14, 1944

On June 23, 1944, after a harrowing four days on storm battered waters of the English Channel, the 3rd Armored Division, 32nd Armored Regiment reached Omaha Beach on the coast of Normandy, France. Stark reality dawned as they got their first glimpse of the mangled tanks and ships, and damaged equipment left behind from the devastation of D-Day. As the 3rd Armored made their way across the beach, captured German soldiers were marching to transport ships as battalions of American replacement soldiers were making their way through the mud to their assigned destinations. The first few days were spent preparing the equipment and getting ready to go.[1]

Once the advance began, the 3rd Armored Division would be engaged in non-stop battle across Europe. They would quickly earn the name Spearhead, because they were always in the forefront of the advance, relentlessly determined to forge the way. While it is impossible to tell from Goodin's letters the exact location or details of his movements and encounters with the enemy, many of his letters align with the detailed map of the Combat Trail of the 32nd Armored Regiment, 3rd Armored Division, which offers insight into a probable destination.

Goodin's original tank crew consisted of Goodin, platoon commander, Roy L. Pearson, driver, Coye F. Hearne, bow gunner, and Ronald D. Gilboe, gunner.

```
Somewhere in France Sunday - June 25 [1944]
Dear Mom - and all,
   I got your June 12th letter last nite [sic] - sure glad
to hear from you in my first batch of mail since I got
over here. Guess you already have my first V-mail - hope
so. Did you call my Lou-girl?? I got 4 lovely letters from
her last nite - sure did my morale a lotta [sic] good.
```

Five. Normandy—Baptism by Fire, the Spearhead Is Born

"B" Company's original SPEARHEAD crew: Roy L. Pearson (back left), driver, John D. Goodin, platoon commander, (front left) Coye F. Hearne, bow gunner, Ronald D. Gilboe, gunner.

> Funny thing war - here I sit basking in the sunlight calmly writing a letter and enjoying life - French wine and cider (the hardest cider I ever tasted anywhere!!) are good - the wine is 10 years old. Had two quarts of my favorite drink last nite. [Goodin is referring to sweet milk.] The horses and cows are the prettiest I've seen since I left home, and the weather has been marvelous - me and my boys are all getting coats of tan, and I think I'm gaining weight on K rations. I've slept and ate and censored mail and studied French - and that's all I've done for a few days!! You asked about the Record [*The Erwin Record*, Unicoi County, TN newspaper] I'm getting it regularly - or I was until we left - don't know when I'll get it again.
>
> I knew you crazy people would be worrying too much about this invasion - but I also know it's no use telling you <u>not</u> to. That blankedty [sic] Lou is too - even tho she's praying and all. However - she don't show it much - bless her heart. Know what?? She says she wants a football team!! Well - I'm just the man.
>
> Had a slight twinge on your mentioning Julia & Ruth - and am looking forward to the day I can take Lou over and introduce her to them!! Wondering how long it will take me to get home with her!! Hmph!! Wish you all knew

Appalachia to Dessau

her more. You know - we are all set to get married, and I haven't even asked her - guess I won't have to - as Liz & Paul said they just <u>talked</u> about it and finally did it. So with us - what I <u>don't</u> like - I'm not excited about it (probably will be when the day comes, tho) and it just seems natural.

Haven't heard from Sis in a long time - but guess I will. Knowing her it will take some time for her to get settled.

Well, tell everybody Hello - and I'm on my way home at last. After 3 years (in a couple more days) I'm <u>ready</u> to start.

Gotta close and get this mailed to you. Love to everybody. Johnny

The shoulder patch insignia of the 3d Armored Division has a distinct heraldic meaning and a proud history in its mixture of form, color and symbols. The basic pattern is that of three interlaced torques, no one of which would be sufficient without the other two. Combined to form a triangle, the device indicates integrity and esprit de corps. The predominating colors are: yellow at the top for cavalry, red on the bottom right for artillery, and blue for infantry. The superimposed black symbols have a more modern meaning: the tank track for mobility and armor protection, the cannon for fire power, and the bolt of lightning to designate shock action. The Arabic numeral "3" is a division designation. The SPEARHEAD flash was authorized by Major General Maurice Rose after his 3d Armored Division had brilliantly led many of the First Army's drives in France, Belgium and Germany, during 1944 and 1945 (3AD.org).

28 June - 1944
Dear Mom -

So!! You think I'm in her grasp?? Ha - honey - I wish I were <u>literally</u> there!! But I aint [sic] - so I'll relax and read your two letters of June 9th & June 15th and drift off into home for a while - with that no good dog, the cyclonic looking rooms, the piano draped in black - and Ruth Moseley's

Five. Normandy—Baptism by Fire, the Spearhead Is Born

picture - hm, I guess it's time it came down, and Lous [sic] went up. But - if God intended it this way - and if I am "hooked" so I can't get out this time - I promise you I'll love it, and maybe the war has contributed another blessing in disguise! If it weren't for the futility of it, I'd marry her by proxy - Columbus took a chance - and so can I!! Invasion - blast you!! Worrying your blooming heads off while I've been having the picnic of my life - sweet milk by the gallon, butter, wine and cider, and living and basking in the sun and the stars (O.K. - so maybe once in a while Stinky does dive into a slit trench with his tail between his legs as things that go bump in the nite sail by!), and only needing mom's eternal need for perfect happiness. These French don't understand my "Chevrolet Coupe' a la king" so well, but I am learning! The French-Canadian in my platoon does all the parlay-vouzing and so far we haven't lacked for cider. The county is beautiful, the sheep, cattle and horses fine and slick, and only the shattered homes - windows shot out, some burned, etc., to show the effects of war. These dumb people sit around as blasé as you please - seems they don't mind getting all shot up! Don't get it. . . .

Call up Marie Saultz & tell her I said Hello - particularly to her Mom - who I think an awful lot of. Please?

Enjoyed the 20th Psalm - sorta calmed me. The Chaplain yelled "Give 'em Hell" as we passed him the other day. What a boy he is.

Had a quiet 3-year anniversary yesterday - but don't expect it to hold much longer. Am getting fat on these rations - if it weren't for digging ever so often guess I'd get lazy with it. Don't get me wrong - but I like the pleasanter things of life. 'Scuse the shortness - but got to tell Pop a few things. Saw this clipping & tho't of you.

All my love, Johnny

28 June 1944
Dear Pop,

And how's the backbone of the Clinchfield R. R. these days? Yea?? Well - good enough.

Am sweating out a telegram, cable, letter or something from you to find out what you did about me. Hope you followed my heart. But guess you did - you'd better get me hooked, & get my nose to the grindstone!!

Just before I left England I met a Fred Taylor who lived on our farm at Austin Springs - also a boy whose last

Appalachia to Dessau

name I've forgotten but you know his dad I know - he used to be an engr [engineer] on the Clinchfield, is a good friend of Jim Vestal's and lives on the old Ross farm on the Kingsport Hiway [sic] just out of Greeneville - and his (the engr.) first name is Andy - & the last Watts - It just come to me. I was supposed to see 'em again, but we moved that nite. This Fred Taylor worked for Uncle Nels Ford & knew all the Fords & Bowmans - we had a <u>time</u> talking about their good eats.

There is a three-day gap in this letter as Goodin, and the 3rd Armored, were in heavy battle June 29–30, at Villiers Fossard.[2] He describes it as "I just put in ten years or so." He tells his dad to "keep praying." He said he had to laugh because "this was the first time I ever sat at an organ with a loaded pistol on me and played for a church service."

A newspaper clipping from the *Johnson City Press-Chronicle* dated Sunday, July 16, 1944, reported the following: First Lt. John D. Goodin of an Army armored division has written his parents, Mr. and Mrs. T.E. Goodin, that he is with the invasion forces in France.[3]

The 3rd Armored Division's first engagement in Villiers Fossard, June 29–30, was a "baptism of fire." This was Goodin's first introduction to mortar fire, which in a later letter he would describe as lethal and deadly, and that the Germans were masters of mortar. The first thing encountered were the impassable and lethal hedgerows, with very few tank-dozers. Openings in the hedges were death traps as they were covered by tanks and machine guns. The 32nd learned firsthand that the Germans were a formidable enemy.[4]

For the first time Goodin heard the screams of the men around him in sudden and violent death amid the ear-piercing, deafening blasts of firepower. Shocked at seeing comrades sliced in half and limbs blown away, Goodin, and the 3rd Armored, were brutally introduced to the German bazooka and panzerfaust teams. There were heavy casualties in the two-day fight, with 1500 yards gained. According to the Official Record of Combat, the 3rd Armored lost 31 tanks, 12 other vehicles, 18 officers, and 333 enlisted men.[5] The regiment would regroup amidst rain, mud, and constant artillery fire, and forge on from Normandy to Northern France, attacking again and again against a dangerous and determined enemy.[6]

The seriousness of the situation is apparent in this letter to his dad, as he begins asking about his life insurance policy. Though he asks them to keep praying, with his usual sense of humor, and keeping things light-hearted for his parents, he jokes about the many uses of a tin can.

Five. Normandy—Baptism by Fire, the Spearhead Is Born

The Spearhead learned quickly that to go through an open hedgerow was suicide, as German guns were trained on the opening. The maintenance battalion designed a Sherman tank equipped with a hedgerow cutting device. Picture taken from the side, showing the blades in the lowered position. 3rd Armored Division, Maintenance Battalion, in the St. Jean de Daye, France, area.

```
2 July
    Well, Pop - I've just put in ten years or so. Been kinda
busy for the past couple of days - getting a rest now
and as usual everything is under control. One of my boys
was cleaning a pistol and shot himself through the knee
this morning - he had just come back from church. My first
"casualty" but can't count him as one, or otherwise I
couldn't tell you about it for 30 days.
    I'm sending you $50 today - we got paid off and I can't
spend money now here. So - you know where to put it. How
much money do I have these days - if and when you get
over $1000 cash - sock the rest in bonds each month as it
comes in - O.K.??
    I also want you to check on my Prudential policy - and
if it doesn't pay off at the end of 20 years - find out
what it will cost to convert it - I may need some cash
in that time to send my football team to school - tho
```

Appalachia to Dessau

frankly, I have sometimes tho't that that football team was a <u>long ways off</u>.

I'm just afraid it's a policy that's paid up at the end of 20 years - and what I want to do is draw it at the end of that time. I can't convert my G. I. insurance into a 20 pay - the best I can convert it to is a $10,000 policy paid up at the end of 20 years - so that should take care of that. In the meantime - it doesn't make any difference. Wish you would check up on it tho.

I also wrote you recently to check up on my voting status - think you have to write to somebody in Nashville to get the dope and sent to me. See Dewey & Bricker are thrown in against F. D. [Franklin D. Roosevelt] - my personal note will go to F. D., as I have no desire to change from a horse to a <u>pony</u> in mid-stream.

We sure do get <u>fed</u> good over here - no kick along that line. Had to laugh the other day - sitting in my tin can, eating out of a tin can, drinking out of a tin can and urinating in a tin can. Don't know what I'd done if I should have had to s----! I was thankful I didn't.

Well, guess that's all for now - why don't you ask Mom if she wants to have Lou down and ask her if she does. You know I can't just write and tell her to go off and see you all. All you'd have to do is call her up and ask her.

Well, keep praying - God is answering our prayers every day now, so I know somebody is doing some good. I had to laugh this p.m. - first time I ever sat at an organ with a loaded pistol on me and played for a church service. But - everybody else was the same way, so it wasn't extraordinary. Must be closing now - so, so long & God bless all of you. Love

                    Johnny

Goodin describes a different kind of fireworks for the rainy 4th of July holiday.

VMail 4 July, 1944

Dear Folks,

Just a note to tell you I am spending a quiet sane and safe 4th of July. I have shot my one firecracker which I have saved for the occasion, in the event we weren't loosing heavier fireworks. I've had my holiday drive, taking a short trip this a.m. to do a bit of civilian investigation of a suspicious character. Ride was uneventful, except for our own artillery. It rained, as usual for the 4th, and I'm now stretched underneath the tank tarpaulin writing a few letters. Not raining for the

Five. Normandy—Baptism by Fire, the Spearhead Is Born

present, but can expect it anyhow. I slept beautifully last nite - through ack-ack [Antiaircraft Gunfire] and everything - so my conscience isn't bothering me any - God is still taking care of me.
    Well - I'm waiting to find out my financial, marriage, and voting status, so loosen up a little. O.K.? In the meantime, just keep your Faith in God - it has been <u>more than justified</u>.

                      All my love, Johnny

The next few days, between June 29 and July 7, the 3rd Armored prepared to Cross the Vire River at Airel while surrounded by the sounds of "planes roaring overhead" and field artillery fire, which was "uncannily accurate." The men learned quickly how to camouflage the tanks and dig fox holes or make use of drainage ditches and high hedgerows.[7]

In this letter, Goodin asks his parents to keep his letters because they are not allowed to keep diaries. He also expounds upon his activities on the 4th of July, of finding a beautiful church, and "chatting" with the priest whose home was destroyed. Goodin also found some fruit, which he says he has missed.

Dear Folks,
   10:00 a.m. - nice, sun shining, planes roaring peacefully (?) overhead and all's well with me at last for the present.

   6 July - '44
   Am enclosing you the first continental issue of Stars & Stripes which I want you to save for me - have asked you before - but just wondering if you keep my letters?? We can't keep diaries - I'd have a heck of a time keeping them anyhow - but my letters would probably serve as a refresher to my memory. On the p.m. of the 4th I wondered [sic] into a very small settlement - straightened out some soldiers & a French salesgirl with my limited knowledge of French, and drank a glass of cider - she was also selling cognac - 12 francs (24 cents) for a thimbleful and getting plenty of buyers - my boys said - "[Rrumph!! - <u>Moonshine!!</u>" Anyway - across the road is one of the most beautiful little churches I've ever been in - and it's [sic] real beauty is unmarred by the few shell shots that are in it - the priest, whose home was destroyed in the fire and shelling, spoke broken English & I had quite a chat with him. A few hundred yards away was a home in which a German general had billeted himself - there were tons of coal in the back yard and plenty (we went into the basement) of hot water - the boiler was rolling - and

Appalachia to Dessau

I expect all our mouths watered at the thought of a hot bath. However, knowing the occupants were pro-Nazi, and darkness beginning to fall, we didn't linger.

In another week or so the apples will be large enough to munch on - I've already eaten a few cherries, and some people had strawberries!! Fruit is about the only major item I miss, and it not <u>too</u> badly.

Have been lazying around for a while - sure is nice not to hear artillery fire - except from a distance. Hot stuff can drive one batty.

      Well, must close for now.
      All my love to all, Johnny

July 8–12, the 3rd Armored crossed the Vire River at St. Jean de Daye and repelled a German attack attempting to cut the Normandy beachhead.[8] Goodin tells his parents that he has "been in combat, lost one tank, but men got back safely." The crossing of the Vire River was under heavy mortar and machine gun fire, but it did not deter the 3rd Armored.[9] It was later learned that troops had been battling the Panzer LEHR division, "which was reputed to be one of Germany's best armored units."[10]

Goodin describes the treatment of people by the Germans who were "living in style," and calls them a "degraded bunch." Goodin describes the men as "brave heroes" and "our infantry must be made of iron." He says he is "amazed at how plain damned foolishly unafraid I was," stating that he lost a tank, but no men.

10 July 1944
Somewhere in France

Dear Pop & Mom,

Just got your June 20th letter - thanks so much. I see at least you arrived at the same conclusion I have. I know if you talk to her [Lou], you'll O.K. her - altho, she's 18 - and she may be a bit shy and somewhat reserved with you. This happens to be the first time I've felt sure of myself and "her" too - and - making a broad confession - she's sure kept me out of trouble.

Your idea of a "maybe" ring sounds O.K. to me - if Mom is willing to risk a pearl - or whatever. I still haven't formally asked her - as I still don't like the idea of putting it down on cold black and white when you can <u>say</u> it. However - we are going right along with our plans - and you might be surprised if you knew how far they have progressed.

So there it is. I <u>am</u> going to marry her when I get back

Five. Normandy—Baptism by Fire, the Spearhead Is Born

and I'm not kidding you. If I don't get married when I get back - I may fall back into my old ways. And that wouldn't be good - would it?? She's the only one I'm even slightly interested in now - which should convince you. Sure there's Anne & Margaret - I've told them about her, and her about them, it's a delicate situation, and one heavy with danger - but maybe I'll be diplomatic enough - AND <u>MAN ENOUGH</u> - to keep the situation under control. As to the ring - ring or not, she'll be waiting for me I know.

Now she has been asked to come to Erwin and visit with a sister of a lady she knows. I don't know when, because she is working this summer - and I don't know when she can get off. So if you can - take off a day - and go up and see her - she lives on 1211 Second St. S. W., in Roanoke. And just tell her the situation O.K.??

Well, I can now tell you I've been in combat - and after it was over - was amazed at how plain damned foolishly unafraid I was - except for God I guess I would be having wings or a shovel now. He sent me down an angel for each tank, and I pulled through all right with no men hurt. I lost one tank to mines but as I said got all my men back safely. The payoff was a couple days later when one of the boys came back from church, started to clean his pistol and shot himself through the <u>knee</u>. But - then, that's life over here.

I milked a cow last nite - they are just wandering around loose every field has one or two dead ones - last nite found two cows & two horses in a building which had been shelled & burned pathetic - but necessary I guess. Have a young filly - she can't be more than a couple of weeks old out here - yesterday she was eating <u>anything</u> sweet - today, she is a damned nuisance won't eat anything but <u>white</u> sugar cubes and bites (or tries to) when you don't feed her. P. S. She won't drink cows [sic] milk!!

Cognac and cider is plentiful - also hundreds of bicycles which the Germans had and our boys are riding in style. The Germans lived in style - with women right with them - with some of the pictures we've found on them, they are a degraded bunch - most of them have been kids or oldsters - some Polish, and other occupied countrie's [sic] lads. But guess you are reading all about it - Ernie Pyle gives a good picture - and cowards are practically unknown to us - so many brave heroes - it's really amazing - and our infantry must be made of iron - they really are good - but you can gather that from the fact I had no losses! Course, some of my friends weren't so fortunate. But - all my men came through in swell shape - and as

Appalachia to Dessau

MacArthur said - there are no atheists out here. Life was funny - tho cheap - I was sitting in a tin can, eating out of a tin can drinking out of a tin can (<u>milk</u> & water from my canteen) and using empty shells for a "urinal" - unluckily once when I pitched out a shellful of ----, it hit some infantryman and drenched him!!

Well - how about getting me fixed up!! And if and when - how about a cablegram?? In case you've lost it - our code is ANOMON. Lou isn't extravagant, and she is not expecting a ring as yet.

Must close - by the way this cockeyed war is about to give me a habit - coffee - but this damp weather - one has to have something hot - and it isn't every day you're back far enough to have a fire.

      Well - so long for now.
      Love to all!! Johnny

Part of Goodin's duties as tank commander is to write letters to the families of his men. He expresses that it is hard for him to know what to say, but from some of the replies he received, he apparently succeeded. This letter is from Mrs. K.C. Pearson to Goodin. Roy L. Pearson, Goodin's driver, was on the passenger list for train #7 under the command of Goodin in August 1943, from Indiantown Gap, Pennsylvania.

Ida, La.
July 11/44

Dear Lt. Goodin,

I just can't express in words just how much I do appreciate your nice letter in regards to Roy. He's a sweet kid, and I really do believe you have picked a good driver, and one you won't haft to worry about letting you down.

For he's got what it takes, if you get what I mean. He loves the feel of a wheel in his hand all the way from a modle [sic] "J" to a Sherman Tank.

Also had a letter from Roy this morning, and wasn't one bit surprised to find him in France. I have confidence in his courage and devotion to duty, and with the help of God you all will come thru O.K.

Thanks, Thanks, a lot for the swell letter. Any words at any time you can write me of Roy will be highly appreciated.

      Good Luck, and God Bless you.
      As ever & All ways a True Friend
      Mrs. K. C. Pearson

Five. Normandy—Baptism by Fire, the Spearhead Is Born

After four days of intense fighting, Goodin tells his mother he is "taking the day off" to read his 19 letters, while he listens to "the ear-deafening crescendo of friendly artillery." Goodin's farming background comes into play in his concern for the animals as he feeds a "filly" and milks the cows to relieve their pain. He describes the chaos, "diving into foxholes and under tanks," and the devastation left behind by the Germans. His description is of an abrupt interruption to daily life with "meals left cooking."

12 July 1944

Dear Mom,

   Got your letter of June 23rd yesterday along with 19 other letters - so you see it is a good thing I'm taking the day off. The weather, as usual, is miserably uncertain, and not too warm. The stench ain't too pleasant either, but it is bearable, as is the ear-deafening crescendo of the friendly artillery in the next field. Amazing - the cows and the little filly don't even flicker an eyelash when it goes off - whereas we jump - and if it's <u>enemy</u>, we <u>dive</u> into fox holes or under tanks. So it goes - laughter - grim maybe, but laughter with blood and guts and sorrow. Don't know if I've told you (time disappears completely as an element) about the little filly - her mother dead, and we fed her a little chocolate the first day, then sugar - and <u>now</u> she's a plain damned nuisance - bowling us over or attempting to when we don't give her <u>cubed</u> sugar, and won't eat chocolate.
   She drank a helmet full of cows [sic] milk this morning. When we got here, the Germans had just left, and the cows hadn't been milked for a couple of days - we've been milking steadily, got the lumps out of their bags, and giving good milk again - which we are enjoying no little. The houses - shot to hell - bear the evidence of war and rush - meals left cooking, a stray cat with his tail shot - just enough to be sore and friendly as heck!
   Wardrobes looted, drawers dumped, pictures all over the place. Wine casks, cognac barrels, cider (250 gal. bowls of it) still here. And the boys - inevitably a couple get a drink too much. Ah me. And funny - the German who was taking a crap reached for his pistol - and never got to wipe!! We have even done a little breeding of the cows while here - we had two bulls available - so we gave each of them enough chance and opportunity to perform their "bully" duties. The city boys are becoming educated. I could roll on and on - but won't. Art is now over here somewhere. His wife's address is

Appalachia to Dessau

Mrs. Arthur W. Meyer
6401 Hampton Blvd.
Norfolk, 8
Virginia

I had a nice letter from her yesterday and so have the address. Don't know where you got your information about <u>escapes</u>, but actually 24,999 who <u>start</u> get through. Besides - I told you George was all right - and we'd rather be <u>dead</u> than have you old hens worrying your life away about us. There's so many of them who have just <u>ceased</u> to live until their Georges or Jacks or Johnnys or Bills came home. Which is a sure sign of weakness - but guess you are living as usual, aren't you?? I know Dad is - his letters don't change any!! And his appetite must be the same.

Look - for the umpteenth time - I'm asking <u>nobody</u> any questions when I get married - and when I announced to you my intentions of marrying one Miss Lou Baker - it bothers me not one whit that she is not a millionaire, she's <u>not</u> brilliant, she's not musical, her family <u>didn't</u> come over on the Mayflower, - or what have you - my life will be half over before I get back and I intend living the rest of it and, or <u>we</u> want to - even if it is on the farm at Limestone, O.K.?? when I wrote Dad - my mind had been made up - and his sizing her up was so much bull - guess I put too much in my letters - all I wanted him to do was to see that she gets a <u>ring</u>. And she'd be tickled to death with a 10¢ one - she's wearing one now that I gave her that was made out of a German propeller, and wearing it on the correct finger. (My tank's name is "Bakers Beau".) She's also at different times worn her Mothers [sic] diamond - but it doesn't bother her any!!

If you want to - Mom dear - I'd like for her to have one of your rings - it doesn't make much difference - just something to tell the 4-Fs that a claim is staked out there - not that I'm worried any - but just that I want her to have one!! See??

Well - I want to drop Pop a note or so - so I'll be closing. It's almost milking time too, and my pet is coming up - darn her she's eating green apples to beat heck!!

If my writing doesn't make sense at all times - blame it on the blooming artillery - for once I've had enough racket!! By the way - my initial combat test against the Germans was two weeks ago today - we did all right, and my men all got back safely. One of them shot himself in the knee while cleaning his pistol a couple of days later

Five. Normandy—Baptism by Fire, the Spearhead Is Born

- but it was a clean cut - no danger of death. The Lord sure stayed with me and - had an angel on each one of my tanks - I saw two miracles in about ten minutes - and 8 lives still good as new. Stinky got excited once, when a sharpshooting sniper knocked out a periscope, but we were too busy to be scared!!

    Well, must close - so long for now, and write again.
    Love, Johnny

12 July, 1944
Dear Pop,

    Got your June 26 letter yesterday, & one from Mom, 2 from Sis, 5 from Lou, one from Tom, and the rest from people in general.
    First and foremost - there's no ifs, ands, or buts about Lou so if you wanted to save any openings - you are barking up the wrong tree. My mind has been made up for some time - or should I say ours has been made up. I don't expect she can get off to come down - she's working this summer, and will probably have to stick to it. I hope she does, as everything she does and says helps prepare me to make our marriage a success. The Good Lord has given me a power of observation - and I don't need any advice - all I want is a little action. If I weren't so damned silly - I'd marry her by proxy - but personally I think it's foolish. We don't expect to live in luxury, but we already have a small account started - we're buying a few records and music and stuff like that.
    Just don't worry about the other girls - that's my worry, and one I'm taking care of. In fact, it's the first time in my life I've done something completely on my own - and if mail was quicker - I could tell you lots of things. Right now - I'd just like for her to have one of Mom's rings - and then we'll be set until I get back. If Mom isn't ready to have her - don't bring her down. Gotta close for now - one more thing - I've got your guts so far as Germans go - and I didn't know for sure till two weeks ago. Good feeling - but better knowing the Lord is with you.
                       Love, Johnny

7724-7th Ave Brooklyn NY 7/14/44
Dear Lieutenant,

    I received your very nice and most welcome letter. You can't imagine what it means to me to know that my son is with your kind of people, people who are interested in their fellow men.

Appalachia to Dessau

I have been hearing from Sam pretty regularly and he writes a nice letter but seems reluctant to talk about his work in the service. Your letter has put my mind at ease for which I am very thankful.

In your letter you talk of Sam's sense of humor and his willingness to cooperate - well here at home he was the very same - always working things out to the best advantage and never let anything get him down.

I know he is a great boy for team work in sports or what ever endeavor he is undertaking.

Well Lieut. Goodin I can never express my real sentiments to you for your keen interest in my boy Sam and hope you will let me know more about how he is getting along from time to time.

I'll close now with these words, "May God Bless and Protect you and all your men through a Speedy Victory."

                      Very thankful I remain yours
                      Mrs. Bilotte

West of St. Jean de Daye, the troops are once again regrouping and preparing for the next move even as the enemy continued to fire on land and from the air. "Rations, ammunition, fuel, and other supplies were loaded onto tanks, half-tracks and trucks." It was at St. Jean de Daye that the 3rd first encountered poison gas scares when they smelled unfamiliar odors.[11] As they waited for the weather to break, the Germans filled the skies at night "dropping flares and anti-personnel bombs."[12]

Goodin tells his parents he is getting good at "jumping into foxholes" and only "dogfights and mines to worry about."

15 July 1944 France

Dear Folks,

Just a note to tell you all is well and conditions are favorable. I am becoming the acme of alacrity at jumping into fox-holes, into and under tanks - my eyes and ears are sharper than I ever thought they could be. Am moving from the land of milk - but may be more up or down the road.

I haven't received my voting ballot for any elections yet - who is running in Tennessee? How about a clipping or so - so I can tell what's going on - is Bob Taylor going to run for Governor??

Life is O.K. here - and we're still plugging. Hope you are praying - it sho do help!!

                      Love to all, and see you soon.
                      Johnny

Five. Normandy—Baptism by Fire, the Spearhead Is Born

Same envelope
VMail dated 17 July 1944

Dear Folks,

Nice short break with only dogfights and mines to worry about - God sure does ride with me every time I get my motors turning over. For which I am grateful. Got your letter last nite - if you have to <u>sit</u> on Dad to make him behave - do it - as apparently my Mom is <u>fat</u> enough to these days. I hope my Pop is O.K. - just watch yourself - to hell with these records of 4th of July - it's 4th of July now here all the time.

Got a letter from Anne with her picture yesterday, & Keith Broce sent me a picture of his mother, wife and baby - cute. He's still in England.

Sorry, in a way, about J. R. giving up his business - it won't be the same - but a lot of us are going to have to face changes at home when we come back anyhow.

I'm feeling fine - Sis's box of cookies arrived O.K., and I'm right on the beam with eats. Had a lovely bath today - cold water - one of the boys washed my back. Keep your chins up and Love to all.

       Johnny

Letter dated 17 July 1944
Somewhere in France

Dear Folks,

I'm afraid I'm going to lose all the religion I got in my first two days of battle if Mom don't perk up her ears and get her chin as high as Dads. "Oh ye of little Faith" - is what keeps ringing - you can pray and pray <u>sanely</u> - without whimpering before the Lord - as one says - it may be a one-way conversation - but He doesn't have to <u>ask</u> questions. Your moans & groans should be converted into something worth while; still if a man like Albert Jackson had a heart attack - guess I can't say anything about you women!! One thing about Lou - if she's got any doubts or worries - she must tell 'em to God!! So - old woman - sit yourself down, & say Lord - give me strength to get up & put on some coffee - and <u>you</u> do the worrying - I <u>know</u> you'll take care of my Johnny - and if you <u>do</u> want him - he'll brighten up your Heaven - or he'll beat Hell by shoveling coal so fast the Devil will give him a <u>furlough</u>.

Pop sick - even if his wings were rustling - <u>my</u> God ain't going to let anything happen to him - at least till I get back - and there's no reason why both of you don't live to be 110 - it ain't very long till you'll be

Appalachia to Dessau

celebrating 50 years - which is more than <u>Lou</u> & I can hope for. You just got to take care of yourself.

Well - I'm sorta behind in my mail - so I'm going to close - keep up your prayers, but get some <u>real</u> religion into you!! (Who am I to be preaching!!!)

       Everything is O.K.!! All my love,
       Johnny

The tension of non-stop battle wears on the soldiers. Goodin says in this letter that his "platoon sergeant got tight as a rusty hinge yesterday."

19 July 1944

Dear Mom,

 Am sending you an "S&S" [*Stars and Stripes* Newspaper] and the general is one of those you salute - he's not over me anymore, but he may or could be. My other general I'm so fond of has been given a Silver Star for bravery, in our first encounter - he saved our necks more than once. Sure got a lot of confidence in that man - almost wish he had the Division!! Corlett & he both are like the rest of us - even to carrying pictures in our pocketbooks!!

 Golly - you know something I've missed in farm life?? - <u>Goats</u>. I don't know <u>nothing</u> about 'em. Yesterday I saw one of the most touching sights I've seen - a little billy standing guard over his dead mother & twin - sister - bawling like a <u>baby</u> and excitedly eating grass & leaves - quite a change from milk. Then the engineers buried his family, and he was <u>really</u> lost. He's too wild to put on cows [sic] milk - and I just hope he pulls through. Still stomping around, confused, amazed, and bewildered - over their graves.

 My platoon sergeant got tight as a rusty hinge yesterday on cider - and he's sleeping it off today. I confiscated the cognac, but cider - it's rather difficult to get that - all of it anyhow. Had a couple more changes in my platoon, but think they're for the better. Naturally.

 I sweat out each days [sic] mail to hear from Lou, Sis & you all. Am now sweating a letter from Lou's Mom - to whom I declared my "honorable intentions" sometime ago. You'd better set down on Pop - it's not his nature to realize he may <u>have</u> to slow down a little bit!! And if you have to put him to bed - go ahead.

 Keep him if necessary. Haven't seen a piano since I've been in France. An organ in a little church is the closest thing I've seen to one.

      Must close - love to all, as always.
      <u>Johnny</u>

Five. Normandy—Baptism by Fire, the Spearhead Is Born

Goodin jokes with his parents that he can't decide which is worse, the shelling or the mosquitoes, and that he is writing his letters from foxholes.

```
VMail 19 July 1944 (France)
Dear Folks,
```
   Just to say hello and everything is "under control." Had a little trouble yesterday, boys got hold of some French cider and "teed off" - all sleeping it off today, and thank God we aren't mixed up in anything right now. Made a couple of changes - hope I don't have to make anymore right away.
   Some girl who visited Bill Lundy's wife (T. Burgendahl) told Lou she talked to my Pop and said she liked him - can't imagine girls liking my Pop, can you??
   Between shelling and mosquitoes - I don't know <u>which</u> is the worst - but between them - I have fun. Nearly all my letters are written on the edge of, or <u>in</u> a fox-hole these days. They're gonna keep messing around until somebody gets hurt!!
   Well - drop me a line when you can. And let me know what is going on. O.K.??

                        Love to all, <u>Johnny</u>

With the continual moving and regrouping amongst relentless enemy fire, it is amazing that Goodin finds time to write these letters every couple of days to his parents, and to the parents of his men. Here he expresses he is unharmed except for his "nerves."

```
VMail 20 July - 44 (France)
Dear Folks,
```
   Just a note to tell you Hello - everything is going good and I've no complaints, except against the weather. Pretty rainy and cool. We've had plenty of excitement in the past 18 hours - but no harm done other than "nerves." Some actually beautiful sights - sky lit up by ack-ack fire last nite - I had just finished playing the Chaplains [sic] organ - had quite a bit of fun. Well - six letters today - no complaints about the mail!! Uncle Sam is doing all right by us men here, and no kicks coming - really. Gotta close and answer a few. Love to all,

                              <u>Johnny</u>

Goodin mentions that he has not received any mail in a few days, and that "we've been doing nothing lately." Goodin did not tell his parents about the poison gas scare at St. Jean de Daye. Unfamiliar odors caused a bit of panic, with soldiers hastily donning gas masks. Nor did he tell them that a weather front had moved in and the 3rd Armored was having to wait it out, while all the time they were being attacked by machine-gun fire and bombing by the Germans.[13] This would be the calm before the next storm.

```
V-Mail dated 24 July 44 (France)
Dear Folks,
  Just a howdy note to say I'm O.K., getting along O.K. -
and no complaints except against ants, mosquitoes, flies,
and the weather - and the sun is out for a change, too!!
  Not much news as we have been doing nothing lately - of
course we get our shows every so often - planes, flares,
bombs, and artillery - and we hold our own "track meets"
in diving and running into fox-holes or tanks. We have
seen several planes shot down - and ack-ack [antiaircraft
guns] fire at night sure is pretty - but this damned 4th
of July is going to be expensive eventually.
  Haven't heard from you all for several days now - just
hope everything is all right at home. Guess it is or I
would hear.
              Well - love to all, and write when you can.
              As ever,
              Johnny
```

Northern France: 25 July–14 September 1944

From July 25 to September 14, 1944, the 3rd Armored would smash and batter their way through rivers and streams, from St. Lô to Stolberg, capturing enemy soldiers, and destroying German trains and tanks. On September 2, they would capture the entire rear guard of the 7th and 15th German Armies. More intense fighting was to come in Mons, Belgium, and Maubeuge, France. Pursuing the enemy across Belgium against constant resistance, they finally reached the German border on September 12.[14]

On July 26th, the Spearhead looked up to see Mustang, Fortress, and Liberator bombers fill the sky and begin relentlessly raining down bombs. Men in the 3rd gazed in awe and wondered how anyone could survive the onslaught of what would be known as one of the greatest air-ground operations in history: the Normandy breakthrough.[15] As the planes began their retreat, the Spearhead advanced forward

Five. Normandy—Baptism by Fire, the Spearhead Is Born

fighting night and day, sleeping in trenches, never removing their helmets. Fatigue set in due to always being on the move, constantly on alert, and fighting all day. The Germans attacked at night. There was very little rest as shells and mortars, called "concussion ghosts," made their way into the trenches all night long, never letting up. "Incoming mail" was a call that became all too familiar to the battle-weary soldiers.[16]

It was during this time that the French people, who were now refugees, began appearing along the roads to cheer on the "American Liberators" by throwing flowers.[17]

On July 27, they attacked north of Canisy to effect and exploit the St. Lô breakthrough under the command of Colonel Leander L. Doan.[18]

They advanced against bitter and determined enemy resistance to Cerisy La Salle and Roncey between July 28 and 29, leaving roads cluttered with destroyed enemy vehicles.[19] German troops advanced through the towns while the Luftwaffe gave support overhead. On July 29, as American fighter bombers blasted convoys, the Germans retreated. Troops killed and captured hundreds of enemy soldiers.[20]

It was during this time, while making their way through the fields of Normandy in north-western France, that engineers came up with a plan to thwart the hedgerows, which were "deathtraps." Maintenance built a "hedge chopper," which allowed the tanks to "punch holes" in the hedges and get through more quickly not allowing the Germans time to "zero them."[21]

Under the command of Lt. Colonel Leander L. Doan, the 3rd crossed Seine River on July 30 in vicinity of Gavray against determined enemy resistance.[22] The 32nd Armored tanks plowed ever forward, gaining ground while leaving behind "smashed and burning vehicles of the Wehrmacht."[23]

The bridgehead was secured across the Sée River on July 31 by fording the stream after building up the bed with rocks.[24] Now inside enemy lines, the tanks rolled forward destroying anything in their path determined to reach the next objective: Mortain.[25]

The *Stars & Stripes*, a military newspaper, dated August 1, 1944, referred to in this letter, reports that "Sherman tanks roared ahead, garlanded with roses, tossed by French civilians whose homes were left unburned," and that "tank units rapidly mopped up German pockets of resistance."

After continuous and heavy fighting for 12 days, and driving through tracer bullets, "strong points were established."[26]

A defensive position was held on high ground west of Mortain

Appalachia to Dessau

between August 3 and 4 under intensive and uninterrupted enemy shelling.²⁷

Goodin does a rare thing in this letter to his parents. While mentioning his fiancée, Lou, he expresses that all he can be concerned about right now is his own safety. The intensity of the situation and his weariness are apparent as he says "after my life, she comes next," with next underlined and two exclamation points added. And to further let them know that things are tough, he tells them his dog Stinky hides and "all you can see from under the tank is two eyes and a torrent of curses and prayers."

```
Letter 5 August 1944
Dear Folks,
    Am enclosing a Stars & Stripes and some personal letters
which I'd rather you don't read, but knowing your curiosity
(both of you!!) well - guess you will read them.
    The months drag on - but we are going almost too fast.
I'm often reminded of Mother as I pass through some towns
- which!! - "I always did want to see !!" [sic] Look Mom
- money is no good to me - I can't spend it. The French
people would give us anything we wanted - but they've
so pitifully little - other than wine cider, cognac, and
stuff like that.
    I'm not worrying about Lou right now - as I told her,
after my life, she comes next!! But we are doing O.K., and
I'm well and happy (happy to be well & O.K.!!) Tell Mr.
Moss hello - and go over & kiss Audrey for me - I only
kissed her goodbye and tell 'em all "Hello" for me.
    Stinky still has his tail up - but often all you can
see is two eyes from under the tank and a torrent of
curses and prayers - oh me!!
    Well - gotta close - keep all this stuff for me - by
each letter, I hope.
                            All my love, Johnny
```

The 3rd kept on rolling having gained nearly 100 miles since leaving Omaha Beach on June 29.²⁸

The bridgehead across Mayenne River of Ambriéres was quickly secured on August 6.²⁹

On August 7, Major General Maurice Rose assumed command.³⁰ Goodin expressed great respect for General Rose in his letters.

Between August 8–12, the Spearhead would engage in battle after battle constantly moving forward toward areas west of Mayenne. According to the Official Record of Combat, British and American

Five. Normandy—Baptism by Fire, the Spearhead Is Born

forces were working together to create a trap around Field Marshall Von Kluge's Seventh Army.[31] In order to achieve this goal, the 3rd Armored was ordered to "drive deep into this Nazi cauldron of elite units in an attempt to close the gap."[32] "The 3rd Armored Division was going to be in at the kill."[33]

During a brief reprieve, the 3rd Armored conducted much needed maintenance. According to a 1943 film produced by the War Department titled "Security on the March—Mechanized Units," there were five main points for tank commanders and crews: advanced preparation, alertness, concealments, dispersion and firepower. To ensure the efficiency of equipment for upcoming battles, specific maintenance procedures were to be followed. Once a halt was called, guards would be posted. Soldiers were constantly on alert because the enemy could approach from any angle at any time, and "surprise is the enemy's deadliest weapon."[34]

As tank commander, Goodin and his crew would first ensure their tank was concealed and guards posted. The tank was positioned in a way that would allow forward movement and ease of escape, with guns pointed out toward an approaching enemy. The type of concealment would depend on the terrain. Tanks must be hidden from enemies on the ground and from the air either by hedgerows, under the cover of trees, or covered by cut tree branches. If no natural cover is available, the tank is to be covered with a camouflage net. Concealment also means getting rid of any tracks leading up to the area. This could mean taking a tree branch and sweeping dusty roads to eliminate tracks.[35]

Once concealment is achieved and the area is secured, maintenance begins. All parts of the tank and equipment must be checked and refurbished as needed. Dank containers were to be kept filled, gas masks at the ready. Gas, engine, track, supply and ammunition checks were to be conducted immediately. Track checks were of critical importance as any type of debris could stall a tank at a critical moment. All ammunition was to be checked, reloaded, cleaned, and undetonated: "Large caliber guns should always have a full quarter. One shell may decide whether you live or die."[36]

Goodin, as tank commander, would also be looking once again at the map of the terrain to familiarize and know all points of possible attack while double-checking to make sure all boxes have been checked for maintenance. Tank commanders had to know the route from Point A to Point B in order to be able to rejoin the column in case of separation.[37]

Appalachia to Dessau

3rd Armored mechanics check out the competition inspecting a German tank after heavy battles in Normandy, August 1944.

Medics pick up soldiers for evacuation hit by German shells in Belgium.

Five. Normandy—Baptism by Fire, the Spearhead Is Born

American M24 Chaffee tanks.

After a brief rest, resupply and maintenance, the 3rd crossed the river at Mayenne and advanced forty-five miles to Ranes and Joue du Bois between August 13 and 14, leaving a smashed trail of burning enemy equipment. Heavy fighting and resistance met the troops. Elements were completely cut off by the enemy for two days.[38] The Spearhead had become used to being surrounded, but now battled-hardened, they had gained confidence they could break out again.[39] Medical supplies were dropped by air.[40]

As the day dawned on August 16, the Spearhead went on the attack.[41] After vigorous and determined fighting against elements of the 1st SS (Adolf Hitler) and 2nd SS (Das Reich) Panzer Divisions, the outskirts of Fromental were reached about dark.[42]

A coordinated advance by Companies A and B of the Spearhead on the road to Fromental was fraught with conflict as "Jerry assault guns and artillery contested every inch of the route."[43] According to the *Spearhead History Official Record of Combat*, "The enemy was everywhere... and many surprise engagements were fought. Tanks and tank destroyers had many engagements at ranges less than one hundred yards."[44]

Tanks were vulnerable at close ranges. A World War II War

Appalachia to Dessau

Department Training film titled "How to Destroy German Tanks," describes in detail that vulnerability:

> A tank is 9/10 blind and stone deaf over the noise of the tank. Because of fixed guns, the tank can only fire in one direction at a time. If the turret is turned to the left, the "dead space" on the right side is vulnerable to attack. The guns cannot cover the ground close to the tank. There is 20 circular feet of dead space around the tank. Firing is limited to 25 feet high, so if there are men on the roof of a house or a high embankment, the tank cannot fire at them. A tank that is out of gas, fouled its track, or stalled due to engine trouble is vulnerable.
>
> All tanks have vulnerable spots, limitations that can be manipulated by a tank hunter. A soldier on foot in the dead space, is a danger to the tank. Vision devices can be destroyed by small arms. Antitank mines blow the tracks off tanks that go over them, smoke grenades "blind" the tank, and rocket grenades are a walking death that can penetrate tank armor and kill the men inside. The walls of some World War II tanks had thin side armor and has been compared to "tin foil."[45]

Fromental cleared of enemy and contact made with the British on August 18, thereby closing the German escape gap to the east.[46] They had been through a battle with the best of the German army, and "they had won by a slim margin." After grueling days of battle with little rest or sleep, the 3rd Armored rested a couple of days before moving toward the Seine River.[47]

Understandably, Goodin had not written his parents for nearly two weeks. He always expresses to them how glad he is to receive mail. He took advantage of the brief reprieve to tell his parents "my gray hairs are increasing." He speaks of losing some of his soldiers who "can't take it under pressure," and that he could "write a book if he had time." The constraints of censoring kept Goodin from elaborating about activities and locations.

```
18 Aug 1944
Dear Folks,

   Sorry I haven't written in so long - but guess you know
and understand I'm getting your mail fairly regularly,
and haven't just had time to write. I'm O.K., and still
getting along all right - altho my gray hairs are
increasing, so the boys say.
   I've been getting your mail O.K. - Pop's letters and
Mom's V- mails - all of which are swell. Don't get so much
mail anymore so I don't write so much. I occasionally
write one of the boys' mothers, telling them how they
are, etc., and get answers from them.
```

Five. Normandy—Baptism by Fire, the Spearhead Is Born

This smoldering tank was a familiar sight in Normandy, August 1944.

> I've lost three non-coms [non-commissioned] in the last two weeks to drinking - can't take it under pressure.
>
> Lou really had competition yesterday - a 16 yr. old red-head who has 9 in the family - twin girls & twin boys - and a build about like Lous [sic]- hair not quite as red. My, my. Unfortunately, we don't stop anywhere long enough to "get acquainted." I almost did, once.
>
> Got a package of nuts from Sis which are going down extremely well. She also writes as often as ever - guess she is home by now.
>
> Well - I could write a book if I had time - but I don't have it. So - until I get back - just take it easy.
>
> All my love to all,
Johnny

Between August 19, and 22, 1944, the 3rd Armored "mopped up" at Ranes-Fromental and began "maintenance and refitting."[48]

In addition to overseeing maintenance of the tanks, the World War II Tank Crew Training Film, titled "Security on the March—Mechanized Units," also describes the many stressful and multi-tasking jobs of the tank commander. One is to stand on alert in the tank turret for 12 to 16 hours at a time. This requires accurate and acute observation of

Appalachia to Dessau

American Sherman tank in a ditch near Fromental, August 1944.

all surroundings for the enemy, in the air, left and right sides, front and rear of the tank. Tanks are vulnerable due to limited vision devises, limited firing ranges, fixed guns that can only fire in one direction at a time, thin side armor, and dead space around the tank that cannot be covered by ammunition. The pressure of imminent danger, as well as having the lives of his men in his hands, takes its toll. The tank commander must also watch for messengers and signals from the platoon leader at all times.[49]

In the book *Spearhead of the West*, a repeated theme is a lack of sleep due to battles enduring for days. Pure adrenaline, loyalty to their comrades, and dedication to their motto "Victory or Death," urged them on.[50] The battles had apparently taken their toll on Goodin as he uncharacteristically expresses to his parents "this Hell over here is changing me."

```
VMail 21 AUG - 44
 Dear Folks,
   Haven't had time to write lately - this is just to say
 "Hello" to you. Have gotten your letters & clippings O.K.
```

Five. Normandy—Baptism by Fire, the Spearhead Is Born

Abandoned German Panzer IV tank, August 1944.

- no time to acknowledge them. Hold up on Lou for a while - I'm afraid this Hell over here is changing me and I don't want to hurt her if I can help it - right now, tho - she & <u>love</u> seem far away from me. It can't last too long, tho - and when we get back to normal - everything will be O.K., I hope.

Everything is O.K. with me - have made a few changes here & there. Went to church last night & played the organ - as usual. Tell Charley Moss & all, Hello for me.

On August 22, the 3rd Armored began moving toward the Seine River. They reached the area just below Paris on August 24, with preparation to cross on August 25. Units would cross the Seine on a 540-foot span bridge built by the 23rd Armored Engineer Battalion.[51]

Crossed the Seine River at Melun on August 26 and attacked to northeast to begin liberating French towns and cities by the score.[52] By August 27, they secured the bridgehead over Marne River at La Ferte Sous Jouarre.[53]

Appalachia to Dessau

Speeding on toward Braisne, two German railroad trains were caught and destroyed on August 28. Battle ensued between four Tiger tanks loaded on one train and our tanks. Enemy tanks were destroyed by tank and direct artillery fire.[54]

The attack on Aisne River continued, and the bridgehead was secured on August 29. General Maurice Rose personally checked a suspected bridge for damage. He received the Distinguished Service Cross for his disregard for personal safety. The 3rd crossed the Aisne River, smashing through small bands of resistance.[55]

On August 31, they received orders by radio to change direction and proceed north toward Mons, Belgium, to trap large numbers of enemies.[56] The 3rd Armored executed a swift 90-degree change in direction and began attacking its way north in less than an hour. "This feat is considered to be one of the most spectacular ever accomplished by the 3rd Armored Division."[57]

```
VMail SEP 1 1944
Dear Everybody,
    Am O.K., well & happy as usual - no news - read the
papers. Have worked with Reconnaissance for a while and
liked it. Can't possibly answer all your questions - but
tell the Carters I am O.K. - Luck to you - & don't be so
damned optimistic!!!
                          All my love to all, Johnny
```

They crossed the Franco-Belgian border at 1615 hours on September 2 and seized Mons.[58] Throngs of Belgians were cheering on the first American troops to enter their country. Seizure resulted in trapping the entire rear guard of the 7th and 15th German Armies, with approximately 30,000 soldiers attempting retreat. Ten thousand were captured by the Spearhead, and many more killed.[59]

Intense fighting raged between Mons, Belgium, and Maubeuge, France, for two days and nights between September 3 and 4 as the enemy attempted to break through and escape. Hundreds of enemy vehicles were destroyed, and more than two thousand enemy soldiers were captured.[60]

By September 5, they began pursuit across Belgium, overtaking remnants of fleeing enemy. Many wagon trains and vehicles were destroyed.[61]

They entered western section of Liége on September 7.[62] The troops were once again greeted with cheers by civilians who showered them with cognac, champagne and ice cream, but the troops had no time to stop.[63]

Five. Normandy—Baptism by Fire, the Spearhead Is Born

The troops moved on to Verviers between September 9 and 11, and continued attacking the German border in spite of increasing enemy tank resistance.[64]

On September 12, they reached German border at Langfeld (south of Aachen) at 1638 hours.[65]

On September 12, the 3rd Armored had reached their destination: the Siegfried Line. Eighteen brutal days of non-stop battles across Northern France and Belgium had taken its toll. Looking into the face of Germany at the formidable Dragon's Teeth, they knew it was far from over. The only way through these concrete barriers was explosives. The men were exhausted from lack of sleep, dirty, and nerves raw from the barrage of deafening noise, loss of comrades, and death all around. There would be no time to rest as General Maurice Rose had already sent men out to determine the best way to proceed.[66]

On September 13, they tore a gap through first Dragon's Teeth of the Siegfried Line, destroying several 88mm AT guns and six concrete pillboxes. Casualties were heavy as the enemy defended their home country's frontier tenaciously.[67]

In the *Stars and Stripes* Newspaper dated Thursday, September 14, 1944, the headlines on page one read: "Yanks at the Siegfried Line Clearing Way for U.S. Armor." On page four an article titled "Siegfried Line 2000 Yards Away—and No Shots Fired," by United Press War Correspondent Robert Richards, quotes Major Gregg McKee's first impression as he gets his first glimpse of the pillboxes: "This is the real McCoy." The articles states that "the boys are eager to start for those hills and they do not seem to care how tough the Siegfried Line is."[68]

The significance of this battle is best put into perspective by a Battle Honors letter, dated April 30, 1945, awarding the Distinguished Unit Badge and Oak Leaf Cluster from the Headquarters of the Third Armored Division for the period of September 11–13, 1944:

> The 2nd Battalion, 32nd Armored Regiment is cited for outstanding performance of duty in action against the enemy in Belgium and Germany during the period 11 to 13 September 1944. During this period the 2nd Battalion, 32nd Armored Regiment, was assigned the mission of spearheading an armored task force in its drive to reach the German border and smash the outer defenses of the Siegfried Line. In three days of fierce fighting the 2nd Battalion, 32nd Armored Regiment, succeeded in overpowering enemy defenses of the "west wall" near Nütheim, Germany.
>
> Vigorous hostile resistance was counter-balanced by an insuperable urge to close with and destroy the enemy wherever found. Undaunted by concerted hostile fire, this unit grimly pushed on killing or capturing the

Appalachia to Dessau

enemy and destroying his equipment. The 2nd Battalion, 32nd Armored Regiment, in spite of severe losses, achieved a glorious victory. Elements of the 105th Panzer Brigade and the 9th Panzer Division offered defiant resistance throughout, employed anti-tank, machine gun, mortar, and artillery fire and fanatically held their positions until either killed or overpowered by the unrelenting pressure. During that period 11-13 September 1944, the 2nd Battalion, 32nd Armored Regiment, distinguished itself in battle by extraordinary heroism, exhibited outstanding gallantry, determination, and espirit de corps in overcoming unusually difficult and hazardous conditions. The skill, proficiency, and complete disregard for personal safety of the personnel of this unit paved the way for more devastating blows against the enemy on German soil despite fierce and stubborn resistance. The

Here and next page: Spearhead faced the formidable, but soon to be proven not impenetrable, "jagged symbols of Nazi Germany, the Dragon's Teeth" of the Siegfried Line, Rhineland, September 1944.

Five. Normandy—Baptism by Fire, the Spearhead Is Born

unconquerable spirit and extraordinary heroism displayed by the 2nd Battalion, 32nd Armored Regiment rendered an invaluable contribution to the Allied cause.

The letter is signed by Command of Brigadier General Hickey.

Goodin's short letter to his parents must have been hurriedly sent just to tell them he was okay, but that he "lost two of my best men." Unable to talk about the ferocious battle he has just been through and the number of comrades lost, he compares his feelings of reaching the German border to those of the Israelites reaching the promised land. Constantly reassuring them, he let them know that mail was "sporadic" and they were "still rolling."

```
VMail September 13, 1944 (Somewhere in Belgium)
Dear Folks,
    September 13th and all is well - I've been looking into
Germany and feel sorta like it must have felt to Israel
to see the promised land. I got mail today - takes it
a good while to reach us now - and definitely in spurts.
Still - it's good if it stays that way.
    I'm O.K., well - a little grayer - I've lost two of my
```

Appalachia to Dessau

best men since last I wrote (that was ages ago) but they
are not seriously injured. We are still rolling - I've
quite a few guns now - if I get them back with me. How is
my mail reaching you now??

        Love,
        Johnny

CHAPTER SIX

"Still Rollin'"

*Rhineland, Germany,
September 15, 1944–March 21, 1945;
Ardennes, Belgium,
December 19, 1944–January 25, 1945*

On September 15, the second and final line of Dragon's Teeth and pillboxes were breached west of Stolberg. Battle-weary men accomplished this difficult job with sheer willpower and in spite of great losses.[1]

According to *Spearhead in the West*, one of the techniques for breaching the formidable Dragon's Teeth was to blow them up with dynamite, then smooth the path with a tank-dozer.[2]

By September 18, they had cleared rear areas of enemy and assisted in capturing Münsterbusch, situated on west edge of Stolberg, Germany.[3]

The 3rd Armored were tired. Tanks and equipment desperately needed maintenance. Reinforcements were needed. The Siegfried line would prove to be a daunting, formidable and dangerous barrier. Piercing the German armor of pillboxes and dragon's teeth would take careful planning, reconnaissance, persistence and courage through the heavily defended area referred to as a "nightmare of whistling shells and heavy mortar fire."[4]

Between September 18, and November 18, the 3rd Armored were in the Rhineland area of Germany, specifically Stolberg and Mausbach-Breinig. They began to "regroup and take stock of losses. That 18-day dash from the Seine to the Siegfried had been successful and very spectacular, but it had cost a great deal in men and machinery." Only 100 of 400 tanks were fully operational, and supplies had dwindled.[5] Goodin's letters go back and forth between Germany and Belgium during this time.

Appalachia to Dessau

```
VMail
25 Sept [1944]
Hi Folks,
```
    Am O.K., well & happy - sent my voters ballot in today - some people I don't know - but that is O.K. Write when you can.

Love, Johnny

Time between September 26 and November 18 was spent defending the sector in Stolberg, Rhineland, approximately 20 miles from the Siegfried Line.[6]

The 3rd Armored controlled half of Stolberg, and Germany the other half.[7] While stationary and able to make use of abandoned homes for living quarters, the 3rd Armored was constantly on alert from enemy fire day and night. There were numerous casualties, little sleep, and with the fall rains, the ground had turned into a "quagmire."[8] Compared to the last eighteen days, all was relatively calm, but the 3rd was on full alert as an order to move out could come at a moment's notice. Goodin and his tank crew knew the dangers of tanks trying to maneuver over the sopping wet ground.

In the next two letters to his dad, Goodin is showing some of the strain of the last few weeks as he talks about comrades lost, but reassures his dad that no news does not necessarily mean bad news.

```
6 Oct 44 (Excerpt)
Dearest Pop,
```
    Sometime since I have written to you down "here" but every so often, I feel it sorta necessary. No particular reason..just..well, just you and me. That's all.

    Have just finished writing a letter to one of the boys in the company's wife. He was killed way back..and she had written one of the sargeants [sic] wanting to know some of the details. The War Dept. won't let us tell anything like that, and it makes it kinda tough on us... as I know what one would like to know in such a case. Anyhow, I did try and tell her a few things about Bill without telling anything about his death.

    One thing...when you don't hear from me, and you don't hear from the War Dept. either...well, you don't have to worry, as they are strictly fast in getting information about casualties and so forth out. One reason they don't allow us to write anything is to keep from confusing people who may hear from them, and then get a letter from one of us.

Six. "Still Rollin'"

Well, gotta close for now. All my love and write when you can.

---

8 Oct 44

Dear Folks,

Sunday afternoon and while I'm waiting for church to start will drop you a line and tell you everything is still o.k. with me..am still in the rest area, and am enjoying life as well as could be expected this close to the front. At any minute, though we may pull out, so we are making the most of the break. I sure have caught up on my sleep for awhile...sleep about 12 hours a night.. not counting the interruptions by the enemy artillery, planes, mortars, and what not. Last night they really started after me...personally, I thought,...but as usual, and with a silent prayer..God and his angels were hovering around me, and I'm still o.k.

No news from here that I can tell you...we've had three fairly good days, days that were nice and sunny and stuff..but still and all, I expect that the winter will be kinda rough over here. Naturally we had hoped that this mess would be over before the winter really sets in..but now we don't know. We may start a big one anytime and not stop until we get into Berlin..but we don't know, can't know...so..Anyhow, I'm not planning on being home before Christmas of next year at best. That way...well, things may break before then...sure hope so. Anyhow..if I get back altogether..I don't care if it's two more years.

Not much mail lately...my last v-mail took 24 days to get home according to the way I figure it..that was 1st of Sept. and you got it 24th. Oh well..it sure gets here in a hurry.. I got Dad's airmail of the 25th day before yesterday..so I sure can't kick about the mail coming in here on time.

<blockquote>
With love and kisses to all,
and best love to you,
Always,
Johnny
</blockquote>

According to *Spearhead History Official Record of Combat,* this period was a build-up time with activity twenty-four hours a days of supply convoys, machine and road repair, and replacements. Abandoned buildings were used for headquarters and workshops.[9]

On October 11, the order came down to take Aachen. Part of the 3rd Armored proceeded to Aachen, while others continued to improve and patrol Stolberg.[10]

Appalachia to Dessau

```
VMail dated 15 Oct 44 (GERMANY)
Dear Folks,
```

   Sunday morning and things are quiet around here (weren't so quiet last night with the Luftwaffe buzzing around being careless and dropping things all over the place) so will drop you a line. I am having Uncle Sam send you fifty dollars for me for this last month, and am sending Sis fifteen dollars...just for what ever she may need it for. I also sent Russell Haynes a check for the church...I haven't made any contributions to the church since I've been over here, and I thought they could use it at the fishery church as well as anywhere.

   Have been getting your letters rather well of late... seems to be taking a long time for them to go out from here, but the airmails and v-mails are coming through in excellent shape over here, and of course...you know how mail is to us.

   Sent Earnest Day my copies of the "record" [Hometown Newspaper, *The Erwin Record*] that I'm getting rather regularly, and got another one in last night. He's up on the front right now, but will get them to him sometime this afternoon.

   Guess everything is going along well with you...wish you would quit worrying your silly heads over me...if you didn't hear from me, and you don't hear from the War Department...there's nothing to worry about...I don't believe there is anything to worry about, anyhow.

   Well, have some little details to attend to right now. Four of my boys that I recommended stars for, have gotten them..all of them bronze..so I'm kinda proud of them right now. Am going to recommend about three more shortly, and hope that they come through. With all my love as ever... let me know when your package arrives.

                           Love, Johnny

With over 700 prisoners taken, Aachen surrendered on October 21.[11]
   Upon entering Germany, a military government was set up: "The 3rd Armored Division was the first united of the Allied Armies to establish Military Government in Germany in World War II."[12]
   Goodin is unusually blunt and straightforward with his mother in her request of him not to hate the enemy. He expresses complete disdain for the German soldiers calling them "machines" and "mass-produced mechanical soldiers," while he applauds the women and children. Goodin is finding it difficult to reconcile what he has to do as a soldier to the Ten Commandments upon which he was "brought up."

Six. "Still Rollin'"

And while Goodin says he doesn't "gloat over the dead," he knows the harsh reality is kill, or be killed, as he points out in this letter. He says, "While retaining the quality of mercy, I still must exercise the law of self-preservation—which may not be God's 1st of Ten Commandments, but is *Nature's first.*" Goodin reminds his mother of what this war is about when he tells her he is willing to "risk destruction in order to save others from annihilation," and that by liberating people he is doing something "real and worthwhile."

```
Oct. 21st - 44
Dear Mom,
    Well tonite - have been moving around today but am
getting a little sleepy - getting good light, tho, and so
- will write you a few lines. Shooting the bull with the
boys, I'm not getting very far - this is all I've written
in 2 hours now.
    Mom - I appreciate you not wanting any feeling of hate
in us - that they have mothers, too - but - if you have
any of your old time fire - I'll bet you'd beat their
mamas up for raising such a stinking bunch of bastards,
now - wouldn't you?? Seriously Mom - I have nothing but
pity - sorta like killing a sheep-killing dog, or an
egg-sucking dog - just can't break them of the habit. The
nearest I've come to God was because I had little enough
sense to leave the comparative safety of my tank to help
a wounded German - but - enough of that. They aren't
human, Mom - they're machines. But - these little kids -
they're darling - a little girl about 3 - the meanest
cutest thing I've ever seen - and steam? Wow. But - a
perfect lady. Hildegard-11, cleaned up our room, washed my
socks, patched my torn jacket. Even scratched my back. It
may be hard for you to realize the tremendous difference
between the German mass-produced mechanical soldier,
and the family he has left behind. These kids & their
mamas go to Mass every morning, are perfectly reared to
be young ladies, are profusely grateful for chocolates
& sweets. No, mummy - there'll never be any hate in my
heart to that extent. I don't gloat over their dead, and
except for the desire to take them prisoner instead of
shooting them - I would not have lost two good men. It
was a bitter lesson for a pupil who was brought up on the
Ten Commandments, and on love, affection and kindness.
But - it's value will not be forgotten and God saw fit to
let me learn without injury to me - so - while retaining
the quality of mercy, I still must exercise the law of
self-preservation - which may not be God's 1st of Ten
```

Appalachia to Dessau

Commandments, but is <u>Nature's first.</u> It is this latter law that makes Stinky whine and hug the earth, to call on the good Lord for strength and courage, and to not be afraid - and a coward. And it is <u>God's</u> will that overcomes Nature's law, and a force from within that drives the physical being into an atmosphere dregged [sic] with danger, fraught with fear - to risk destruction in order to save others from possible annihilation - and the Almighty with his Angel of Death (who has been called a veritable prostitute because she sleeps with all, takes anyone promiscuously - and her price is the same to all) held in check, graciously allows us unworthy souls to continue our living - or existing, from day to day. But gives us the courage to smile, even as Death looks at us - not conscious perhaps that we are still impudent and ungentlemanly enough to smile at anything in a skirt, and to flirt with any angels - or wink slyly at just any girl!

So it goes - Mom, my dear. One of my greatest joys in France and Belgium was to smile, wink and tip my hat to some old lady (or gentleman) who sat back from the howling, screaming, adoring crowds of liberated peoples - and occasionally blowing them a kiss. I somehow felt the glow that sprang in their hearts - and <u>could</u> see the twinkle in their eyes - and thanked my Heavenly Father that he has so graciously spared <u>my</u> Mom from the horrors of occupation. And - I'm proud - tho you would never know it - that I'm a part of their liberation, that I have sacrificed in sweat and blood (99 44/100% sweat!) for their freedom - that I'm doing something real, worthwhile - even wonderful. You must know the feeling - of releasing a trapped animal, taking a splinter out of a dog's paw - pulling a nail from a child's foot - (might I even say milking a very tired old cow whose "Mo" neglected her - you <u>did</u> help Mamie, didn't you????) it's the same glow of self-satisfaction from practicing the Golden Rule.

And yet - I wonder about my insatiable love of hunting - is it the feeling of freedom of doing as I want, in hunting what game I want, the thrill of perfection as a shot finds its mark? Or it is the lust to kill, to demonstrate man as all-powerful and ruler of the lower kingdoms? Or matching wits with Nature's own children, learning their tricks - as the wily, squeamish squirrel, or the 'possum? Again - is it the confidence one receives - knowing that if necessary, one <u>could</u> live on the game of the forest, and successfully manage to live if all vestiges and clothes of civilization were thrown away and primeval conditions were forced on one?

Six. "Still Rollin'"

>   Many questions, Mom, dear - which in my youthful ignorance
> I could not imagine to answer satisfactorily. But you -
> (who are wise) your letter - I quote - "now that they know
> I'm <u>crazy</u>" - ha! - you who dropped so many little pearls
> of wisdom - (yea, verily - almost before swine!) - perhaps
> in your communions with God, you have found the answers
> to my feeble brains [sic] questions. I am not at all
> convinced that the good people who wrote "young men shall
> dream dreams, but old men shall see <u>visions</u>", made a mistake
> in <u>not</u> including <u>old women</u>. Sometimes I find myself taking
> strolls into the hills with you, or sailing madly off
> some mountain top - "4 wheels and no brakes" and I wonder
> what it would be like to have you here to witness the
> liberation of a just proud people and the conquering of
> an arrogant array of Aryans. But, I must content myself
> with my musings and hope that, the Good Lord willing -
> sometime soon I can sit down and discuss things with you.
> And - I have your dear - welcome letters to me - always
> a comfort as you have been writing <u>quite</u> frequently -
> sorta like a gentleman who imbibes too much beer and finds
> it necessary to make frequent "trips" - finally, pouring
> his beer into the can so as to cut out the middle-man - I
> hope to cut out the middle man soon - and talk straight
> to you, and vice versa. And now, my dear Mom - it's after
> 1:00 and your Johnny must have his beauty nap - gray hair
> may be distinguished looking - but the face under it must
> remain awake.
>
>   With all my love, as always,
>   Johnny

In the next few letters, Goodin apparently has more time to write, as the letters are quite long, and he mentions he's "sorta jittery, doing nothing for so long." He gives much more information about his situation and events taking place. He jokes with his mother about her worrying about the "concrete teeth." He tells her the "Germans are the masters of mortar, and it is deadly, as you can't hear them coming in on you." He mentions the public abuse heaped on French girls who were "mistresses of the German soldiers."

Goodin expresses his admiration for all of the brave generals who have "led them through hell" and "the bravery of General Maurice Rose, who is now in charge of their division." He also applauds the Air Corp and the "Forts and Libs" and how they should be the "ideal of every American Boy." He is excited to tell them that General Rose, a man he greatly respects, has now become their division leader. Goodin applauds all of the leaders who "led and followed them through hell."

Appalachia to Dessau

Oct. 22nd, 1944

Dear Folks,

   Well, whatta you know...here it is Sunday afternoon, and after a night of riotous living during which I won all of 7 marks (70 cents), I finally got to bed at the grand hour of 5:00 this morning. I wasn't drunk..not even drinking... not even so much as a little beer. But..sorta felt jittery, doing nothing for so long...beginning to itch again..and that isn't good, is it?? Haven't been to church today, but am thinking about going later this afternoon. Ferguson isn't back yet, but at least we go and have a few prayers and sing a few songs and carry on half way..in fact, his assistant is doin[g] a darn good job taking his place, though of course, our bitching to him does not do so much good as it did with Ferguson.
   No mail last night...but maybe I'll get some tonight. I sorta feel like I'll catch it up sometime. I am also getting caught up on my mail..have answered most of my mail now, and try to get you a letter now and then.
   Had to laugh at Mom's sweating out our going through the concrete teeth..it wasn't bad really...our boys got through that all right...it was then that we ran into a little difficulty...but the teeth, once they were blown through weren't too bad. It sure is a sight to see all that wasted labor gone up in some sort of monument to German stupidity and failure in dreams of world conquest. Some of the pillboxes were excellently equipped...we got nice comforters out of them, weather coats, wine, brandy, whiskey, arms and ammunition, to say nothing of sweets and candies. We had real lemons, preserves, butter, and delicacies we hadn't enjoyed for some time. Some instances, they had left cooked meals which we got in in time to finish for them. My first day across the line..we ate like kings.
   No, Mom, the artillery fire is not quite the worst but it runs a close second to mortars...the Germans are masters of the mortar, and it is deadly..you can't hear them coming in on you. Artillery, makes a hum that gives you warning..some times not much of one, admittedly. Anyhow, right next to the mortars, comes the artillery airbursts ..which our army has developed to a very high degree, also, these don't give you much warning, either..but more than the mortars.
   You don't want to see the firing squad of the French traitors..perhaps you would not have enjoyed seeing French girls who had been mistresses to German soldiers getting their hair cut completely off in public squares,

Six. "Still Rollin'"

in most cases having all their clothes but a G-string cut or torn off of them. Then paraded through the streets to the jeers and frenzied cries of a wild mob. Some of them were lucky they weren't killed. And I don't doubt that in some instances, they were. Some collaborators were brought out on the spot and bumped off..in the worst instances...give the French credit they at least were honest enough in most cases to give them a trial. The Belgians..well, they weren't quite so given to red tape to say the least.

General Rose has now been listed as our Division leader ..and what a man...a driver and a leader..we have more guts in our brass than ever before in any war..our Col. Doan, Blanchard, Whitlaw..General Rose and my beloved of all beloved Generals Doyle O! Hickey...leading us through hell and us following them through hell, and trying to emulate their example in our small way, our small effort to keep things running smoothly and efficiently.

And the air corp..the 47s. <u>diving</u> into hell, while we pause and hold our breath to wait for them to come out, and then let it out as they zoom up graceful as a bird; the magnificents Forts [Fortresses] and Libs [Liberators], moving relentlessly through the flak, unshaken by the flak that envelops them sometimes into magnificent balls of fire.. ghastly, yet magnetic..the frantic diving for field glasses and binoculars and the little white dots of the parachutes are meticulously, painfully counted..1,2, 4,5..another and another, and finally the souls of those great ships give up the ghost, and dive in long spirals earthward, incredibly slow appearing,

General "Doyle O!" [Hickey] and Colonel Leander L. Doan in the center are flanked by Barnwell and Hidalgo. Goodin extols the virtues of both, stating that Hickey is his beloved general who led them through hell.

Appalachia to Dessau

because of the height and the distance; or one seems to explode literally in midair, no time for getting out.. yet, out of the smoke, the clouds, the flying particles of metal, playing aimlessly in the sunlight, miraculously parachutes appear..not all of them, even God does not save all of his Daniels from the fiery furnace, and we are grateful to see the few that do appear. And those great silver twin ships..having two of everything but the pilot..diving and bombing with split second precision, leveling off and climbing back up into the sky at tremendous speeds..then a spurt of flame, temporarily blown out by the wind as the pilot dives the ship at top speed..then more smoke, and he levels off, pulls up into a vertical position and parachutes into the great void.. as the mortally wounded bird suddenly nose dives to the earth, colliding with a huge explosion of dust, smoke, fire,...death.

And the pilot swinging in the breeze floating down, maneuvering his chute as best he can in the wind, drifting..trying to reach friendly lines...some times they do, some times, they don't.

Guts, nerve, courage,..they should be the ideal of every American boy as they carry out the traditions of our heritage in every detail.

The old devils who want to go so bad...I'm surprised at you. You who have always wanted to do things, different things, see new things, explore..criticising someone who would want to be here..it <u>is</u> a great adventure..dangerous, surely..but you could never accuse a man of J.R.'s stature of lacking courage..and I, for one, <u>vividly believe</u> he would want to be here..no..J.R. would never run...and he would be like me (there are lots of things I try to pattern myself after him in), he would enjoy the good parts of this saga and appreciate the finer things, the same as I do..sweat out the enemy, certainly, but at the same time..when the opportunity came...to take advantage of the chances and things that are worth seeing. Surely.. there are parts that are shot up, but there is a lot of beauty left here..picturesque, old, archaic..ancient, even medieval cities left..with life in some parts of them no different for the marks of the ages on them. But, I must be closing..so be good and write when you can.

                    All my love and kisses to all,
                    and don't send me anything for
                    Christmas..we have everything.

        Johnny

Six. "Still Rollin'"

Oct. 26th 1944

Dear Mom,

According to the papers, the boys have had their first snow, and it looks like a winter campaign against the enemy. I can see you are worrying over me now...well, honey, I have three pairs of heavy long johns and wool socks, a nice big mackinaw, and as far as that goes... when we aren't actually in the front lines, we are staying in houses, and will be I guess for quite a while. So, darling...please don't worry about me. I'm sleeping in a nice bed..all to myself, covers and all..and I open the windows at night and get plenty of fresh air, and things that ordinarily would get me down don't bother me anymore. I have a <u>grand</u> (not a baby grand) piano upstairs, a fire and hot water to wash and shave in (had the loveliest hot water bath...just got soaked and soaked in it..best bath I've had since I left home, and no kidding). We have hot meals (lovely hotcakes..tonight we had the best hamburger) hot drinks..and well..Mom..for a war to be so short a distance away..it doesn't seem real at all.

Got another bronze star for one of my boys tonight... still am sweating out three more...I now have 5 for them, and several Purple Hearts. I have three others in for them, but they haven't received them as yet. Today I wandered down to the front...the houses are all shot to hell, and the pictures you see and the stories you read of ghost towns, are just what I see. No one around, a dead cat in a doorway, baby clothes hanging on the lines, windows shot out, glass all over the place, a tank knocked out. German machine guns shot up, gas masks and other stuff laying around..where they (Jerries) had been shot or captured. A helmet..hole through it, bicycles, wheels off; wires stringing everywhere...broken up, twisted..houses all the same. A church steeple banged to pieces..yet standing majestically viewing the countryside and the vacant streets.a puppy...vest pocket size, wandering around..he'll make a good Allied pooch when he grows up.. he certain [part of letter cut out]!! A civilian gal being led, unceremoniously particularly [part of letter cut out] out of the restricted area. Shops all torn up...people wandering in the permitted zones..and wondering why the hell we have to [part of letter cut out] with them, their smiles, sometimes smirks. The lovely gals..already we have cases of venereal diseases because some dopes can't control themselves. As some one says, if they aren't trying to kill a German, they are trying to kiss a German girl. (There is a beautiful little brunette next door to us here.)

Appalachia to Dessau

But so much for that...I think of my own little home town. The *Erwin Record*, the show, the drug stores, A. R. Brown Stores, Unaka Stores..the Y, Hale's Hotel Erwin... and Johnson City...me, me. A cold morning on top of the mountain picking up a maple tree and brin[g]ing it home. The old Howells at the line...and their whiskey and trimmings!! My, my. And the many little things that we did together..a joy of living that made more love between just you and me than thousands of miles, millions of people, and 24 hours a day of action cannot wipe out..and the very picture of Death herself cannot wipe out, obliterate, or even mar or scar to the slightest degree. That same love, Mom, that enables me to bring you and God together and we have a talk together ever so often..just to see that I don't wander too far away from my peacetime thoughts, ideals and principles. The <u>love</u> that says Johnny, you know right from wrong..and <u>that</u> is wrong; or maybe a compromise is worked out. Sometimes..I don't think you'd exactly approve, but you'd understand it all...and maybe that is best. And I look forward to the time that I can get back and tell you all these things that I want to tell you, and I can't tell you now — as we sit in front of a big fire, eating potatoes with <u>2</u> pounds of butter, and a gallon of sweet milk.

Well, Mo..it's getting a little late and I think I'll go to bed. Write me when you get a chance and I'll try and write you more often from now on.

All my love from your, Sookcalf!!

Goodin laments about people who have died at home, many in the Clinchfield Railroad family, and the many lost in the war.

31 Oct. 1944.

Dear Dad,

Seems as though every time I hear from you lately there is some one else missing from our Clinchfield family of men that have helped to raise all of us. I guess I really knew Mr. Page lots better than I did Mr. Mac really, but at the same time...the two of them almost at the same time must have been pretty rough on all of you. I have thought of him often..wondering where Louis is and if he is still on the road..so many of the people have gone, that I wouldn't be surprised to learn that he was gone also to the services of some sort.

But, Dad...guess we all have to go..with you, it is old friends, men you have been associated with all your life and feel that they are a part of your existence. With

Six. "Still Rollin'"

me..it is a casual friendship, or maybe some fellow who has saved my life along the way..someone who has safely guided me through danger..through 88s, through mortars, through mortar fire..or through all of it. And the deaths here are rather horrible..some of them...but we get used to it, because it is so frequent, and because we expect it. I have lost several of my good friends over here.. killed, wounded, and Missing in action...but none of them quite affected me like learning of Sid Patton, Mr. Mac, and W. Page...its [sic] just that here, we don't think anything about it, don't let it bother us...and well, they were all men that meant a lot to me. Men like them don't come along every day and it takes years to become men like them, too, I suppose.

[This section of the letter is damaged, and many spots are illegible.] But, Daddy...as I wrote to Harry Mac... men have lived honorable upright lives, like Mr. Mac, Sid and W. and Charley Moss...for their spirits...who give themselves to service...who have self control, and a bellyful of guts...sometimes...all in all...I have a heritage that has been wonderful to me over here...a confidence of Faith in God that has carried me through.

And..not drinking or smoking has enabled me to hold up physically much better than a lot of them have. And some of the windbags faded out of the picture rather early when the going got rough, and once in a while one goes now. I could name a dozen things I have gotten from men who could carry me through when the chips were down, and the ones I did pick...have all come through...mostly with Bronze stars, and not only their, but our, lives.

Tom has just about picked my position out..but then guess you have known approximately where we were since the time we were taken off the secret list.

Well, Dad, must close for tonight. I want to write to Lou yet tonight..haven't had much time lately...busy with a lots of little things, and haven't had the chance to do it.

      Write when you can,
      and take care of yourself.
      Love as ever,
      Johnny

In this letter, John is concerned about his mother and feels that the family is withholding information from him. He makes an observation about war to his dad, saying, "war would a wonderful experience if it wasn't for people getting killed."

Appalachia to Dessau

2 November - 1944.

Dear Dad,

Got your Oct. 19 letter today, along with the *Knoxville News-Sentinel* clippings of Dewey and so forth. I am convinced he is <u>not</u> the man for President, but neither am I convinced Roosevelt <u>is</u> the man. But, it makes no difference now - does it?

I rather doubt Anne Carter's seriousness about me - we are close and she would worry about me and we've known and gone through a lot together - so it is natural she should be seriously interested. I am not at all sure where you people get the idea I may not come back home after this mess is over. Do you lay awake a nite dreaming up such things?? I still believe some people have little to do to worry about some of the things they do.

Winter <u>is</u> definitely here - and wonder if we are going to be stuck here. I'm sorta disgusted - would love to sneak away from here and go hunting - but, too much artillery - almost nailed me this morning - but, God is still with me.

Am particularly glad you all are receiving my mail now - it was difficult for a long time for me to write, but now, well - I can write 3 or 4 times per week.

How's everybody - Mom must not be too well - but I don't know what's wrong with her. No more information on Uncle Pyott selling the farm - Tom says he thinks he may not be wanting to anymore. Well - must be closing for now. Everything is O.K. - had steak today for dinner - real potato. We sure are eating very well up here - but I would rather spend winter at home.

Have been out watching an attack - the planes have raised a smoke cloud over the moon - war would be a wonderful experience if it weren't for people getting killed.

      Must close for tonite.
      All my love to all,
      Johnny

6 Nov. 1944. (Excerpt)

Dear Anne,

Sorry little girl..but damnitall, if you are on my mind...and I have the time, I'm going to write to you..so don't be surprised.

Anne..Mom is in the hospital, or was the last I heard from Pop..and I don't know what is the matter with her, and they won't tell me..Dad and Sis have both written to

Six. "Still Rollin'"

me, and neither have said anything..primarily because they think I'll worry about it. Luckily, I have one of my high school sweethearts who is waiting on her and I may be able to find out from her what is up. Damnitall. If they would only realize that I am a grown up, and a man, and slightly mature. But they will never realize that, I guess.

Have done very little today...those darned people keep you on your toes just watching for stuff to happen.

Must be closing for tonight. Am waiting for a letter which I know will or must be on the way soon. Hope you are keeping your head in this muddle of mine...I always have been able to depend on you to...and maybe you won't let me down this time.

So..honeychile..be good, and careful..and don't let things get you down.

      Johnny

Germany, Nov. 6th, 1944

Dear Dad,

Got your letter tonight, and it warmed my weary heart no little bit. You know...I feel better than I have felt in some time.

First of all, there has been that feeling of the disunity at home, the knowledge that things aren't too good (I don't know yet what is the matter with Mother..Sis just mentioned it and nothing more, and then tonight you finally mentioned it a little...I don't like knowing what is going on and not knowing just what is the matter..so if anything ever does happen..want you to cable me the whole story immediately.), and yet I know there is a feeling between all of us that is stronger than anything else that could ever possibly come between us.

As you know now, I have reconsidered the farm possibility, and know that it isn't the thing to do right at the present time anyhow. I'm trying to save up enough money to get married on..and I shouldn't be thinking about farms and such things as that, anyhow..at least for not a while. I am fully realizing finally, though, what you meant years ago by seeing the world before you get married and settled down. That's one reason I'm not too sorry about being over here. As a matter of fact, it could turn into a pretty good thing...only I want to go home, and not spend too much time here. I don't want to stay..that is for sure. But there is something about getting around in the foreign countries that gets me. I don't know whether I'll be able to see all that I want to

Appalachia to Dessau

or not...but at any rate...it will be worth seeing what the rest of the world is getting like. I held a royal flush in spades last night with the aid of the joker.. made all of a 45 cent pot on it. Held a straight flush in hearts tonight.

Getting back to me and the war..it looks like I'll be here for a while and there's nothing, of course I can do about it.

Anyhow..the way things are going up, I don't figure the price of living is going to be easy to get along with.. particularly at first, along with the fact that I won't have this dough coming in steady every month...this cockeyed army could ruin a man if he would let it. But I'm trying not to let it influence me too much. I also know and realize that I have a job to do right at home when I get back..I've been trying to read between the lines, and I think I'm beginning to get the picture. It has taken several months of it...Sis is the tightest-lipped I've ever known her..she doesn't tell anything anymore, so I know that something is wrong...more so than usual. So..I won't be surprised too much at most anything. I also got a honeyed letter from my sister in law..and naturally, as usual, she didn't have much to say.

Did you send Mr. Baker a check for my bed roll? You can draw it off of our account..I am also sending you a card to mail for me..along with a check..I have no blank checks anymore..it's for a magazine subscription I'm sending to Mom...If I get to take my pass..I'll have something for all of you at Christmas, but don't know when I'll get it to you.

It looks like you and sis are going to have a problem on your hands..Sis is sorta the forgotten man in our family, if you come right down to brass tacks..she has always done most of everything for all of us, and maybe we haven't appreciated it as much as we should have...and now, I guess she is about all you have to fall back on..as well as Mother...I know the family traits of all the rest of them...so I know they aren't doing anything to help out. Or if they do..it is nothing short of a miracle.

Anne Carter said Mrs. C was worrying about Lou... that she asked a thousand questions about her all the time. Sorta amuses me in a way..and yet deep down in my heart..I know that I am well pleased over her worrying over me. If I were some people..I'd marry one and love the other one on the side. On the other hand..I may be loving both of them. Funny what ideas a man will get around a place like this. Well, Dad, I'm going to close for tonight. Not much I can really tell you. How about asking sis if she won't get herself a P.O. box.

Six. "Still Rollin'"

Must close..love you as always, and wish I could be with you, if only for a little while...but we'll both have to wait a while, I guess..

All my love, Johnny

P.S. Just enclose check for 3.75 made out to *Newsweek* in this envelope with the card in it. Thanks!!

As Goodin describes the beautiful country of Belgium, he also talks about the state of mind of the people, and frustration at their feelings about democracy. He says, "It is rather hard to jam democracy down someone's throat at the point of a bayonet."

10 Nov. 1944 (Belgium) Excerpt

Dearest Annie,

Whoof!! I'm back agin!!

Belgium..Anne, what a country that is. The most beautiful vivacious girls..the most unusual people. And yet the Nazis have succeeded in sowing the seeds of distrust, hate, malcontent, jealousy..so much that I don't know how the heck they will ever recover. They have no feeling of democracy as we do..they accept our principles..and let it go at that. They are so concerned over nationalism that they just can't see what it takes to develop a feeling of security...they admit that our freedom is real..and yet..they will never accept our form of it...rotten as it may appear to be sometimes. Don't know..this mess is going to be rotten regardless of the outcome..of course.. we'll win..but if the French, the Belgian and other "liberated" countries are so torn between themselves... it is no place for us, and we might as well stay out of it. How that is possible I don't know. It is rather hard to jam democracy down someone's throat at the point of a bayonet.

Sorry, Anne, to have bored you like this. It is just that I can't see so many things that are happening, in my ignorance, I can't fathom the present results.

All in all, if one really wanted to rest and relax, it was o.k. though. We had steak for dinner..served on tablecloths and silverware, water glasses, coffee cups with cream pitchers, and sugar bowls. Belgian girls waiting on us, smiling, their omnipresent breathless "Silvousplait" every time they hand you something. Not much English spoken..I know enough to ask for what I want whether I get it or not. Same for stores. I managed to find a thing or two floating around at strictly out of this

Appalachia to Dessau

world prices. But what the hell..doesn't make much difference in case I should get shot does it?? Time out for a minute..am opening my first Christmas package..a lovely fruit cake from a girl in Erwin...another lovely creature - far from beautiful..yet a heart of gold and a character that makes all who know her love her...You'll like her, Anne, if you ever get a chance to meet her. If you have met Love and Bill by now, you can ask them about her...her name is Kat Morgan.

Well, took a break and had the fruit cake and got into a political discussion...seems that is all I'm doing lately ..I'm going wild trying to find a solution to all this damnable mess, and so far it has only antagonized me to a hopelessness that is maddening. Opinion would seem to be that the people at home are waiting for us to return to straighten out the problems there, and refuse to accept the problems or the responsibilities, and that doesn't help us any. One thing about fighting, you don't have time to worry and think about other things.

I don't know yet why I worry you with such junk. Guess you must be the one to suffer though..maybe I can repay you someday for this..but don't know when even. <u>if</u>.

So, Annie I now come to the end of this letter and guess I should go to bed..I'm about half sick..I got cold this afternoon and I'm still not happy, still dissatisfied, and have that feeling one has when the opportunity to visit heaven has presented itself and has passed away. So..I don't know..I like to think that when I write to you, I'm just sitting down and talking to you..sorta musing along waiting for an answer from you, and if none comes, just think that you may be pondering over what I'm saying, and letting it go..so many times you have done just that, and I've continued..maybe boring you, maybe not..I never know. I haven't heard from you in some time now, and would like so much to do that.

Goodnight, Anne, dear..and please forgive me if I overstep my bounds.

      Loving you, Baby
      Johnny

The 3rd Armored, recuperated, resupplied, and regrouped, were awaiting orders for the next offensive.[13]

17 November 1944 (Belgium)

Hi Anne!!

Really don't know what to say to you tonite - loneliest, most miserable I've been. I'm "way back" in Belgium now,

Six. "Still Rollin'"

in a hospital - and think I'll go AWOL back to my boys tomorrow - it's easier to have one malady there than 2 here, and I sure am homesick or worried as something over them. I'm the only platoon leader left with any experience, and I feel I ought to be up there. Oh damn these wars anyhow.

As to me - in 10 days no 2 medics have agreed - so here I am. Frankly think one or two old injuries are back to haunt me, or maybe 2 1/2 years as a tanker is finally catching up with me. Damn again.

So much I'd like to tell you - so full is my heart and yet I feel that old restraint coming back on me again - that lonely self-contained desire to be miserable by myself. Never could understand the paradox that went around in my clothes. Nor why so often that paradox turned loose so freely on your broad shoulders - but, oh well.

Now - Anne, guess your humble Johnny will be closing. G'nite - God bless you,

                    Johnny

Letter dated 21 November [1944]

Dear Folks,

Hello and how are you?? Yesterday I met a Major Parrish from Johnson City who worked with Bill Elliott and knows my Daddy and nearly everybody on the Clinchfield Railroad. Had a long chat with him - he's originally from Roanoke, married an Andrews from Johnson City - and loves hunting - have no fears I'll be hunting him up after the war. A few days ago I met a Mr. Hoover - a warrant officer from Chattanooga - He's a civilian specialist and may be returning home soon - he also is quite a hunter - knew Bill when he was Attorney General - and a fine fellow despite his name.

Wrote Mr. Moss yesterday - there's not much to write about these days - I'm just waiting - will, no doubt, have plenty to write about when this phase is over. If the good Lord continues to bless us with good weather -

Still no mail for a while!! But once again, as back in France - when it does come - it will probably be with a bang!! Don't care much - as there's not a great deal of time for writing now.

Must be closing - take care of yourselves and as always - write when you can.

                All my love,
                    Johnny

Appalachia to Dessau

Between November 24 and 30, the 3rd Armored anticipated an attack to eliminate German salient in the vicinity of Nothberg.[14]

```
30 November 1944
Dear Mom,
    The sun is out, the air is crisp and for me - I'm a
little melancholy thinking of home, hunting rabbits, big
fires and long wintry nights - snow-bound perhaps. But it
is great to be alive these days and I am grateful to be
fully and wholly so!
    Not much doing at present, sweating it out, and trying
to get a few letters written now and then - mail is
coming in swell once again and packages are due most
anytime now. I am not doing too badly anyhow!!
    I think the "Fountains of Youth" must have been hundreds
of young girls!! Saw a good movie recently and I felt
younger just seeing kids on the "screen." I still think
I allowed the best years of my life to slip away from
me because I had too high a moral standard - but maybe
that's why God has spared me so long - so maybe I haven't
missed anything. Guess so??
    We are still sweating out the end of the war by Christmas
but I rather doubt it. Incidentally I haven't done anything
"bloody" in a long time, so hope you are happy therefor
[sic]. Not much chance, tho - as we have been kind of
quiet. Hope my packages are arriving O.K.
    Well - must be closing. Love and kisses to all - and
especially my love to you.
                          'Night now," Johnny
    P. S. I am really enjoying myself eating French Fries
(actually Belgian "Fries"), actually Fry while writing,
so don't mind mistakes.
                          Love again, Johnny
```

10–12 Dec Attacked a well dug-in enemy from Langerwehe to Hoven, driving the enemy across Roer River.[15]

Goodin finally mentions the weather in this letter, which was wreaking havoc in their attempts to move forward. Deep mud was bogging down tanks, and causing general mayhem as the troops tried to advance. "Recent rains had swollen every marsh and stream in the battle area and high ground was soaked so thoroughly that attacking armor wallowed hulldeep in the clinging stuff."[16] Blown dams flooded their bivouac positions in Nothberg, and there was no letup in Langerwehe. Taking on heavy fire from tanks and artillery during this slow trek through the mud, the company finally reached Obergiech.[17]

Six. "Still Rollin'"

12 Dec. 1944 (Excerpt) Nite of the 11th, <u>rather</u>.

Hi Ann!!

What a day - continued mud, slop, rain, with intermittent sunshine at rare intervals. Same old story - our bombers in day time and at dusk, here comes theirs. Some of the fireworks I've seen I'll <u>never</u> appreciate 4th of July again!! But - what the Hell!!

I'm really enjoying the bedroom slippers - I wear them constantly - even to slipping overshoes over them when I go out now, so I won't have to take them off!! Did take them off when I went to church yesterday.

Say angel-puss - would like to have more letters from you - I really enjoy them, you know. Maybe I feel safe in "crying" on your shoulder - when I get back - well, maybe I won't take 5 years for me to make up my mind.

The boys all say many thanks for the cards - they've initiated the first deck - one kid lost $5.00 <u>he</u> doesn't think they're so good!! But, on the whole they appreciate them, too!!

12 Dec. 1944

Dear Mom,

Just a note tonite [sic] - sorta tired, light isn't too good, fire low - but the coffee is boiling - did I ever tell you that I've <u>learned</u> to drink coffee since I've been over here?? You can pin a medal on Sgt. Ronald D. Gilboe as he is the one responsible. So - when I get home, after I get my fill of <u>milk</u> - I'll drink coffee with you, O.K.??

Have done hardly anything for ages. Got me some different equipment which puts me off of the front now for a while. We are a little more optimistic [sic] now, by the way!! Well - just wanted to say Hello and I'm all right - trusting in God and saying my humble prayers at nite, asking forgiveness for my many sins.

Hope everything is O.K. with all of you. All my love to all of you,

<u>Johnny</u>

In-mid December the 3rd Armored was preparing for Christmas. The weather had finally cleared, and passes were being given to Verviers. Goodin had taken a much-needed break in Verviers in early November. The Spearhead was hoping for a peaceful Christmas break, but it was not to be. On December 16, the German counteroffensive "erupted in an action that shocked the allied world."[18]

Maj. Gen. Maurice Rose, Commander of 3rd Armored Division, enters an Army vehicle as he prepares for a tour of the front lines.

Suddenly, they were ordered to return to Belgium to halt German Ardennes offensive on December 18.[19]

This surprise attack was launched with the full fury of the Nazis, and they intended to "take no prisoners." This was their last chance for victory, and the "rule book had been destroyed."[20] The Battle of the Bulge had begun.

They fought over a very wide front (from Manhay to Marche) between December 19 and 29, beating down numerous enemy attacks and halting the German advance.[21]

Confusion due to little information, mud, fog, which caused low visibility, bitter cold, fire coming in from above and on the ground, and vagueness of the location of the enemy, did not stop the 3rd Armored. They had faith in General Rose, and they would not be disappointed. But there would be no peace on earth this Christmas.[22]

Goodin tells his parents the "Good Lord is still watching over me."

Six. "Still Rollin'"

Dec. 25 - 44.
Somewhere in Belgium
Dear Folks,

At best, this has been one of the most different Christmases I have ever spent - anywhere. We were to have turkey, but our kitchen truck had a flat tire or something that it didn't get to us, so guess will have "much turkey" tomorrow. We did have fresh eggs today which I enjoyed very much.

"Bakers Beau" is no more. [Goodin is referring to his tank.]

I haven't had much time to write lately, hope you are not unduly upset - but it has been zero weather, lots of snow - but not today - which was good. I am now situated in a nice home, plenty to eat - and can stay warm. Ann Carter sent me a pair of fur-lined bed-room slippers and they have really saved my feet. I put on two pairs of socks, the slippers and put my overshoes over them. Haven't worn any shoes for a week now!!

Saved one of my packages till last nite - two boxes of candy, and a fruit cake. Might interest you to know that I've gotten several nice packages from some of my boys [sic] families. Fruit cakes and candy - lovely!! (I ate so much fruit cake while we were still in Germany that I got a touch of dysentery - but a little cheese fixed me up!!)

Typically, I was "up" on Christmas eve, waiting for "Santa Claus" (awfully glad he didn't come!!), and took my Christmas nap this p.m. - probably be up tonight for a while!!

Using a hedgerow for concealment, U.S. infantrymen keep a wary lookout for Nazis on the outskirts of a Belgian town, December 29, 1944.

Appalachia to Dessau

    I have no news for you - the good Lord continues to watch over me and take care of me - so I can't complain about anything. We don't have it too easy, but - we are so much better off than so many. Personally, there is so much to be thankful for we can't complain.
    Haven't had any mail for some time, but when it does catch up, there will be plenty.
    I've gotten so much from home - I haven't been able to keep up with what I have gotten - apples, candy, peanuts, fruit cake, etc., it must all be coming through all right. Must be closing for tonite.

                          Love & kisses to all!! Johnny

Goodin expresses his feelings to his friend Anne saying the "Jerries are hot as hell, God and my luck are still carrying me through, a bit subdued and someday you'll know why."

26 Dec. 1944
Somewhere in Belgium
Dearest Anne,

    Well, sweetheart, in the past few days your bedroom slippers have done quite a job - and not in any Mademoiselle boudoir, either. I have put on two pairs of socks, the slippers, and my overshoes over the top of them - my shoes and boots were too cold - and this did the trick. The weather has been zero, with snow - and the Jerries hot as hell - God and my luck are still carrying me through. Christmas was the most different I've ever seen, naturally, but details for you will have to wait because of censorship regulations.
    Anyhow, kiddo - I hope you had a pleasant Christmas, and New Years as well. My own - I'll pray for my luck to last.
    I'm expecting lots of mail from you, if and when it catches up to us. I've had no mail for a week and a half now - so you see when it does come there should be plenty of it for us. Providing of course - it gets through!
    There certainly is some beautiful country over here - better than Germany - lots of hills and mountains and woods, and the snow, under other conditions would have been beautiful. But - if I ever get home again I have no desire to see this again, as I think we have everything a person would (or at least <u>should</u>) want right at home. Why people want to leave - I'll never know.
    One thing about this place is the fact that what civilians there are here - we can talk to and "fraternize" with. I think some mademoiselle could twist my arm right now!!

Six. "Still Rollin'"

>Seriously Anne - I'm <u>still</u> not overly optimistic and the days going by are bearing out my pessimism. I'm still of the opinion people at home don't know there is a war going on and there is no way to convince them. None at all.
> Nothing else, Anne - afraid I'm a bit subdued at the present. Someday you'll know more why.
> Hello to your folks when you write - tell 'em I'm O.K. and getting along all right.
>
>>Love & kisses,
>>Johnny

After a battle with the 2nd SS Das Reich Panzer Division, the 1st SS Leibstandarde Adolf Hitler Panzer Division, and the 12th SS Hitler Jugend Panzer Division, the 3rd Armored was "pulled out to rest and refit." According to *Spearhead in the West*, they won this battle because they "fought to the last cartridge and the last drop of blood and gasoline."[23] They launched an attack against Germans salient (bulge) in snow and mist north of Lierneux between January 3 and 25, 1945. Gains of 1000 yards a day were made against fanatical enemy resistance in most severe winter weather. The attack continued until relieved at Gouvy, near the Luxembourg border.[24]

The winter of 1944–1945 was one of the coldest and most severe on record. Bare skin touching the side of a tank could be ripped off from the cold. Goodin mentions the "weather being zero" and that he put on "two pairs of socks, bedroom slippers and overshoes, because his shoes and boots were too cold." In an article in the *Elizabethton Star*, dated December 16, 1984, titled "Battle of the Bulge Remembered," Goodin and Ray Lyons, tell J.D. Greene of the *Star* staff that it was "misty with low clouds and there was plenty of snow and ice," and that "more men were lost from frostbite than were killed in battle."[25] According to *Spearhead in the West*, the icy mist was "paralyzing," and even the tanks "skidded alarmingly" on the roads. Add to this "ceaseless wind," and the next six days would be pure hell for the 3rd Armored, but Lierneux was theirs.[26]

In keeping with his lighthearted relationship with his mother, Goodin writes this letter on whimsical stationery with a border in red and blue that says, "What's cookin: good lookin? What's hitten: Kitten? What's clickin: chicken? What's fresh: Presh? What's buzzin: Cousin? What's doin: Cooin? What's ruff: Fluff? What's steamin: Demon?" Goodin displays the sense of humor he shares with his mother in the letter when he says he has "been busy as heck."

Appalachia to Dessau

10 January 1945 (Excerpt)
Dear Mom,

Sorry I haven't had time to write - have been busy as heck - as you know - but with God and my luck - I'm still O.K., and rolling along. S. M. Anderson wrote me and sends his love & regard to you- he's O. K., too!!

The last few days have been rough - 8 inches of snow, Germans everywhere, concentrated artillery, and always Death lurking in the foreground. But I have come through so far and see no reason why I shouldn't continue to do so. I'm not so foolhardy, reckless, and carefree as I was - but I'm still me.

Yes - Bakers Beau [Goodin's tank] is gone. Somewhere on the Bulge. Wish you could be here in Belgium with me - feeding and milking the cows, sheep, horses amidst [sic] artillery fire - eating huckleberries and hot food for a change and generally getting thawed out.

Must be going to bed. Goodnite, [sic] God bless you and I love you all.

      Johnny

Goodin mentions in this letter that he is "moving." This photograph in the Goodin Papers dated the same day as this letter describes the following: A dead German soldier lies in a ditch along route of the Third Armored Division advance near Langlir, Belgium. The U.S. Army provided the information for the photo.

As the snows begin to melt, Goodin tells his dad he has "licked the winter" and "Christmas Eve was rough." According to *Spearhead in the West*, "frenzied German soldiers" attacked hard and furiously twelve times, and twelve times they failed, but casualties were heavy on both sides.[27]

13 Jan. 45 (Excerpt) Belgium
Dear Pop,

Just a short note - Mr. Moss wrote me a very nice letter and sent me Mr. Mac's last letter. I sent it home to Mom.

I am getting along O.K. - still O.K. and moving. Feeling better than I have in a long time. Have licked the winter, except for slight cough, and am getting over that. Wear plenty of clothes!!

Got your Christmas letter, along with Sis's of the 25th - so know about your Christmas. Christmas Eve was rough, but everything cleared up.

      Best of everything -
      and watch your step!! Love,
      Johnny

Six. "Still Rollin'"

A dead German soldier lies in a ditch along route of the Third Armored Division advance near Langlir, Belgium, January 13, 1945.

Goodin is a bit dismayed that the snow has started again but thrilled to finally start getting mail again. He wishes his mother a happy birthday and tells her he hasn't even had a "substitute bath" in over a month.

```
15 January 1945

Dearest Mom,
     After 2 or 3 days of no snow, and complete sunlight,
snow has started to fall again, covering up the tracks,
the mud, the dirty roads, and so on. I'm conveniently
located in a Belgium farmhouse (there is no other kind
of house) and the fire is low, as is the light, and I'm
slightly chilly. Yesterday made 1 month since I've had
even a substitute bath, and don't know when I'll get one
- if all my friends could see me now (as long as they
can't smell me - guess it's O.K.!) By the way, you might
notify the Carters I'm O.K., and call Kat Morgan. I had
an awfully nice Christmas letter from Pauline. And today
```

During one of the severest winters on record, military vehicles are covered in snow in the Ardennes, December 1944.

Downed Jerry plane at Soy, Belgium, Ardennes.

Six. "Still Rollin'"

Sky over Ardennes Forest is cross-streaked with vapor trails from high-flying bombers over Belgium en route to Germany. Infantrymen of the 3rd Armored Division, partly obscured by fir trees, patrol the "Bulge." January 14, 1945.

I got a <u>Thanksgiving Greeting</u> from the Pastor - timely as some of the Christmas Cards I'm getting. Also reminds me - if you have time, call Leann Cornett and thank her for remembering me - I simply don't have time to get letters written to people anymore. I've had awfully nice letters from Mrs. McIntyre, Bill Simpson, and Russell Haynes. Got the *Erwin Record* - a little late, but enjoy it thoroughly - tho these "kids" who are going off to war now seem like babies and I don't know any of them. Betty Ellen must be singing here, there and yon. Still don't wear any shoes - my bed-room slippers, thanks to Anne Carter plus 2 pairs of sox [sic] and overshoes are doing the trick. I'm not getting fat, but I'm getting along O.K. Things have improved steadily since the 24th of December for "us" and me, in particular. Glad everything is coming along allright [sic] with you. It's nice to start getting letters from you again. Sis must not write as often as she did - Dad writes fairly often - I write when I can - which isn't often.

Appalachia to Dessau

I got a red neck-tie for Christmas!! Guess you must be about 63 now aren't you? Happy Birthday!!

     Love to all, Johnny

18 Jan., 1945
Dearest Anne,

 Hi - Elusive! Just a quick note to tell you Hello & that God is still taking care of me altho - sometimes I've wondered if my Faith was going to hold out with my luck. Haven't heard from you in ages - not mail much from anyone - have no heart to write to anyone, either - damn this confusing chaos!!

Effect on Sherman tank of German 88MM armor piercing shell is examined by Capt. Hollis L. Towne, of Aberdeen, South Dakota. The shell from Tiger Royal Tank went through corners of two buildings, then completely pierced tank armor in Belgium. 3rd AD DIV, 32ND REGT.

 Can tell you now that things didn't go too well for my lads on Christmas Eve and we had more fireworks than I've ever had before on a Holiday season!!

 How I'd love to have a bath. One month, same clothes - and I can hardly stand myself!! Still - I'm alive, so what the Hell!!

 If I ever meet you in Washington (that is for more than a few days), as soon as the "preliminaries" are over - there's someone I want to entangle you with for a long discussion. Mood of the moment - so don't be surprised it falls through. By the way - heard from Billy Wilkins at Christmas - or did I tell you? Well, this is it for now - will write you again when I get the chance & time.

  Bon chance, Johnny

Six. "Still Rollin'"

A Signal Corps cameraman points to a hole in his steel helmet, made by enemy shell fragment as he was photographing action of 3rd Armored Division troops in Belgium. He was bandaged on the scene by medics and continued the mission. January 16, 1945.

Catching up on his mail, and in his typical humorous style, Goodin tells Anne he "forgot to duck last week" but that he is okay but fatigued. He expresses how much he loves her letters. He has adopted a "shell-shocked pooch" who is a victim of war. He also mentions a scare of moving out at midnight in a "blinding blizzard, cold miserable" with the fear they had blundered onto a Russian front.

```
Sunday - Jan. 21,1945. (Excerpt) Belgium
Dearest Anne,
   Got your Jan 1st letter. Your letters, Anne - penetrate
beyond words - should I say, with no attempts at flattery
- they stimulate me - mentally, and morally - so much of
what I need. You can't realize Anne - how much they do
mean - you'll probably never know. But - lacking a physical
love - something which was never considered, certainly
never encouraged by either of us - I find myself more
```

Appalachia to Dessau

strongly bound to you - with each letter...and Anne you have been my anchor - the rock on which I stand to fight, kneel to pray, and flatten out to dodge the hell that comes our way (I didn't duck far enough last week - but I'm O.K.).

Gosh, Anne - the years are rolling by us, and I'm doing nothing, NOTHING worthwhile! The best to wipe out the evils - to kill, to harden one's heart - its so--unnatural. The brittle course laugh at the suffering - and yet the crimes, the atrocities they have committed and are committing every day - Ann, darling - we aren't made up that way. (I feel like I'm almost unloosing my very soul to you tonite - and I shouldn't!) And yet, day in and day out - the number of the originals drops and falls and the odds go up. Some days you notice it, others you don't.

Sometimes, the feelings, the foreboding of impending disaster rest heavily, and yet you grin and take off. Some day - I wonder - if pent-up passions will burst forth unchallenged, and what. Sophistry and hypocrasy [sic] will be much smaller obstacles than before the war...If I seem apologetic at times, Ann, for my muddled letter, please forgive me - because maybe my mind which is putting the thoughts out is alright, but the one which is putting them on paper may be a little dazed. I know for a fact sometimes my subconscious mind will be clicking perfectly, and yet the other one is ringing with explosives, hearing the detonations, seeing hell & destruction, feeling the vibrations and even smelling the powder - perhaps have after the real thing. By trying to write you now and then - when the opportunity arises - you may catch the outward me, or perhaps the "inward" me - I never know - some times I can't remember what I have written to you. But - that's war.

Mind if I digress a bit from the beaten path?? Yesterday - I adopted a pooch - a smart intelligent - looking, yellowish wolfish pup. Shell-shocked, dazed, hearing gone, and utterly beaten. Suspicious, temperamental, afraid, gun-shy, starved for food and water - and human-conscious. I finally coaxed him into the house, fed and watered, babied and pampered, pleaded - softly swore, too, I expect, and finally calmed him down. He cowed every time anyone entered the room, and dove for the table, bed, chair, or what not. At any rate, the guard changed about midnite, and he had been asleep - in come a G I and "YIKE" what a racket. Anyhow I woke up, calmed him down (he still barks at anybody who comes in) and was about to go back to sleep when he whined and scratched the door - nurse-maid Johnny got up, and we went out in the

Six. "Still Rollin'"

drizzling blinding snow and after the mongrel's kidneys were relieved he snorted and back we came.

Today he has stayed in except for Natures calls - I'm getting quite a kick from it. At 9 tonite I asked him if he wanted to go out, and off <u>we</u> went. Amazing, too, he understands my French which is more than the natives do. I want to take him with me but doubt if I can coax him into being a tanker!! Anyhow - he breaks the monotony and the loneliness, and he seems to appreciate a little kindness.

Look, Ann - my mind is wide awake, but the old body is howling with fatigue, so - with deference to future happiness I'm going to have to close for tonite. I can lay back and think but - I'm just tired - baby - just tired. And, as usual cold. Nite before last we moved at 12:00 - 4 miles in a blinding blizzard that overwhelmed everything, cold miserable - I thought we had lost our maps and got on the Russian front. But come daylight, I found a better place, and warmer. Luckily we moved, too, as beaucoup shells came in that p.m. - lucky. Hm.

Well, baby, I'm going to bed with dreams of ham sandwiches and necking parties on divans

       G'nite
       Johnny

P. S. Could you write just a wee bit oftener??

Goodin tells his dad "The only happiness you get in life is doing things for others, and he has "learned things some people will never learn if you live another 67 years."

23 Jan. 1945 (excerpt) Belgium

Dear Pop,

Just got your letter of Jan. 1st and as always, thoroughly enjoyed it.

And, once again - Sis comes into the picture - <u>please</u>: I'm putting all my money in an account which you could wipe out with <u>one signature</u>, and I'm not <u>worried</u> about it. And - if I want to give Sis $10,000 - the part of it I have earned by sweat and <u>blood</u>, over here - I'll give it to <u>her</u>. It matters little if they are making 50 times as much as <u>I am</u> - you seem to forget that I'm now nearly <u>28</u>, and at least credited by the <u>army</u> <u>as</u> having a brain of my own, and on occasions using it - so I don't have to be told that they are better off than I am. In 65 years, Dad - I'm surprised you haven't learned that the only happiness you get in life is doing things for others

```
- but then you never lived in a Hell like I have for the
past few months.
    I may not live through this mess - but if I do - I've
learned things that some of you people will never
learn - if you live another 67 years. I'm not being
"holier-than-thou," but at least - I'm learning - and it
took you 52 years to realize money isn't everything in
life.
    We pulled back yesterday for a rest - movies, hot meals,
clean clothes (haven't bathed or changed clothes since 18
of December) and a few hours off here for writing, reading,
and sitting in front of a fire. For the first time in my
life, I've seen snow constantly for 2 months - never saw
anything like it!!
    Beautiful - but damn - it's awful - we moved at 12:00
one nite in the worst blizzard you can imagine and you've
seen 'em out West!! But - we made it - and that's what
counts.
    Well - everything is O.K. - write when you can, and don't
worry about me. By the way, Kraft (you met him at Pickett
when he was helping me) was killed about a month ago.
    Must close for now.
                            Love, as always,
                            Johnny
```

The Battle of the Bulge ended on January 25, 1945. According to the National Veterans Memorial and Museum, the Battle of the Bulge was "the largest and bloodiest single battle fought by the United States in World War II. In total, it is estimated that over 1 million Allied troops fought in the Battle of the Bulge, including 500,000 Americans. Approximately 19,000 American soldiers were killed in action, with 47,500 wounded and 23,000 missing. It remains the third deadliest campaign in American history."[28]

Goodin's relief of a reprieve is evident in this letter to his dad where he says, "it is nice to sit back out of that racket."

```
Jan. 29th 1945 (excerpt)
Dear Dad,
    This morning there is lots of wild confusion...we are
on a rest and the peep sheets are flying thick and fast,
ranges, decorations, instructions, shows, showers, mov-
ies, schools by the dozen.
    Things are looking up a little for us...we get official
credit for stopping the German drive and smashing it back
into Germany...don't know what our next mission will be,
```

Six. "Still Rollin'"

or where..but right now, it is nice to sit back out of that racket.

All my love, Johnny

During this brief respite, the 3rd Armored was refitted with new equipment, including the latest guns and tanks.²⁹ After a brief rest, the 3rd Armored returned to Stolberg, Germany on February 9, and remained there through February 25, crossing the Roer River, which was swollen due to the dam being blown by the enemy.³⁰

Goodin tells his mother he is mailing home his Purple Heart.

```
Feb. 16-45
Dear Mom,
```
Just to let you know I understand the "German bulge," and I got your Valentine - in time!! Everything is going well with us for the present and I'm sleeping in a bed, having hot meals, and getting a bath once in a while. The pen Sis sent me is doing pretty well. We have the winter licked, I think. Tell Mrs. Swingle to keep George's Purple Heart for him - but like the rest of us, he probably won't wear any of them when we get back. <u>Write as you feel</u> - to hell with whether its "cheerful" or not - if you try to color things, you waste your time in writing. I may have some pictures soon. It's too cloudy right now.

Love, Johnny

16 - Still

Just got another letter from you and Dad - of Feb. 7th so it's good time, plus. A few questions - I'm still in 1st Army, 3rd <u>Armored</u> Division - I can't tell you where I am except by country, there are four men in my tank. What I do: In summer time I break out in a cold sweat, in winter I <u>freeze</u>, and still sweat - same difference. I try to tell 4 other tanks when to go, tell my gunner where to shoot, my driver where to go, my company commander where I am, and shoot my own gun - all at the same time.

No - I <u>don't</u> know <u>who</u> I am - and I do know what you're thinking about.

Took a few pictures late this afternoon - maybe they'll turn out all right.

Spring is here - the flies and mosquitoes are buzzing around the dung-hills, and the sun is shining - but there are no birds, no rabbits, no animals - nothing left but waste and destruction - and armored vehicles and grim men who ride in them.

Must close for now - Love, Johnny

Am mailing you my Purple Heart tonite.

Appalachia to Dessau

16 Feb - 1945.

Dear Dad,

  Got your last few letters O.K. - last one <u>Feb.7</u> - haven't had too much time to write. Have been in infantry, tanks, artillery, and now - engineers - we are reconstructing some of the roads preparatory to using them - the hard way - with man power and little machinery. Sure sorry to hear about Hugh Webb - was thinking about him the other day - guess he was getting way up in years. But deal is to keep on working as you say.

  Tell Cleve Reedy & Jim Range hello and all the others - I think of a lot of the men, but couldn't <u>begin</u> to name all of them. Be sure & tell Mr. Mc & J. J. McLaughlin hello for me.

                That's it for tonite -
                Love, as always,
                Johny

Goodin received a Bronze Star Medal for heroic achievement in action against the enemy in Germany on February 26, 1945.

    Between February 26 and 27, the 3rd Armored crossed Roer River and attacked well dug-in enemy on Cologne Plain.[31] By February 27, they had forged across difficult Erft Canal in a surprise attack and established a bridgehead.[32]

1 March, 1945

Dear Dad,

  Got your Feb. 12th letter a couple of days ago with all the clippings - sure enjoyed them all. Didn't know Hilda Parsons was in the Red Cross - guess she'll see a lot of Erwin boys in New Guinea.

  Paris?? For you? <u>Certainly</u>! They tell me that it doesn't make any difference <u>how old</u> you are that you'll still enjoy it! "Cause - a man loses 10 years off his life, but haven't heard anyone who regretted it."

  Am really living in style right now - after 3 days & nites - no sleep, we rested last nite and are today - I just finished eating ham and eggs - I'll be sick probably from all the meat I've eaten lately - for 12 hours I've been feasting royally. Slept so soundly last nite that planes, artillery and prisoners didn't wake me up.

  Remember Coons who helped write a letter recently?? He's on his way to England again. Probably home later. Awful good boy.

Six. "Still Rollin'"

```
Well - gotta close for today. Papers back home sure are
optimistic - would like for some of them to see what I see!!
                    Love, as always,
                    Johny
```

On March 2, 1945, Goodin was wounded in Germany. He was hospitalized in Paris, France. Having previously been awarded the Purple Heart, he was awarded the Oak Leaf Cluster on March 22.

The following telegram was sent to the Goodins on March 19.

```
WESTERN UNION TELEGRAM
Washington DC 209P
MAR 19 1945

THOMAS E. GOODIN SR
    THE SECRETARY OF WAR DESIRES ME TO EXPRESS HIS DEEP REGRET
    THAT YOUR SON 1ST LT GOODIN JOHN D WAS SLIGHTLY WOUNDED
    IN GERMANY 2 MARCH 1945 CONTINUE TO ADDRESS MAIL FOR HIM
    AS FORMERLY OR UNTIL NEW ADDRESS IS RECEIVED FROM HIM
                    JA ULIO THE ADJUTANT GENERAL 245P
```

An article in the *Johnson City Press-Chronicle*, dated Sunday, March 25, 1945, titled "Lt. John Goodin Suffers Arm Wounds in Europe," stated: "Lt. John D. Goodin has been wounded in action in the European theater of operations and now is in a hospital in Paris for treatment of injuries to an arm. His parents, Mr. and Mrs. T.E. Goodin, Sr., have received word he was awarded the Purple Heart."[33]

The official report, dated March 22, 1945, from the John Goodin Papers, is from Army Headquarters stating Goodin received the Oak Leaf Cluster, which is awarded to those who have already been given the Purple Heart.

```
HEADQUARTERS 40th (US) General Hospital APO 350 U.S. Army
GENERAL ORDERS:
22 March 1945 E X T R A C T No. 61
II - AWARD OF OAK LEAF CLUSTER:
    1. Under the provisions of AR 600-45, the following
officers, having been previously awarded the Purple Heart;
are awarded the OAK LEAF CLUSTER, for wounds received in
action somewhere in Germany on the dates set forth after
their names:
    John D. Goodin, 0-1010821, First Lieutenant, Tanks
United States Army, wounded 2 March 1945
    By order of the Commanding Officer: 40th GENERAL
HOSPITAL OFFICIAL SEAL
```

Appalachia to Dessau

Goodin mentions being in the hospital and his treatment in several of the following letters. He tells his mother he got a "slight scratch again."

```
3 March 1945 Germany Vmail
Dear Mom,
    Just a note - everything is O.K. with me, and still O.K.
got a slight scratch again - you may hear from the War
Department on that deal.
    Am writing you an airmail along with this - so don't
get worried about it!!
                        Love to all, Johnny
```

The 3rd Armored assaulted Cologne and completed its capture by reaching the Rhine River between March 5 and 6.[34] (Goodin was still hospitalized during this battle.)

```
Mar. 8-45
Dear Mom,
    Just a note - everything is O.K. with me - arm is a
little sore - but I've been playing the piano for a
little, reading, flirting with the nurses, drinking Coca
Cola (by the 1/2 gallon!!), and enjoying myself while I
can. Yvonne - a French nurse, washes my back, head & feet
- tho of late I've been doing it. She's a nice kid - but
unromantic, particularly when there are so many nice
American gals around here. The Red Cross is still the
shining light of Europe for the soldiers.
            All for now - Mom - a bridge game is on.
            All my love,
            Johnny


16 March - 1945 Paris
Dear Dad,
    Was reading a story last nite and was still thinking
about it (when the lights were out) and a slight parallel
between and you and me - I think I'm almost as headstrong
as you are sometimes - and yet there must be some of your
patience in me too. You see, I remember now how patient,
how easy you were with me when I was in my low spots - in
1938 and in 1939 when I let you down in school, and other
times when less-explosive parents would have booted me
out. Possibly it was part of your determination I would
amount to something that gave you your patience - but
whatever it was, I can appreciate it far more now than I
ever could have then. At that time - I would not ask for
```

Six. "Still Rollin'"

Goodin receives Purple Heart from Lt. Col. Walter B. Richardson, Major Bill Martin, Greenwood, South Carolina, assisting near Stolberg, Germany.

Lt. Harry Hittler, Capt. John B. Owen, and Lt. John D. Goodin receive the Purple Heart, Cluster and Purple Heart, respectively.

your patience if I exploded, but now - particularly after being off the front for 2 weeks, I realize I was under a lot of pressure, and my reactions were not up to normal. Someday, when I can get back and talk to you - maybe I can explain what I mean. But - in case I don't, and I don't know God's will, I hope you'll realize that the troubles and hurts I've caused you were not intentional, and often-times had I had time to stop and think before acting, they would not have happened. Maybe we kids never do grow up altogether!

Had my stitches out yesterday - really a neat job and guess I'll be leaving here in a couple or three days. Sure have had a vacation here - hot water, hot meals, showers, clean sheets and beds, and so on. Have gotten out a couple of times as you probably know by now. Paris is wild, but I'm a bit afraid to take a chance on some of these gals - some officers have been reclassified already. An enlisted man married a French girl here yesterday - so chivalry is not completely dead in all Americans.

Met Major Bob Spillman of Knoxville (former President of Appalachian Mills, Inc) here, a Hultins boy from Kingsport, a McChester from Bristol, and a Mathison boy from above Elizabethton. Quite a bunch here.

Must close for now.
All my love,
 Johny

Goodin, left, labeled this photograph "Me and my favorite tank driver, Roy L. Pearson, Ida, Louisiana. My driver while spearheading through France, Belgium and early part of German campaign."

By March 20, Goodin was released from the hospital and had rejoined the 3rd Armored.

They crossed Rhine River in Remagen bridgehead area at Honnef and attacked north between March 20 and 22, assisting in clearing enemy from area south of Sieg River.[35]

Six. "Still Rollin'"

Preparing to cross the Rhine, March 1945.

Rhine Bridge at Bonn, Germany.

Appalachia to Dessau

Momentary pause along the Rhine...all houses are gutted. Three miles or so north of Remagen, Germany.

```
20 Mar. 1945
Paris
```

Dear Mom & all,

　Just a few notes to say Howdy - am still getting along O.K. - I played the piano for about 2 hours tonite - intended to quit early & write a long letter but didn't quite make it.
　Our "dirty dozen" is fast disintegrating now - 2 gone, 1 to England, 2 more going out tomorrow morning - sure has been a swell bunch to be with.
　No news - spring nites [sic] here are lovely and I'm sorta lonesome & lonely - it is such a nite as - but you wouldn't understand - and it's hard for me to realize some things now.

```
            Well - goodnite [sic] or now.
            Love & kisses to all.
            Love,
            Johnny
```

CHAPTER SEVEN

Dessau: Victories and Atrocities
March 22–April 25, 1945

The 3rd relentlessly marched, engaging in battle after battle taking Asbach and Hachenburg, then racing to Paderborn, advancing 90 miles in one day. This "proud, triumphant achievement" by the 3rd Armored, under Major General Maurice Rose, was the "greatest one-day advance in the history of mobile warfare."[1]

Between March 2 and March 24, Goodin had been in the hospital recuperating from a wound received in Germany. He sent a note to his parents letting them know he was reporting back for duty.

```
Envelope dated MAR 24 1945
  Note: Going back to duty today - feeling good - went to
Versailles yesterday - had a swell time!!
                   Johnny
  Enclosures 10 postcards from Versailles, France
```

A pre-dawn attack pushed off in vicinity of Asbach, which surprised the enemy. After two days of relentless fighting between March 24 and 26, enemy positions crumbled and a breakthrough was achieved.[2] Hachenburg was captured and bridges on Dill River at Herborn seized on March 27.[3]

The race to Paderborn began on March 28, advancing 90 miles on first day. Hundreds of enemy trucks and supply vehicles were overtaken and destroyed or captured.[4]

Bitter battles with SS Panzer Training Regiment took place along approaches to city of Paderborn.[5] After 100 miles of hard-won battles between March 30 and 31, the 3rd Armored approached Paderborn. It was here that they would suffer a devastating loss.

Appalachia to Dessau

On March 30, 1945, the esteemed General Maurice Rose, a beloved and courageous leader referred to as a "soldier's soldier," was gunned down by a German tank. According to *Spearhead in the West*, "He fell at the head of his men, away up front where general officers, according to popular belief, are not supposed to be."[6]

They entered Paderborn on April 1 while elements moved 25 miles westward to Lippstadt, contacting elements of 9th U.S. Army. This was the first link-up which formed the envelopment of the great Ruhr industrial area.[7] This is referred to as "one of the great drives of World War II."[8]

```
Letter dated 2 April - 1945
Dear Folks,
    Still sitting in a Reinforcement Depot waiting for the
war to end, or to get back to the outfit - so far we are
just fooling around. Rode across the Rhine in a tank/
truck and got a few pictures which I hope will turn out.
I have several pictures in now for development & should
have them out by June anyhow.
    These towns are not badly shot up - tho the Air Corp
has torn up all the railroads and yards - they are a
mess. Civilians here are typical - either stonily silent
or grinning from ear to ear - still have the same opinion
of them. We caught some prisoners here in our "backyard"
today - silly war. We're so far inland we've had no news
for a couple of days now, and the war may be over, but
I sincerely doubt it - just yet. Maybe by the time this
reaches you, it will be over.
    Picked up a couple of helmets today - think I'll send
'em to the Carter boys - If I get a chance to send 'em.
    There's also lots of good "loot" here - but it is
forbidden, altho there are quite a few choice items
leaving their regular places. Funny, too, how the regular
Nazis take off to beat heck when we come in. Nearly all
the rest stick around, and look forlorn. I'm still hoping
for a leave to England at some near future date, and in a
way I'm afraid of it - at least when I have a week of it.
Ummmmmm!

                    Well - it's getting dark,
                    so will have to close for tonite.
                    All my love to all,
                    Johnny
```

An official letter from Army Headquarters was sent out on April 4 by Brigadier General Doyle O. Hickey, Rose's replacement, mourning the

Seven. Dessau: Victories and Atrocities

loss of a great general, and lauding the achievements of General Rose. This was a heavy blow to the morale of the 32nd Armored Regiment, but they were encouraged to "maintain our glorious record and standards set for us by General Rose."

```
Airmail Envelope APR 17 1945
(Two documents enclosed)
4 April 1945

HEADQUARTERS THIRD ARMORED DIVISION
Office of the Commanding General To:
All Members of the Division
   It is with a heavy heart that I assume command of
this great Division, stepping into the shoes of our lost
leader and my very warm, personal friend, MAJOR GENERAL
MAURICE ROSE.
   The high standards that GENERAL ROSE set are ingrained
in the Division. Our record, known throughout the world,
is a result of his exacting demands upon every individual
and every part of our team. His faultless tactical handling
of all the troops under his command; his personal drive
which instilled in us the desire to close with the enemy
and ruthlessly destroy him, regardless of the cost; his
personal bravery and insistence that commanders be with
their forward elements in order to better maintain the
forward impulse; all, should inspire us to even greater
deeds, as a tribute to him - our fallen leader.
   With complete confidence in every member of our Division,
I know that, individually and collectively, we are
resolved to maintain our glorious record and the standards
set for us by GENERAL ROSE, in order that we may the
sooner destroy the Nazi armies opposed to us, and achieve
the victory and peace for which we are all fighting - for
which GENERAL ROSE made the Supreme Sacrifice.
                      DOYLE O. HICKEY,
                      Brigadier General, U.S.A.,
                      Commanding
```

They attacked to east and fought stubborn German troops along Weser River between April 5 and 7,[9] then crossed Weser River at Veckerhagen and began racing through the heart of Germany on April 8.[10]

Goodin tells his parents they "ran into a little trouble." He is referring to the difficult crossing of the Weser, where the Germans, "stunned by the swift approach of American Armor," were "blasting every span which might aid the invader."[11]

Appalachia to Dessau

He also tells them he is just now getting some Christmas mail.

```
Letter dated April 8th, 1945
Somewhere in Germany
```

Dear Folks,

Another Sunday morning and a beautiful one at that...we are now in a little town just beside a river, and waiting to get across it..had beautiful luck coming in, only one man slightly injured, and he is not from our outfit, luckily. Anyhow, the planes were on hand, and everything cliked [sic] to perfection. The night before we ran into a little trouble, but that turned out all right too, because they took off, and left us the town with no trouble..but I almost froze..despite all the clothes I had on.

Did I sleep last night?? Whooee..slept the sleep of the dead...and thousands of beautiful women down in the cellar below me, but I was tired!!

I finally got all my mail from you people...amazing...I got a letter from Dad that was dated Dec. 8th...so you see our mail is not always so prompt...had several Christmas cards...and thanks to all the people who sent me get well cards and Easter cards and what not...don't know if I'll ever get caught up on my mail..but will try and keep you folks posted as to about where I am.

Tom seems to have the idea that if I get thirty days off, I can pick where I go..home or England..well, if I get thirty days off, I assure you I'll be home..but I don't expect to get it to begin with, and now then, the seven days rest that we get is spent down on the Riviera, quite a resort in peace time, near Nice, Cannes, and so forth. But there are still few passes to England....I'll be lucky if I get three days to go back to Paris now. But one never knows, do we?? One of my sergeants is going home soon, and I think that he will call you up. If Alex didn't call you...just remember that telephone calls are hard to put through, and just that thirty days is awfully short in one's life. One boy spent all of his at home, and another only stayed one day at home...so you never know what they are going to do when they go home these days.

I'll have just as much trouble in England as if I go home...cause I sure intend to see Kay..AWOL or one way or another, and Sheila, and the Wren...and Scotty has been writing some nice letters too of late. Her sister left for India about two weeks ago to join her husband, leaving Joan with another sister...You have a picture

Seven. Dessau: Victories and Atrocities

of Joan somewhere at home...Eileen says she has really grown...so maybe I won't have to wait too long for her!!!!

Had a nice letter from Mrs. Francis, said that S. M. Anderson had written to me, but apparently our addresses have messed up some how or other since last summer, as I haven't heard from him and I've written several times, too. Mrs. Francis sure is swell..she tells me everytime that she is saving chicken and eggs and milk for me when I come home.

Can hardly believe all my neices [sic] are growing up, but guess that they will be well past the prime of life before I get back. Silly damned war isn't it??

Got the clippins [sic] of J.R. signing the TVA agreement ...guess that is one dream that he has seen fulfilled... he fought for it long enough..they should elect him Mayor or something or other of J.C. he sure has done a job and done it well for them.

Well, must be closing for now..will try and get you a few lines tomorrow, or when ever we stop again. How do you like my "liberated" typewriter???? It works fairly well!

Love to all, Johnny.

Soldiers use a Sherman dozer tank for cover, 1945.

Appalachia to Dessau

PFC Mayer Waddell, Houston, Texas, 3rd Armored Division, U.S. First Army, fires on fleeing Germans in the outskirts of Cologne, Germany, March 1945.

They captured Gieboldehausen and began the drive to cut off Harz Mountains between April 10 and 12, while far to the rear, the towns of Osterode and Herzberg were being cleared of the enemy.[12]

On April 11, Nordhausen was taken, but it was not the battle that would be remembered by the 32nd Armored Regiment. The shock and horror of the atrocities in that town would forever haunt their memories. The stench of decomposition assaulted their senses, as their eyes could not believe or comprehend the skeletal bodies of live human beings intermingled with the bodies of the long dead. Acres of corpses on the ground, barracks crammed to capacity with those alive and dead, bodies strewn haphazardly in heaps like garbage. Faint whimpers could be heard from those barely clinging to life, the emaciated bodies and sunken eyes, seeing nothing.[13] This atrocity fueled and reenergized the tired and weary 32nd Armored Regiment more than ever to defeat Hitler and the German army.[14]

Seven. Dessau: Victories and Atrocities

These two tank destroyers were abandoned by the Nazis in their flight from the 3rd Armored Division outside Oberpleis, Germany, March 1945.

A 3rd Armored Division tank passes burning debris at a factory near Marburg, Germany. Led by General Maurice Rose, this one-day advance of 90 miles was listed as the greatest in the history of mobile warfare.

Top: Ready to continue forward, crew members remount their tank after they stopped to fire on a village near their objective when enemy resistance was met. 3rd Armored Division, March 1945. *Above:* SS Panzer training regiment resistance outside of Paderborn, west of Weser River, Germany, March 30–31, 1945.

Seven. Dessau: Victories and Atrocities

They crossed Saale River in the vicinity of Könnern, assaulted that town on April 14, and continued attack to northeast.[15] Next, they entered Bernberg on April 15 and fought elements of Hitler's new home defense, Scharnhorst and Von Hotten divisions.[16]

Widespread fighting occurred over a wide area from Bernberg to Jessnitz between April 15 and 21, beating down several German attacks.[17]

Battling their way through three more towns, the 3rd Armored finally reached Dessau.

Goodin tells his mother that they are liberating prison camps and sugarcoats the horror.

```
16 April, 1945 Germany

Dear Mom,
    Am trying to get caught up on my mail again, and will
try and answer your letters..or a part of them..in the
mess I haven't been able to keep all of them, but have a
few of them..and can tell you hello if I didn't have any
of them. Seems that you have been able to get out again
and walk and ride around again (I had to laugh about that
tire going flat..doesn't it happen to us every time???) and
guess everything is under control.
    You silly people——if I were home and broke an arm..I
would tape it up and go about my business, and no one
would worry about it..and here, all I get is a scratch
(the Purple heart was for a scratch down in the bulge
that I wasn't even evacuated for) and I get all the way
back to Paris with it..so don't worry about me..and if I
got hurt seriously..it would be the same..the time I left
the tank to help the Jerry..I didn't get touched, but it
wasn't because they didn't try..so that wasn't the same
time!!
    And the picture of the "forgotten tank driver" is our
mess sergeant who used to be one of my drivers, but has
been back in the safe rear areas for quite some time..
don't worry about him either..that big Texan will come
along all right.
    We are liberating quite a few prison camps now, and
getting a lot of prisoners out..haven't run into anyone
we knew, but have plenty of British, Poles and Russians..
the Russians are funny..they organized and beat hell out
of the Germans..then cleaned up a couple of towns for us
saving a mean job...they don't mess with the civilians,
though occasionally the guards get their throats cut,
and fights break out between the Poles and the French, or
```

Appalachia to Dessau

Goodin labeled this photograph "trouble." It appears to have been taken from inside his tank, 1945.

just anybody...they all get the fighting spirit once they are out..and it does them good to blow off steam...just human nature. Course, there are the pathetic sides too, the skinny beatup, scrawny guys, the sick, wounded, diseased, and what not.

Hope that George Swingle is o.k., but you never know what the Germans are going to do. He might have been lost in the bunch that moved.

Your trip to Limestone is one that I want to take when I get back..leisurely, no hurry and nothing to worry about..to hell with everything and everybody and do what I want to..stopping here and there and playing around. Haven't enjoyed any of your letters quite as much as I have that one...course it was long and that always adds

Seven. Dessau: Victories and Atrocities

Crossing the Weser River, Germany, April 8, 1945.

to the help of a letters interest. I always seemed to sleep better down there myself.

Yes, I got your letter about the farm..and the most I can say, I'm coming back, and I am guaranteeing all of you, that when I do, you, Bill Carter or no one else will see much of me for quite a time..I'll be around, but I'm not doing anything but the things I've been missing..and loneliness here is not the same as in the woods by yourself..there is something about it. Hope Tom hasn't worn out my 22.

Well, no news..I'm gonna close for tonight..just don't worry about me..I'll be home some of these days...may be by the way of the Pacific, but it will be some of these days, anyhow. G'night for now..love to all,

      Johnny.

17 April, 1945

Dear Dad,

Will try and answer a few of your letters which I have here...some go back to Dec. 10th..so don't be surprised if it is a little late in news to you of what you want to know.

First of all, wish you would write just a little bit larger..your glasses must magnify these awfully large... and as I don't carry mine with me, I sometimes have a little trouble making out words which you run together.

A tank travels through Aschaffenburg, Germany, 1945.

Walter H. Coons and John Goodin at Mösbach, Germany, 1945.

Seven. Dessau: Victories and Atrocities

You also appear to be in a rush that you used not to be in when writing.

I will want to take about a two weeks tour or vacation with you and J.R. when I get back and then I'm going to take myself about a months vacation...and maybe after that I'll take off on a honeymoon—you people seem rather convinced that when I come back I'm going to hit the harness immediately.. well, I'm giving you fair warning now..I'm not.

About the loan on that farm of Bills... think it would be a good deal just get it somewhere where it is safe. If you can sink 5,000 in a Bldg and Loan Assn. where it

Goodin at Mösbach, Germany, 1945.

can be pulled out immediately, that will be good, too... half and half ought to do it, I think.

Maybe you are like Pa was with you...you are hoping that I reach 30 without getting into jail!!! Funny..

I've thought a lot of times how I'd love to kick the traces (really did day before yesterday...but it would have reminded you of your younger days on the road... no..it didn't have anything to do with women or whiskey).

I got the JC [Johnson City] paper of some time ago... and really enjoyed it..lots of people and incidents that I knew of.

Not much news over here...we are scrapping every bit of the way, and it is far from over. I am convinced...good men are staying here permanently every day, and sometimes my faith fails and like Peter, I sink into the water. I'm convinced of a lot of things I haven't been before..but it is kinda rough sometimes.

Appalachia to Dessau

Arthur E. "Pop" Goodwin rear left. John D. Goodin front center. Eppertshausen, Germany, 1945.

I now have two new big tanks with a lot of additional firepower, but unfortunately, no more armor. What a life.
Guess you are upset over Roosevelt...I am too..and just like I said, they put in a Vice-President who is not big enough to handle the job..he'll be lucky if he lives through the rest of this term without a breakdown. Might be a good thing...Stettinius seems a pretty good man.. and those damned fool politicians over there may wake up some day to the fact that there are a good many men left who can handle these jobs and do something about it. They don't mind bungling lives, so why bother about a little thing about a country...but I'll quit soap-boxing for a while.
Burns me up though...Dewey probably had more qualifications than this bird.
Well, don't know when nor where...but I'm taking it as easy as possible. I'll be relieved when it is over, but

Seven. Dessau: Victories and Atrocities

Ronald D. Gilboe and Arthur E. "Pop" Goodwin, 1945.

```
until that time..there is no relaxing. Another of my
best friends is gone for good. Walt is in the hospital in
England and writes that he is getting along o.k. for the
present.
   Take care of yourself...and when the war is over..you
and J.R. start your plans..for it looks like I'm going to
have to go to the S. Pacific before it is all over..and
that may take another couple of years or so.
                    Bye for now...write when you can.
                    Love to all, Johnny.
```

The 3rd Armored assaulted Dessau between April 22 and 23, capturing the city and advancing to the Elbe River.[18]

```
Germany, Apr 23rd, 1945
Dear Dad,
   Just have a few minutes..don't know what is up, but the
rumors are that Joe is near here, and I guess that soon
I'll be moving from right here. There are a thousand
things that are going around and nothing that we can
believe definitely.
   I'm enclosing a couple of letters for Sis and a couple
of pictures..the letters are for Sis. Thanks for the
```

Appalachia to Dessau

clippings, and guess that they are good stuff..I never could speak very much stuff...wish that I could speak some more.

Glad to know that you are all right and that you are keeping in trim playing cards..I'll take all of you on when I get home...wish this thing was over..and it looks as though it might be over soon now, at least for us... wish that it would.

I got a very nice letter from Mr. Moss..wish that I had time to answer him, but tell him that I'll write when I get the time. O.K.??

       Hope that this finds all of you well and happy,
       With all my love,
       Johnny.

According to the *Spearhead History Official Record of Combat*, "the 3rd Armored Division completed its 221st combat day on the continent of Europe on 24 April." They were relieved by the 9th Division. Between June 29, 1944, and May 12, 1945, an estimate of 6,751 enemy vehicles and equipment were destroyed, of which, 1,794 were tanks. Losses to the 3rd Armored was 1,832 vehicles and equipment, of which 780 were tanks.[19] Personnel losses were as follows:

KILLED IN ACTION	2,214
WOUNDED IN ACTION	7,451
MISSING IN ACTION	706
TOTAL CASUALTIES	10,371[20]

Relief effected from the line around Dessau on April 25, at which time the Russian forces were 21 miles to the east.[21]

Between April 24 and May 13, the Division began occupation and governing duties as they waited for the Army Redeployment Plan.[22]

In April, after the pullout from Dessau, John Goodin became acting Burgomeister (Mayor) of Greifenhagen, Germany. Goodin's hometown paper, *The Erwin Record*, reported on Thursday, May 17, 1945: "1st Lt. John D. Goodin with our military forces in Germany said in a recent letter that he was mayor of a German town, but spoke no German and they couldn't understand anything he said."

Chapter Eight

The Fatted Calf
April 28, 1945–September 10, 1945

Goodin had written a letter to his parents in early December 1944, telling them the war would be over by Christmas. Then, in April, he told them that the general news was that the war is *not* over and he may have to go to the South Pacific first. Goodin would wait many uncertain months before he would be sent home, writing 11 more letters of transfers and changes of address, expressing his exasperation, and eventually his capitulation, that his release was still unknown. On September 8, 1945, Goodin wrote a letter to Kay telling her he was in Le Havre, France, "waiting to be shipped out tomorrow." During this time of frustration at the lack of things to do, Goodin would become explicit in his letters to Anne as to exactly how he was feeling about the war and the world.

Goodin tells his parents they are withdrawing from the front and mentioned Roosevelt's death.

```
28 April 1945 (Excerpt)
Dear Dad,
```

Have gotten about two or three letters of you of late, but haven't had a chance to answer them as we have been withdrawing from the front and are now in a rest area... just wondering if it is going to be an occupational area ..but of course, we never know. The news tonight is very good, and it may be that we are kind of through for this part of the world. All I have to do now is sweat out the Pacific, and the war Dept is talking of releasing the men with four and 5 years service in the army...but say nothing about the officers, so I don't know really just what the score is now.

Have letters from you of the 14, 17, and 20th of April.. so you can see that the mail is pretty good at times..at other times, it isn't too good, mainly, because it is so hard for them to keep up with us.

Appalachia to Dessau

Our battalion is supposed to receive a Presidential Citation for breaking the Siegfried line, but we haven't received it as yet, and don't know when it will come in... things are always messed up somewhere.

Well, at least God didn't think Roosevelt was indispensable... though the Republicans couldn't find a man as good as he was...and I'm surprised at you getting so soft--we realize his loss, but we can't let that stop us from fighting...and you confessed to the same feeling when Mr. Mac died..so it isn't the first time since Ma [Grandmother] died that you have felt that way..not being mean...really..but I read all your letters pretty carefully...and the length of time between them to me is not much..not near so much as it is to you. Anyway..we'll make the most of it as always...

What kind of jackass is this Hubert Brooks??? [Goodin is referring to Senator Hubert Brooks from Tennessee who introduced a bill to ban red lipstick.] Any simpleminded sonofabitch who has no more brains that to suggest such a measure as he did in concern to womens lipstick should have been rode out of town on a rail... surprised at the good women of our district not doing it...or maybe they consider the source in such a case.

Have been getting the J.C. [Johnson City] paper regularly now..and see where our deal with Smith make the headlines... well...at least the front page anyhow. Rather interesting.. I was wondering one night about Fred Muhleder..the German boy who lived across the street from us in J.C., and in the next days paper, I saw where he had been visiting there..is a now a St/Sgt. in Virginia somewhere.

Goodin was mayor/military governor in Germany after the pullout from Dessau in April 1945.

Eight. The Fatted Calf

    Got a big birthday card from Mom from Burnsville..we all get a kick out of it..just hope I am home next year. Tell CDM [C.D. Moss] thanks for the letter.
                      Love, Johnny

Germany surrendered to the allies in Reims, France, ending World War II and the Third Reich on May 7, 1945.

HEADQUARTERS THIRD ARMORED DIVISION, APO 253
Offices of the Commanding General
8 May 1945
TO EVERY MEMBER OF THE THIRD ARMORED "SPEARHEAD" DIVISION

    I offer to each of you my sincerest congratulations today on "Victory in Europe", the one we have all been awaiting. To each of you who has bravely and tirelessly carried on in order to make this day possible I, as your Division Commander, express the thanks of a grateful nation at home.

    The accomplishments of our Division and its record against the enemy are well known to the entire world. As long as military history is studied and armored warfare is recounted, each of you may have the knowledge that your part in its making has been surpassed by none. I repeat to you the remarks of our Corps Commander when he said, "There have been a few <u>great</u> Divisions in the war and The Third Armored is one of these <u>great</u> Divisions."

    Let us not forget to pay tribute to these brave comrades of ours who have made the supreme sacrifice or who remain in hospitals, in order that peace might once more reign.

    May a Divine Providence continue to keep you safe in order that you may once again, and soon, be with your loved ones at home.
                  DOYLE O. HICKEY,
                  Brigadier General, U.S. Army Commanding.

Letter dated May 10th, or there abouts!!!

Dear Folks,

    Guess you are all happy now the war is officially over and don't think that I'm not too--I was in Paris on three day pass when the news broke though..we hadn't been fighting for several days then, but nevertheless it was kinda nice to know it was over. I promptly settled down to some steady celebration with about 14 other people who also enjoyed a good beer or so. Unfortunately it wasn't official so we couldn't' get skunk drunk then. That night

Appalachia to Dessau

I left and came back. Now we are on the move again in what may or may not prove to be occupation...I don't care much one way or another. Am just waiting so see if I'm going to have to sweat out the Pacific or not.

I have several letters from you all here...Mom has been to Burnsville, Limestone and points north east south and west. Got the letter with Dads picture in it...you don't look nearly as old as I feel. Got a letter from Tom... asking how it felt to be 29!!! Oh well....it sure is nice to hear from you anytime..if just to know everything is all right.

Sorry to hear about all these people dropping off like they do as, particularly now...when it is almost time to go home...there are going to be so many faces missing anyhow.

I didn't get a chance to see Keith Broce...inasmuch as I didn't get a leave to England and consequently, that is where he is. I might accidentally get one yet, but doubt it...as I'll probably be home before I get another chance to go.

Am afraid that I may end up in military government over here inasmuch as there is a huge shortage of available personnel, and they may give that to us in lieu of the Pacific...which I would take..as I don't feel like my luck would last that much longer!

Haven't much else to talk about..I'm still tired from that Paris trip...it seems a thousand miles down there now..and the town itself is something else..oo-la-la....

Write when you can, and I'll try and hurry home some of these days now!!

Love, Johnny

17 May, 1945

Dear Folks,

Have umpteen letters from you again..and again I'm behind in writing as even after peace is declared, we still have to wander all over the country taking care of this and that..or nothing at all. I have 87 points, but doubt if they will do me any good, as in the regiment alone, there are 35 officers with more than I have, and 7 tied with me..and I doubt if they will release us right away anyhow..ah me..what a life.

As I told you, I was in Paris when the shindig was over..and except for not being sure it was the real thing...would probably have extended my pass..and maybe have gotten into trouble or something - Don't guess I'll ever get back there now, though.

Eight. The Fatted Calf

Well, with all the enemies that Wallace had, it looks (from what I can gather from over here) that it might have been a good thing that Truman was vice-President as the people seem more than willing to try and cooperate with him. I just hope he shows some judgment in knocking hell out of the bureaus that we are getting so many thousands of these days.

Don't' know if I thanked you for the pictures or not.. if I didn't, I am now,...it is the first picture I've had of any of you in six or eight months now. These Harrisons aren't any beauties, are they? Well, I gotta stop and go over and eat some supper..we have been having iced tea and lemonade down here...it is really warm.

Mail call, three letters, an announcement, three JC [Johnson City] papers and one from Erwin. Wanting to know more about George....am getting worried about him, as I thought Ben Emmert was in the same camp with him. But maybe he isn't...will just have to wait a little longer I guess until the final news comes out one way or another.

Am still waiting for some pictures to come back, but haven't as yet..they have been in for a long time, since before we crossed the Roer river at Duren..but then that is the way things go..fast service one day and then none the next day.

Not much news now that we aren't doing anything. playing a few games, keeping equipment up to snuff, turning in stuff like gas masks and other useless items, catching up on the things that we have wanted to do for a while, and in the meantime just drifting along waiting for the war department to make up its mind what it wants to do with us. Has been a long 10 months but it's over...lidedi!!

Seems mother is getting around plenty..Burnsville, Limestone, Burnsville, Limestone again...and so forth and so. Bet you will be flirting with St. Pete when you enter the gate (may stand you in good stead, as these characters who think you are such a "good woman" may not be there to tell him how good you are!!!!!..maybe he is susceptible to the wilds [sic] of a woman..and he could certainly be to yours!!) Will be good to get back and take a trip with you here and there again. Sure appreciated the gum and candy..got it when I got back from Paris..and we celebrated some more with it. I didn't find any woman with a gold necklace..at least I didn't kill any of them to take one off of them..Probably should have..saved one more kid or two that will have to be bumped off later.

Tell Tom I'm only 28, please...and its [sic] bad enough being <u>that</u> old. Sorry about all the peace rumors...we had troubles with the real one too..but I drank about 10 good

Appalachia to Dessau

cool weak beers, went to the can, says "Come on Mickey" and down the Champs Elysees we took. Still think a man ought to marry a girl who has been here, because nobody else will ever understand us..or at least a part of us, anyhow. Well, that is all for now..am going to try and finish up the rest of my letters tonight..so I'll be completely caught up one time. Goodnight, and take care and write when you can...I may be home some of these days now..regardless of when..it won't be as bad as when the war was on over here.

     Love, Johnny

27 May 1945

Dear Folks,

 Sure glad to know that my pistols arrived safely..I hope that Perason has gotten a discharge now..he was my platoon sergeant, and a hell of a good man..glad that he got them through o.k. I still have several others here...better give the big one to Tom and let him clean it up for me, because it is in bad shape probably now, and he can clean it up..it's not a permanent deal, I just want him to clean it up for me, and keep it till I get home. So you can let him know. The little one has the cosmoline (grease and oil) on it and I think it is in good shape.

 Sure was glad to know that George Swingle is back in France...if I could get back to France, I could find out where he is and maybe see him..but if at all possible, he has already been flown home, and is probably home right now...just hope that he is o.k.

 You people sure are getting anxious...you know that the army is a strange thing, and I'll be lucky to get home for a long time. I'm not expecting to get home early, because the news is now that the officers will not be getting out for some time, as there is no point system that we will be getting discharged under.

 Wonder whether Reg is going to the Pacific or not...bet he is sweating, since Arnold and Eisenhower have said that the entire force was going to be concentrated in the Pacific...sooner the better..but I'm not too sure that certain parties in the states want it to end as soon as possible.

 No news yet..I played piano, and an organ in church today..played in two churches for two different sermons. Played my first big organ in church last Sunday..not too good..a 75 had gone through and knocked out a couple of pipes in it, and those didn't play..but I enjoyed it nevertheless.

Eight. The Fatted Calf

    Have started a slight course of conditioning myself for myself now...doing a little running..surprising how ten months of this stuff will get you out of condition...and I have really gotten out of condition.
    Gotta close for tonight....so long and take care of yourself. Love and kisses,
                    Johnny.
    Had a nice letter from Ann Rosenbaum today.

In this letter Goodin tells his parents that while his dreams are calming down, he expects to have nightmares for the rest of his life.

The Third Armored "Spearhead" Division Letterhead
4 June 1945
In Eppertshausen, Germany

Dear Folks,
    Sure hate to disappoint you in not getting home right away, and I know you know that I'm as anxious as you, but only those that are getting discharged and are going to the Pacific are all that are leaving right now..and I sorta hope that I'm not in the latter. Our points are going to have a different number, naturally, and so you can readily see that it may be that I will be slated for the army of occupation over here. It will be better than going to the Pacific, unless I might go over as some sort of something or other..like Bubber, that wouldn't mean front line fighting..I've seen all that I want to see for quite a while, I'm afraid..Even now the dreams I have at night are just beginning to calm down a little bit. And guess that all of us will suffer from nightmares the rest of our normal lives, to say nothing of perhaps the hereafter.
    Am trying to get a leave to England at the end of this month...will know more about it tomorrow. If I can get a plane ride over there, I'm going to go. Otherwise, I'll have to wait until a quota comes out that will allow me to go over on their time insteyd [sic] of my own. Beats me...wish that I could get something done, before I go crazy doing nothing. Course, we do some little petty gambling to pass the time away, and guess I'll continue to do that until such time as comes when there is something to do. I had wanted to go to school in England, but guess that may be out for a while too, until I can find out what is going to be done with me...this prison life is not a good one, under any conditions.
    How do you like our paper? [Goodin is referring to the

Appalachia to Dessau

letterhead.] We just were issued it today, and so far have been unable to get the rest of it..are hoping to have envelopes to match before long. Still..doesn't cost us anything, so can't kick too much, can we...

Guess things have calmed down now with Sis gone...what is she going to do with Stoop Inn? If she leaves it...I wouldn't mind having it myself...if I get around to getting married and settled down within the next ten years or so..

Gotta be closing now..take care of things, and be easy.. may be home some of these days soon. But don't get any ideas I'm flying home on the next plane...and please try and realize that John D. Goodin is not the only soldier over here. Some of the letters I got after V. day seemed to think that I would be on the next boat home...just as if there weren't any others over here at all...

      Some people...what small worlds they live in.
      Love to all,
      Johnny.

Medals, which added to point accumulation, were slow in being awarded. Goodin mentions this in his letter dated June 22 to his parents. This excerpt is from a four-page notification, dated June 8, 1945, which lists medals for September 1943 and 1944. Goodin is awarded a bronze star from February 26, 1945.

        R E S T R I C T E D
  HEADQUARTERS THIRD ARMORED DIVISION APO 253

8 June 1945

  IV. AWARD BRONZE STAR MEDAL

Under the provisions of AR 600-45, 22 Sept 1943, as amended, and under authority contained in Memorandum Number 94, Headquarters Ninth United States Army, 8 September 1944, as amended, the Bronze Star Medal is awarded to the following officers and enlisted men: 1ST LT JOHN D GOODIN 01010821 Inf (Armd), 32d Armd Regt, for heroic achievement in action against the enemy in Germany on 26 February 1945. Entered military service from Tennessee.

(Goodin was one of 29 soldiers to receive the Bronze Star Medal)

11 June 1945 Still...in Germany.
Dear Folks,

  Just a note...as you know, there is no news these days. Just sitting around not doing a lot of anything, and

Eight. The Fatted Calf

sweating out the time when we will return home or do something.

I have gone back from the hospital today, where I had a checkup...nothing wrong with me says the doc, that getting married and settling down wouldn't do for me!!! Quite a laugh under the circumstances, but wouldn't be surprised if I did just that some of these days...

From your letter, Sis must be safely settled in South Carolina by now..ho hum....bet that all of Tennessee and South Carolina are relieved that she and Reg are together again..

How is Uncle Pyott, haven't heard anyone mention him for some time..guess he is all right, though or I would have heard from you. I don't hear from many people now that the war is over..very easily explained..I don't have anything to write about, and neither do they. All my points avail me nothing. As I'm hooked for the duration, and six months I'm afraid. Unless some miracle happens to me. I'm still toying with this military government idea inasmuch as if I have to stay over here I might as well be in that as anything else. Beats me..honestly it does!!!

I have stopped my allotment at the bank..so you can tell them not to look for their usual check at the beginning of each month. I don't think I'll need it..but would like to have a statement, and also a checkbook from the bank...things have eased up a bit, and I might end up in Italy or somewhere and need some money..one just never does know. To say nothing of landing in New York, some of these years and wanting to write a check and having to see some woman in order to get money!!! Whoof...some of the thoughts one gets to having over here!!!

Well, not having any other news..must close. Hope that you aren't expecting too much mail these days, as I have no ambition to write, not going anywhere to write about, and not doing anything worth repeating..much less telling the first time!!

                        Love and kisses to all, Johnny.

Tell Geo..Swingle when he gets home that I want a word from him at least..if nothing but a post card...and let me know how he is and how he got along...

            Johnny.

In this frank letter to Anne Carter, Goodin gives God the credit for coming through the war, and expresses disgust at dishonesty, "corruption and petty politics," and concern about the direction of the United States as it is "rotting internally."

Appalachia to Dessau

13 June, 1945.

Dearest Anne,

Three years ago, I received my commission as a 2nd Lt. in the Army of the United States, and today after three years of being an officer, still have some periods of regret. Unfortunately, it is impossible to be an officer in time of battle and then revert to an enlisted man for peace time, it wouldn't be bad.

Unfortunately, too, my idea of an officer and gentleman has collapsed, too, after seeing some of the things that run around in uniforms with various degrees of rank stuck on their shoulders.

The phases of a war are what change one, Anne, and cause perplexity. In preparation for the war to come, one puts aside personal grievances on the ground that teamwork and coordination and unity are all-important; in battle, one does the same thing for the evident necessity of things; but now, with the peace, at least here, when one takes stock of trade it is disgusting to find the shortages. People who let their personal dislikes of someone affect their military evaluation of their execution of orders; others who will not give credit for fear of detracting from themselves; finally those who <u>take</u> credit for achievements that they know rightfully belong to someone else. Regimentation at best is none too good, even for the suppression of would-be world dominators, but when petty things are allowed to control that regimentation...it is more difficult for those of us who retain some semblance of the ideals and principles on which our once-great country was founded.

I am in great fear of our country, Anne. I have no fear of death, as such; I face it, experienced it, defeated that fear within the past few months. I well remember after our first engagement, when with my best buddy (an 88 got him in his last engagement and he is now home recuperating) I went into a little beat-up church in Normandy, and we knelt in silent prayer. I prayed not so much for life itself, Anne, as I did for Divine Guidance, and that I would never show cowardice; those prayers were answered, Anne, as is evidenced by the extremely low percentage losses of the men and vehicles under me—and pure luck would never have gotten us through of itself.

Our country, Anne, is in my opinion rapidly approaching the condition that France was in before her fall in '40. I have recently read in *Readers Digest* Senator Byrds castigation of the bureaus and their evident abundance of man and woman power, and notorious lack of business.

Eight. The Fatted Calf

Yet there is a crying wail of shortage of secretaries, shortage of men for war plants, shortage of Red Cross workers, in short shortages everywhere except where there should be. I know in our army there are many who admit openly that they are on a gravy train, have little or nothing to do. I know that in Infantry divisions that there are small handfuls of men who in battalion and company strength fought the war on their fronts; in tank divisions of single tanks who bore the brunt of the advance; I know of the supreme courage and self-control required to lead those columns day in and day out; I have sensed the feelings of those P4 pilots who dove relentlessly on enemy tanks and guns to make our task easier, and each of their silent prayers that they would come up again after such dives. These men, Anne, represent a small portion only of the fighting men, and a very low percentage of the men necessary to win the war. I am not the only one to criticize our armys use of man-power, or its internal mechanisms. And the other branches of service are just as full of corruption, petty politics and what have you.

In substance, Anne, I am afraid that like France, we are rotting internally; i. e., her army, even now, while composed of some brilliant leaders, and in some respects having policies that are to be preferred over our own, still retains the old bugaboos which led to their downfall in '40. Our liaison officers are frank to admit that they perceive how France was unable to stem the German invasion. Be as it may, France's sickness was internal in government and its branches..and I fear that with a continuance of conditions as they are now, we are in France's danger.

The first bright light I have observed was the refusal of a prominent man to accept a Supreme Court position offered to him by the President on the ground that he was unqualified. The second and most hopeful proposition is that of the President to wield the axe on many bureaus in Washington. If he is able to do this..however minutely his success, it will be a big step in our recovery. If this policy is carried out, the morale and confidence of returning veterans will be boosted to a point inestimable. They are not all of an irresponsible nature and many of them are now taking active parts in catching up with national trends before returning home.

Another hopeful sign is from Senator Byrd: you, as well as anyone perhaps, know that I'm hardly a New Dealer, though I believe strongly in the principles of the original Democratic party, and lean a little towards

Appalachia to Dessau

liberal-Republicanism, as it now stands. Senator Byrd, to me, represents a combination of these, and I hope will eventually become the standard bearer of a party that will arise out of this chaos and lead us back to normalcy. He has stuck his neck out to the point of openly pointing out the deficiencies in our bureaus, though one of our own Tennessee Representatives a couple of years ago, attempted to get an investigation committee, and failed. However, Byrd might do the trick, and more power to him.

Perhaps, nationally, we will arise from our passiveness and evolve into something great again. Unless we do, internationally, we face the fate of the man who created a mechanical man and then was destroyed by the mechanical man. Perhaps you will understand that better if I only point out to you that in Prague, the Russians marched in completely equipped with American equipment. I cannot understand why our State Department made the same mistake with Russia in this war as it did in the last war with France: to bluntly tell them what was expected while we had the upper hand (in France's case, she was dependent on American gold, yet was able to force Wilson to back down after she had gotten it) and not wait until peace was declared and the nations put on a basis of equality.

Particularly in view of the fact that while Russia is our most powerful ally, potentially she is also our strongest enemy-with <u>known</u> nationalist ideals that are diametrically opposed to our own. Even now, it is alleged that Russia is taking people from Poland using them as slave labor in Russia in much the same manner as the Germans did Russian and Poles..and others.

I cannot help but feel that our trend is towards world chaos, that there is no place on the globe that is free from the worry, the potentiality of another war in which literally, everything will be destroyed. Except for my own conscience, and the debt I feel I owe for the 25 years of happy carefree life, I would be well-tempted to retire to Tibet (which no one wants or would have because of its barrenness, bleakness, etc.,) and become a nomad or hermit. But, being reconciled to the law that you can't get something for nothing, and that my part in this war will hardly be classed as payment in full, I cannot quit now, though doubtless my part in clearing up this muddle will be little or nothing.

I'm afraid this letter rather got away from me, but doubt if you mind too much. From the enclosed clipping, you can gather some of the whys and wherefores of some of my remarks. There is no end of bitterness over such things as that. While in Paris at the hospital, I was

Eight. The Fatted Calf

no little disgusted to see officers on their way to golf courses; others running around here and there with French girls, some Americans, but still running around with reckless abandon; at the front we are forbidden any waste of gasoline yet back there there seemed to be no shortages; it did not mind that shoe polish was sent by boat from the states, and used for polishing floors for inspections by generals; there was no excitement over base officers bringing in their civilian friends to their mess, when others could not get in with American Wacs or nurses; there was no curb on a single jeep or other vehicle going many miles to pick up one escort for a dance or party; nothing extraordinary in a colonel in a hospital having the most beautiful of French girls working for him, on government expense. Even now, despite the honor involved, and the prestige, we are rationed on gasoline, yet 1700 airplanes of all types, British and American, honored Montgomery and Zhukov by flying formations over Frankfurt; airplane travel to Paris and to London has been discontinued indefinitely without reason - resulting in many of us not getting to go back that would have otherwise. There is space for 1000 English girls to go to America, with 25,000 more waiting to go over, yet only a dribble of high pointers are going over. There are still silly would-be benefactors who suggest sending families over to us; the number of silly suggestions that come out of our Congress is a disgrace. Bonus bills have skyrocketed out of all reason, and if they continue will result in this bunch of veterans being the most pampered group the world has ever known, and the results will be felt when the responsibility of running a country is thrust on them in their later years, and they will wonder why they are unprepared to handle that responsibility.

Am I completely unrational in my thinking? Am I alone in my convictions? In the latter, I know I am not. The former, I am not sure of. One can never be sure here.

In regard to the clipping, I would say that I believe a rest period, as the coffee hours, is beneficial, but not carried to the illogical extremes as painted here: a fifteen or twenty minute break is beneficial to the maintenance of a high peak of efficiency. Otherwise, I am not shocked, astonished, or unduly surprised at the article. I am pleased with his bland, blunt, and brave manner of revealing his knowledge. As an officer could never make such a public statement, regardless of its truth, without running risk of being shot or such other punishment as the court saw fit.

Maybe if the perseverance of men like Moore, Senator

Appalachia to Dessau

```
Byrd, Winchell, and even yes - - Pegler holds out, some
people will wake up yet.
   I wonder.
                  As ever,
                  Johnny
```

(Article published on Saturday, June 9, 1945. Title: Ex-Officer Scores Brass for Coffee Hours, Bucking by Phil Bucknell, The Stars and Stripes U. S. Bureau)

Excerpt:
   A former public relations lieutenant who spent this war in the Zone of the Interior, and who also is a veteran of the last, has let down his back hair in an article in this week's Liberty Magazine. His beef is that too many soldiers don't fight.
   Concerning the duty hours, the ex-officer [Herbert G. Moore] says: "For days at a time, our program consisted of coffee at ten in the morning; lunch, possibly followed by an hour of pool or pingpong at the Officer's Club; and coffee again at three in the afternoon. The coffee hour is a fixture at most Army administration installations from the Pentagon Building down – and I believe the Navy follows the same social custom."

Germany
June 14th, 1945

Dear folks,

```
   Got your letter mailed June 8 today..so guess that the
mail at least from there to here is coming in rather
good...certainly no complaints from this side of the
pond..
   Have a letter from Art, and he says if and when I get
home to give Mom a big hug and kiss..so I'll send it now,
and enforce it when I get there, o.k.??
   I didn't get my allotment stopped this month in time,
and I am going to a "Rest camp"..a hotel, turkish bath,
and summer resort area down in Belgium, "Spa" it is
called and is not far from Liege and Verviers. So to
finance said deal, I borrowed money from one of the lads
and to save a lot of red tape, wish you would send the
money to his sister..writing your check on my account for
one hundred and ten dollars ($110.00). If you are
wondering about all that, remember I haven't had a
terribly big celebration over here yet, and the main
thing is I am going to have to fix myself up in a nice
dress uniform (Eisenhower jacket with ribbons and all
that junk). The letter, check, address is:
```

Eight. The Fatted Calf

Mrs. Oscar Adams
1 South 9th St.
Chickasaw, Alabama

Got it, thanks.

Got a letter from Fred Whitlow today and he is only about 50 miles from here, so hope that I will be able to up and see him within the next couple of days or so...I've been closer to him several times, but not in contact with him at those times....hope that I'll be able to make it this time.

Not much news over here. We are still just waiting around. Sorry to hear about my old bootlegger...did Doc Whiteheads going have anything to do with that? They were awfully close you know. Gosh..no bootlegger, no dentist, what will I be coming back to, anyhow?? I sent a large box home day before yesterday, and there is not much in it..though there may be some sentimental value to some of the things...there is a liner for my raincoat, which I hope will not be needed till I come home and can use it over there. The little white sweater was knitted for me by an elderly Belgian school teacher who has designated me as the love of her post-menopause period..lovely old lady, but slightly daft. Also the scarf is a gift from her. They were knitted for me last Christmas, but the battle of the Bulge intervened, and so I didn't get them until late. There is also a shaving kit that I bought that I don't know who can use right away, so I'm saving it for the time that I come home and may be able to use it for A Christmas present (doing it early this year!!)

Well, this is it for this time...happy landings and write when you have the time...everyone seems to let off after the war is over, and we still like to see mail come in though. I'm getting the JC [Johnson City] paper rather regularly now...sure enjoy it.

                    Love to all, Johnny

22 June 1945
Dear Folks,

Am back from a wonderful (literally, too) pass which I unfortunately extended a few hours, but don't guess I am in too much trouble, at last not yet. I spent close to a hundred dollars, something very unusual, but I at least got away from Germany, and put off my going crazy for another few months, at least.

My mail from home is coming through in good shape nowadays...seems funny not to have mail a month and a half old anymore.

Appalachia to Dessau

I sure was happy to get that clipping on Allen, as while I was on pass I was told he had been killed during the battle of the bulge, and then when I got back it was nice to hear that he was still not only living, but even back home. Quite a nice lad.

So far as I know, of our group up at Knox that came from Wheeler, only one is dead and he was killed in our division. I finally wound up with 107 points with the addition of the two battle stars that we have been waiting for a long time. Have no idea of when I will be home though. Am now in the Seventh Army, after another reshuffle. I am still at the same place, and getting along very well here. Got rid of my two disgusting characters, and have a new captain in who is a peach apparently, though I'm reserving judgment until I see just what he really is. He is starting off swell, though.

As to my watch, just keep it for me for now, as I hope that I will be home some of these days now...and I can use it to good advantage. If Gladys can have a baby at 40, there is no reason why I shouldn't be able to come through with at least one in the next ten years..or sooner!

Have no other news for you...met a swell guy from the air corp who may take me up for a few spins some of these days, and might get to see some more of Germany that I haven't seen...I have some pretty nice pictures of Paris on my way home, and may get some more if they turn out any good.

Must close for tonight, as I still have some letters to write...seems that in a weeks [sic] time, things can certainly get behind...

Love and kisses to all, Johnny.

P.S. The docs said there was nothing wrong with me that getting married wouldn't cure!!!!!!!!!!!!!!!!!!!!!!!!!!!!!!!!!!

27th June 1945

Dear Folks,

Got your letter of June 20th last night...not bad time at all, is it?? Anyway, glad to know everything is all right with you all. Thanks for the checks, and hope that I won't have to use them right away, anyhow. I had a terrific time in Paris again...visited a lawyer I had met last summer (did he have a nice blond secretary?? Whoof....) ran around to different places, and generally just enjoyed life without too much worry except being over the hill. Rode back in a three star generals plane, and it was fixed up like a Streamliner. Hope no one finds out too much about that trip...ooh. Sunday I am being

Eight. The Fatted Calf

transferred to the 6ᵗʰ Armored Div. as the 1ˢᵗ step in our deployment towards home. Will still probably be about months and months and months before I get home, but if I don't have to go to the Pacific, I won't worry too much about it.

Its raining to beat H--- here, and we are all getting ready to move out Sunday..almost as bad as leaving for somewhere else.

Well, I am going up to see if I can find Fred Whitlow this afternoon, and see if he is still here. So will close for now, until I come back.

      Love and kisses,
      as always, Johnny.

Later....well, Freds outfit has gone home and I didn't get to see him. They said that he had left about two weeks ago, which must have been only a couple of days after he wrote to me...so you should run into him at home on a furlough before too long now.

      Love again, Johnny.

How do you like the picture???

    HEADQUARTERS THIRD ARMORED DIVISION
 Office of the Commanding General APO #253, U. S. Army

30 June 1945

Subject: Departure From Third Armored "Spearhead" Division.

To: 1st LT JOHN DO GOODIN 01 010 821 Co. B, 32d Armd Regt

Within a very short time you will leave our Division and start on the redeployment portion of our Army. I wish that it were possible to see and talk to every man that is leaving us at this time, but I regret I will be unable to do this.

You are one of about 6,000 stalwart men of this Division that has earned sufficient points for a return home. You may have earned this privilege through the willingness of the men of this Division to relentlessly pursue and destroy the enemy across France, Belgium and into the very heart of the Reich. Day after Day and night after night, without pause and without rest, the men of this division carried on in the highest traditions of our military service to enhance the glory and reputation of this great fighting unit. I am taking this opportunity to thank you for your personal efforts. As a member of our great fighting team, you, and the men like you have

Appalachia to Dessau

HEADQUARTERS THIRD ARMORED DIVISION
Office of the Commanding General

APO #253, U.S. Army
30 June 1945

Subject: Departure From Third Armored "Spearhead" Division.

To : 1ST LT JOHN D GOODIN O1 010 821 Co. B, 32d Armd Regt.

    Within a very short time you will leave our Division and start on the redeployment program of our Army. I wish that it were possible for me to see and talk to every man that is leaving us at this time, but I regret I will be unable to do this.

    You are one of about 6,000 of the stalwart men of this Division that has earned sufficient points for a return home. You have earned this privilege through the willingness of the men of this Division to relentlessly pursue and destroy the enemy across France, Belgium and into the very heart of the Reich. Day after day and night after night, without pause and without rest, the men of this Division carried on in the highest traditions of our military service to enhance the glory and reputation of this great fighting unit. I am taking this opportunity to thank you for your personal efforts. As a member of our great fighting team, you, and the men like you have skyrocketed the name of the Third Armored Division across the entire world, and its deeds of valor and accomplishments have been equalled by only a few, and surpassed by none.

    You may rest assured that whatever the future holds in store for our Division, the men that take your place will be instilled with the same fighting spirit and esprit de corps that you have had, and if it should be our fortune to again occupy a role on the field of battle, the standards that you have helped in setting so high, will not be lowered.

    I congratulate you on this well earned opportunity to return to the United States and to your home, and it is my hope that every good fortune will continue to be yours.

Sincerely yours,

DOYLE O. HICKEY,
Brigadier General, U. S. Army,
Commanding.

A letter of departure from the Third Armored "Spearhead" Division to John D. Goodin, signed by Doyle O. Hickey, Brigadier General, June 30, 1945. This letter is typed into the manuscript.

skyrocketed the name of the Third Armored Division across the entire world, and its deeds of valor and accomplishments have been equalled [sic] by only a few, and surpassed by none.
  You may rest assured that whatever the future holds in store for our Division, the men that take your place will be instilled with the same fighting spirit and esprit de corps that you have had, and if it should be our fortune

Eight. The Fatted Calf

to again occupy a role on the field of battle, the standards that you have helped in setting so high, will not be lowered.

I congratulate you on this well earned opportunity to return to the United States and to your home, and it is my hope that every good fortune will continue to be yours.

                Sincerely yours, DOYLE O. HICKEY,
                Brigadier General, U. S. Army,
                Commanding.

        HEADQUARTERS HQ 6TH ARMD DIV
            APO 256, U S Army

9 Jul 45

SO 182

  1 of 16.

  16. Lv of absence for seven (7) days, effective o/a 9 Jul 45 is granted 1ST LT JOHN D GOODIN, 01010821, Inf (Armd), 68th Tank Bn, for purpose of visiting Soissons, France. Auth: Cir 20, European T of Opns, US Army, 1945.

                JAS S MONCRIEF JR
                Lt Col, GSC C of S

BY COMMAND OF MAJOR GENERAL CROW: OFFICIAL: Victor E. CELIO

20 July 1945

(Excerpt) Dear Folks,

  Have just gotten back and recuperated from a 7 day leave that carried me down to Soissons, Paris, back to Reims and the vicinity for about 35 to 40 miles each way...had an emergency leave since Kay is leaving for the Pacific and I had to see her before she left. It sure was grand seeing her again, and although the MPs picked up my peep while I was down there and I got a nasty report on it, it still was wonderful and we had a swell time. Went swimming seeing the country..went to Chateau Thierry, Belleau Wood, and a couple of cemeteries, champagne factories, swimming in the Marne, ate C rations which I had brought along, and met friends and people from all over. Bought a few souvenirs, and except for having to have her in at 11:30 at nights, had the best time one could dream of over here.

  Got back to find several letters from you, and glad to know that you are all well. You are apparently right on that probably home in September or August of this year, but right now there are nasty rumors floating around that

Appalachia to Dessau

this battalion and another one will be placed on detached service for army of occupation and may stay over here for a little while longer. In any event, I should be home by the first of the year, or anyhow, by next summer, at latest.

I have a very nice letter from Ruth Moseley after she returned home and said she had talked to mom for a long time. As to what you told her, I guess it was the right thing all right. At least it was the truth, and I suppose there is never too much harm in telling the truth. Don't guess it will ever die, though it may grow awfully dim, and finally drop into obscurity. Told Kay about her...some of these days I hope you all get to meet Kay...I think you would like her very well.

I sure get a kick out of mothers exploits to the Billy hole and peeping around...aren't you a little ashamed of yourself, peeping like that???? Tsktsktsktsktsktsk!! And chopping poor little snakes heads off.

And the Doctor didn't say I was <u>not</u> to get married—he said I had <u>better</u> get married <u>soon</u>—or do some fraternizing...which once again says that some peoples ideas of modesty and right and wrong may be all wet for all their idealism. We are not doing much of anything right now..as you know I'm not in the 3rd anymore, but am happy over here..some of my boys came over with me, and others, well..went to the four winds, some of them have flown home, and one or two might drop in to see you or call some time or other.....

Sorry that George D. hasn't come in yet...if I had known he was in France in a hospital, would have tried to find him when I was on leave...ooh...what fun...even Steinway grand pianos along with everything else.

Must be closing for today. Just wanted you to know that because I haven't written for a week or two, I'm not on the way home, tho I'd like to be.

Love to all, Johnny

Enclosure:
Newsclipping announcing Goodin receiving the Bronze Star.

The *Johnson City Press-Chronicle* reported on Sunday, August 5, 1945, Headline: "John D. Goodin, Erwin, Receives Bronze Star."

First Lt. John D. Goodin ... has been awarded the Bronze Star medal for heroic achievement in action against the enemy, Army headquarters announced. Lieutenant Goodin is the holder of the Purple Heart medal for wounds received in Belgium and Germany. He has been in the 32nd

Eight. The Fatted Calf

Armored Regiment since June 25, 1942, and fought in the battles of Normandy, Northern France and Belgium, through the Siegfried Line, in the Ardennes, and into Germany to the Elbe River. The lieutenant is a tank platoon commander in one of the Third Armored (Spearhead) Division's armored task forces.

The letter below indicates that Goodin is still presiding over court martials while waiting to be shipped out.

R E S T R I C T E D
HEADQUARTERS 68TH TANK BATALLION APO 256, U. S. ARMY
21 July 1945.
SO 53
    1. A SCM [Summary Court-Martial] is aptd [appointed] to meet at this sta [station] at the call of the President thereof for the trial of such persons as may properly be brought before it:
DETAIL FOR THE COURT:
[Names are listed.]
TRIAL JUDGE ADVOCATE:
1ST Lt JOHN D GOODIN, 0-1010821, Inf
    All unarraigned cases heretofore referred for trial to Special Courts Martial appointed by par 1, SO 32, this Hq [Headquarter], 9 May 45, as amended to pars 2, 3, and 4, SO 39, this Hqs, 8 Jun 45, are hereby transferred and referred to this Court for trial.
    By order of Major SMITH:
                    JOHN C. BEACHAM, Capt, Inf. Adj.
                    OFFICIAL: JOSEPH H. EXHER, CWO, USA
                    Asst. Adj.

Despite their tumultuous relationship and the constant back-and-forth hashing out, or attempting to define, what their relationship actually is, Goodin refers affectionately in this letter to Anne putting the stamps upside down on the envelope, which meant "I love you."

22 July, 1945 (Excerpt)
My dearest Anne,
    Well, honey, I have your first letter written to this new address, it arriving last night much to my pleasure and delight. Have of necessity had to postpone the phase three letter of my last one to you, as the conditions at present are not right for it, and I am getting Americanized again to the point that maybe I won't let it bother me too much. Much has happened to me in the past couple of days:

Appalachia to Dessau

Saturday the huntmaster (game warden back home) of this Kries invited the officers up to his little lodge which overlooks the whole of the surrounding country, even to seeing Frankfurt, Aschaffenburg, and Hanau, as well as numerous lesser towns.

There we met his wife, a very charming frau, his son, and his majestic looking dog. Whilst the others were being toasted in cognac and schnapps, yours truly was downing considerable fresh cider (with disastrous results yesterday morning early!), and was idling over the keys of his baby grand piano. This bit of heaven was the wonderful added attraction. It doesn't, however bode good, though as there are now furnished us as companions, several English speaking frauleins (I can hear you swearing ever so softly, Anne, dear!) who were doubtless a part of a small counter part of German resistance to the Nazis. This I say, since the lad who obtained them was three years a prisoner of the Nazis, and spent the last few months at Buchenwald..and still looks like one of the corpses come to life. His stories are the same, if not worse than those we know so well now, and which still burn us up not a little. Nevertheless, Freddy has found these girls, who befriended him early, and made his life a little less miserable. As yet, I am too obstinate to become interested, and as one of them told me, I would never love anyone or anything as long as I had a piano. It is grand, Anne, to have one completely at your disposal again..it is almost like my own at home. Anyhow, we stayed up till nearly three Saturday night, eating and drinking and singing and playing. We also made plans for a wild boar hunt for last night, and that we did. Yesterday I did nothing, absolutely. Then last night, we were off, with the huntmaster, and another of the same from a neighboring town, and spent several lonely hours on our "stands" which were miles from nowhere. I personally did not have any luck, not seeing anything to shoot at, but some of the boys did have a little sport. And we plan on going back again, sometime soon. It is ideal, and well worthy of consideration for a honeymoon..though one wonders when the hell or why the hell such a thought would come up.

Anyhow, as you can read, I have not been faring too badly around here, and have no complaints to make as of now. Wish I were coming home again, but now, it seems that our battalion is a separate tank battalion, and may not come home for some time yet, as we are only temporarily attached to the 6th Armored.

What a mess things can get into. Oui??

Eight. The Fatted Calf

I apologize profusely for not getting you a letter about your birthday time...though I'm still looking for a suitable present. Thought I had found one, but I'm still looking for something just a bit more special than average. Know what I mean?

Forgive me if I assume this big brother attitude about you at times?? Sometimes, it seems that is what I feel, and when I feel it, it is necessary to write that way or not at all..and that would never do...right? Anyhow... sweetheart, suffice it to say, that whether it be as a big brother, or just as yours-to-be (who can really tell??) the last year has found the bonds being drawn closer and closer, despite the obstacles which necessarily have been thrown in our way. I sincerely hope that by the time I do see you, and I do have my mind made up, that I will be able to put the past behind me and let it go. Can't seem to get much ambition to write to anyone these days...do manage to get you a fairly long letter once in a while... but just can't seem to write to Sis, or the family, to Marg, or to lesser lights..including Lou.

How did Mom get around to losing 20 pounds? Sounds out of this world no less!!! I am happy to hear it though.

Kinda pleased to know that you missed me just a little bit when you were home..and even in a mood to put the stamps on upside down when you mailed the letter, Angel!!!

Well, this is all for this time...will try and write again tomorrow, particularly if something new pops up in the meantime to be worth writing about.

Love and kisses darn you...and you had better get a good look at your apartment for the next couple of months.

                Johnny.

26 July 1945

Dear Folks,

Just a fast few notes to let you know that all is well, am getting along ok, working like heck right now, and hope to soon know whether I shall be one of the lucky ones to come home right away or have to wait around for a little while longer. There are being some more changes made around here and I might be stuck, but no one knows as yet...so guess it is just as well to wait on it.

Kat Morgan wrote me that George D. was home now, and awfully glad to hear about that. Think I told you that I see Cecil Keesecker about every day now, and I am sure that he will be one of the 6th armored that comes home soon.

Theres really not much news here..we are busy getting

Appalachia to Dessau

ready to move, don't know where nor nothing, but still busy and yet have enough time for a little relaxation now and then (I have two pianos at my disposal). Be glad when I get away from these people though..tis kind of bad..I still don't and never will trust them completely, I guess.

Must close for now..write when you can and keep your fingers crossed for your Johnny. O.K.???? Tell George Swingle to drop me a line when he gets the time..know he will be plenty busy for a long time though.

                Love, Johnny.

          R E S T R I C T E D
     HQ 6TH ARMD DIV APO 256, U S Army,

27 Jul 45

SO 200

15. Following named officers are reld [relieved] from further asgmt [assignment] and dy [duty] w/68th Tk Bn, and are asgd to 748th Tk Bn. (EDCMR: 29 Jul 45). Auth: VOCG XV CORPS, APO 436, U S ARMY, 26 Jul 45.

1ST LT JOHN D GOODIN, 01010821, Inf (Armd), 107-Q

31 July 1945

Note New address (748th Tk. Bn.)

Dear Folks,

Just a note to tell you hello, and that maybe I may make it to the states before Christmas yet. I have been transferred again...into a special GHQ Tank Bn., and supposedly it is a good deal. The 68th Tk. Bn. which I was in is going to stay over here until next year some time, and this one is supposed to go home some of these days.

Am sending you a couple of shots, they are strictly no good, but then...the subject is not too hot either...so there!!

No news worth writing about...am just sweating out going home. The nights are getting cool again, and the days are reverting to typical German days again. Things are not too bad here, but we are on a pending move again, and that is no good..one never knows anything when one takes off in a move.

Mail will never catch up to me now, as it has to go through four changes of address, and if I don't hear from you will not be too surprised. Have had one letter in a week now, but that is because of all the changes.

                Love and kisses, Johnny.

Eight. The Fatted Calf

5 August 1945 (Excerpt)

Dear Folks,

  Just a few notes this Sunday morning to tell you hello and that I am all right, and still in Germany and not having much chance of coming home soon. Think that I told you our shipping date has been postponed for another month or two and we don't know when we will be on our way home now.

  Things are about the same, the weather is pretty right now, and not as cold as it was for a few days. Still haven't had an opportunity to get a suntan this summer as I had hoped for a while. But still...may get around to it some of these days.

  All of you amuse me with your speculation as to where and how I am coming home...the army is so definite about things, you don't know what I won't land in New Orleans or in Florida or some place like that, and may not even come home by way of New York, Washington, Roanoke and so forth...but guess it passes away the time for you to think how I might be coming home.

  No letter from Sis of late...don't know what she is doing. Still doesn't look as though I'm going to get to England before I leave over here, despite the fact that I wanted to very badly. I still don't think that I'll ever come back here for that purpose...but then one doesn't know... its only a few hours by plane, and with a bit of money on my hands, I might want to take a short vacation some day and float over there.

  Well, must be closing for now...hope everything is all right with you and maybe some of these days I'll get back there....although they say conditions are pretty hard there now!!!!!

                      Love and kisses, as always,
                        Johnny.

Company "D", 748th Tank Battalion APO 256 U S Army

5 August, 1945 (Excerpt)

Dearest Anne,

  Just got your letter of the 28th a few minutes ago... oooh! Hope I am out of the doghouse by now, as that was the correct period for you not to hear anything from me, coming on the wave of that wild confusion between changes and of course my leave to Reims which I told you about. So, by now you should know that I am not pouting, and certainly, the fraternizing isn't so heavy that it will ever stop an epistle to you once in a while.

Appalachia to Dessau

I am now, also, Trial Judge Advocate..which means I am the District Attorney for this District (the Battalion). The first case never came to trial, as I thought the guy was crazy, and investigation has at least gotten him under proper observation to see if I am right. If so, he won't come up for trial..at least not here.

I don't expect to find a great many things as I had left them, but there are still certain pre-requisites and ideals that I insist I will cling to. I don't think I can go wrong by thinking that, even though it may mean a slackening of that feeling of indispensability I wrote you about.

But, maybe, again...I should stick to what I originally said: Wait until I get home and find out first hand what I want, and what I want to do with it after I get it!!

And why shouldn't you be able to get anything you want? I would almost concur with your mother on that notation. As to Jack not being good enough for you -- you may have a hell of a time finding a guy who is that. I had an idea one time I might be, but I'm too much of a cynic, idealist, and certainly too damned narrow-minded (in a broad sense) to ever make your remaining lifetime happy (and that I consider to be the most important thing in life - the quest for happiness and attainment of it). Coldly considered, it doesn't look good for me. But so much for that.

Our shipping date has been postponed another month (we don't know what the original date was, but it was, as you said, allegedly in October), and with the new policy on discharges for the Pacific coming into the news, it may be some little time. I am getting totally fed up with this existence. Bored is not the word for it, and my vocabulary doesn't contain it. In the meantime, we parade for George Patton, legendary hero, we go swimming, we tell stories, we try AWOLS, we play the piano and sing corny tunes; we carry drunken characters home, cajole others into going into bed, and swap the foulest jokes that we can remember. Mostly, though, all session, regardless of where, usually end up in telling experiences of the war, at this town, that village, those woods, and during specified seasons of the year. It has finally dawned on most of us that maybe there are more things in life to talk about than women, which before the invasion usually was the chief topic with its allied (???) subject of the monster who was always rearing its ugly head. Maybe there are more benefits from a war than appear on the surface. But enough of that tonight, too.

Look sweet...box or no box, I do love you - damnit

Eight. The Fatted Calf

-- and it is with tears in my eyes that I must ask you to save it, for I fear that it might not reach me in time before I sail. On the other hand if you want to take a chance...well, o.k., as it would certainly be a pleasure for a change. But mail right now is a very indefinite thing these days, and it is very difficult, and will continue to be (I have had three changes of address now) until everyone knows my correct address.
 I'm sorry you are discontent -- maybe not too long yet??
      Love,
      Johnny

9 August 1945
Dear Folks,
 No news as yet, but hope that sometime soon, that I may have some for you. We hear nothing but rumors anymore, and not very good ones at that.
 Have not heard much from anyone of late, but guess that it is because the mail is probably screwed up now beyond all hopes of redemption, and well..if I get home some of these days, don't guess that it will make much difference.
 Am now engaged in court martials, which at least gives me a little to do once in a while. The first case I had I pitched up to division and the man will probably be given a discharge for psychoneurosis, or something..at least he is under observation...
 Have had several tragic accidents of men waiting to go home..they drown, get shot, and even have car wrecks and get killed...just like in civilian life. Still say that when your time comes it comes..and it makes no difference where you are or what you are doing..
 Had a long letter from sis for a change..but not much news in it, which is typical..as Dad used to say all she writes in a letter she could put on a postcard....
 No plans or nothing..finally heard from Keith Broce, a very long letter, and then lost it before I had a chance to answer it.
 Think this afternoon I shall take a nap...this life is going to ruin me before I get back to the states...
 Chins up, and hold your hopes a little longer.
      All my love to all of you,
      Johnny.

Enclosure: Battle Honors Letter from Headquarters Dated 30 April 1945 [Letter in Chapter 5]

Appalachia to Dessau

10 August, 1945.

Hi, Darling (maybe?)

Gee, you mean to say that I remained consistent for as long as a period of the 9th to the 22nd? I must be slipping for sure!!! But, you kind of got inconsistent yourself in the last letter, didn't you? Well...of all those itemized dangling ends you have collected, guess we both will have plenty to worry about for a long time when Johnny gets home.

Fraternizing, as such, amuses me. It is very easy for you, at home to sit back and say what you would or would not do. But when men relax from an emotional strain from say, expecting death...if you have read your psychology, you know that there [sic] resistance is at its lowest ebb, and besides, in case they aren't that type, all men are wolves, whether they would be in Japan, Germany, or what not. And there are those who are going to give way to their beastly passions and instincts wherever, or whoever. And besides that, dear one (this really is not intended as a defense altogether), you must realize that there are among us many damned good soldiers who have been out of Germany only 10 years, and they are more at home with the Frauleins than the rest of us. Too, there are those frauleins who willingly admit they have been wrong, some of the them attempt almost to make up for the damage they have caused. And for fraternizing purely and simply...there are many, many young girls who have been married just long enough to get the taste of candy, and now with their husbands dead for different periods of time, they are still young and want sugar. I'm afraid, angel, it will be slightly impossible to beat human nature. Your conjecture that if we lost, you wouldn't go out with <u>them</u>, is purely hypothetical...you don't know actually what you would do..and honey, God knows you have never been as food hungry as some of these people are right now..and soldiers still are human enough not to let people starve in front of their eyes. And sympathy must inevitably lead to more than that. (Only this morning, a lad in the company came to me--his girl friend missed her routine, has a husband somewhere in Russia, we expect to leave soon...and yet he has something of the cavalier in him for he wants to contact some medics somewhere who can help her out. He has no legal obligations to her). Another thing, baby, lots of these boys are letting go with inhibitions that they have had for so long..and they know once they return to America, they will have to return to our old ideas and conventions.

Eight. The Fatted Calf

Exceptions notwithstanding... it is quite a frolicsome picnic. And they are making quite an impression on the girls...even the mothers and some fathers cry when another bunch leaves town.

Contrast Americans to Russians..who come in, and take what they want..whereas the Americans, shall we say, make them want what they (the Americans) want...does it make sense??..A woman would rather be loved, maybe.

On the other hand, there are the usual camp-followers, the gals who play for pay, and always those who want something, whether it is food, clothes, or special considerations...it will take years and years for these people to ever regain a moral sense of honesty, for it is almost gone in the lower classes, and when you get higher up, they are in a confused state. I rather think there are a few thinkers left....and Gertrude Stein said something rather important, I think, when she said that the Germans are the best that the Americans have met. They are cleaner, in all their destruction, than the English, French or Belgians. There are no urinals on the streets, though the evidence of cows may always be in your nose (they waste no fertilizer in this country..not even human), and what is left over here shows evidence of having been kept very neatly. The whole damned place is a field of confusion, in thoughts, acts and words...and the only thing consistent is its inconsistency. The remaining thinkers are deathly afraid of communism, and some point blank say it would have been better to have wiped out Germany completely than to suffer her to fall to communism.

But enough of them. One more thing, though...to add to the inconsistency of things...there is a young girl who does our washing for us who was raped by the Russians, her husband killed by them (now lives with her husbands parents)..and living with us is Freddie, who was in Buchenwald for two and half years...and he has no hate of the German people at all..only for the Nazis and SS..who broke all his toes, killed his family, and subjected him to other tortures that I won't shock you with..God, if I can get out of here before I go crazy.

Down to serious business...I am not in the least worried about staying true to one woman, once I am married to her. I hope frankly and seriously, that I never reach the point in life that women do not fascinate me...however slightly because if that time comes, I will be ready to die. Perhaps you do not know, but if a man doesn't possess that quality, his wife is the one who suffers the loss!! If that appears inconsistent, file this letter with

Appalachia to Dessau

your itemized dangling statements, and I shall attempt to prove the point...back to your original statement, though..best to wait. If you think I can't resist that fascination......................

I have a court martial this afternoon, have four awards to slam, literally, through channels, in an effort to get them approved and give some guys deserving breaks, must write to Sis, get some of my junk sent home. Rumors are flying around of another move again.... this time to France, I hope.

For this time, honey, so long....hope to hear from you again soon..helps me keep my head when I might lose it.

        Love and 22 more kisses for the jackpot.
        Johnny.

15 August, 1945 (Excerpt)
Bettingen, Germany

Dearest Anne,

Gawd, Honey, but I'm tired..but your letter makes everything o.k. again. Have an awful case to try tomorrow.. don't feel happy about it, because I'm prosecuting the damned thing and at heart my sympathies (aren't they always??) are with the accused. But, will worry about that tomorrow.

The news has us all excited naturally, and we are waiting with somewhat justifiable anxiety for the final official report. Of course by the time this gets to you, it will be final. And then we start sweating it out. There is a rumor now that the low point division are being held up pending final statement, and if it is final, they will be kicked off the boats and high point men loaded up and sent home. Tis quite a deal if it all works out. Well, I'll still consider myself luck[y] if I am able to get home by Christmas or shortly thereafter.

About Red Cross, Anne..yes, you could take it all right, but you would never be the better for it. The sights you see don't hurt, and not often do you see things you shouldn't as far as battle goes...but it's the other things that are revolting, to your nature at least, that are not for my Annie. I'm not saying they are right, and I'm not saying they are wrong..that is for each individual to say for himself...and not for one individual to judge. Particularly one like me. On the other hand, there are many of us who have agreed that the best insurance for a happy life would be to marry one of these girls who know and feel more closely what we have been through than

Eight. The Fatted Calf

anyone at home ever could. We are, and always will be partial to nurses and Red Cross girls over all others in this war because they have been with us and know what it is actually. On the other hand it is going to be difficult for them to go back to humdrum existence, too, for over here, not one of them that hasn't been showered every attention man could give to the one or two women per thousand men. Back home, they will become ordinary girls and women again, and I'm not convinced that it will be easy for them.

Yes, Anne, dear..I do realize that fortunate bit of luck that happened to me when Pop says "I want you to go to law school if you never practice a day", and three years later another stroke of luck when I found another home in your home. But Anne, dear..that same independence for me hurts when I realize how few of these poor lads are going to have that. I hear of it now, and I know it is not good...it fills me with disgust, and I'm wondering how long it will be before "comes the revolution". It is not good for capital to be in complete control, and yet labor is driving down the road to a split in its own ranks by their foolhardy reckless acts. But then..what the hell.. the world will come to an end in 1991 anyhow...I sure have wasted the past years of my life.

Thanks honey for the box, you will have my curiosity knowing no bounds now, waiting for it. But I won't complain...I just hope it gets here with in the next couple of weeks or so..otherwise, things may be hopelessly screwed up. I would say some things that you could say to that postal clerk, but since he finally relented, I'd better keep quiet.

No news. Sitting here twiddling our thumbs, sweating. Had a premature VJ [Victory Over Japan] party a couple of nights ago..ugh. Drunks still disgust me. Nuts. Pretty good time on your letter..mailed the 9th and I got it today..the 14th..see you do that again!!

Love and 28 kisssssssssssssssss + 10000000000 more.

Johnny

[A handwritten note at the bottom of this typed letter says in large writing "Final score – it's over, Honey!!"]

15 August, 1945 Bettingen, Germany

Dear Folks,

Another day gone by and still no news. I am awaiting, like most of us over here, for the final news of Japans capitulation, but as yet there is nothing final.

Appalachia to Dessau

In the meantime, we are still doing nothing. I am acting as Trial Judge Advocate of a small court over here, not many cases, and don't mean anything either...just one of those things. But have to have something to do to keep my mind occupied and that is good as anything to keep me from going crazy while I'm waiting for the news.

Had a swell letter from two people today and it looks like my victory march home is going to be interesting to say the least. But then, there are few minutes in my life that have been altogether dull, even at that!! Right now in this house there is more excitement during the day than should be. We have people streaming in and out all day long, complaining, seeking favors and such things and stuff. Then regularly here, are t[w]o girls, one of them's mother in law, and father in law, and then an endless stream of other people who want to do washing, and what not. The help situation over here is really bad. They practically insist on doing everything for nothing, or even very little. And one must fight them off with sticks almost. Same thing at home, no doubt.

Have heard from Sis that she should be back at home soon..will try and get her a letter some of these days soon.

Had a long letter from Keith Broce, or did I tell you about it. He is in England yet, and it looks as though I won't get to see him now. I'm pretty mad..he was over there for five months while I was and if I had known it, I could have looked him up some of the times that I had off over there. But then, one never knows about those things.....such is life.

Well, no news so guess I'll be closing for now. Don't expect me home till you see me coming because everything is screwed up till we don't even know how long we will be here now, much less move to France.

      Love and kisses to all of you,
      and take care of yourselves. Your,
      Johnny.

Note at the bottom of letter written in large letters in pencil: YIPPEE – IT'S OVER!!!!

Though September 2, 1945, is the official V-J Day, August 14 was celebrated as the end of the war.

18 August, 1945 (Excerpt) Still here. Pet!!
Hello, Fatalist!! [Anne]

Latest interest in getting ready to leave here. Have received orders and you probably have read that we are

Eight. The Fatted Calf

due to sail within 26 days now!! The only thing I'm sweating out is a school in England that I signed up for when things were hot and it looked as though we might be here for some time. If you are in it, you must finish it, but if you are out of it and just waiting to go, I don't know whether I have to go or not...I'm just sweating!!

I think and "hope". Orders are to tell people to stop writing to us, but doubt if that will help much. I'm not doing anything till I find out about that ?!'OAU:_($%!! school.

Sorry I spoiled you on the letters..really nothing to write about these days...nothing! These screwballs got plastered last night drug me out of bed at 3 in the morning and I had to play the piano for an hour before they would go to bed...what a crew. Our little girl who the Russians did a job on had a nervous breakdown but is back visiting us again today. About the really nicest thing I've seen over here for morals. 'Fraid my general opinion is that these people are helpless as well as hopeless.

Well, honey, I'm closing for today..am going to take some pictures up to be developed..may have some for you afterwards...they don't do too good a job, but better than none, maybe???

Be good, careful...and write until I tell you "No more". Add 17 more to the jackpot.

                Johnny.

P.S. Thanks for the stamps upside down.

Handwritten note at top of letter: Something else to file for our bottle!!

20 August, 1945 (Excerpt) Still here.
Dearest worth-being-a-hero-for,[Anne]

I expect to be home in September, Anne, but that is for your consumption only..I don't know nothing else and that is only a surmise. I got my school in England cancelled, though I rather surmise that will be regretted the remainder of my life since I don't ever expect to return over here for purely business or social reasons. I don't know where I will be - my leave (if any) from, or if I will even arrive at NY. If I do, I shall see you shortly. And honey, please don't expect me in on the first boat that has 6th Armd Divn. on it, for in the first place, some of these divisions have been split up, and some of their units [did] not arrive for a month after the first one got there. And it would be my luck to be stuck on a cleaning up detail on one of those ships...I got it coming over, and may get it going back.

Appalachia to Dessau

One just doesn't know. Also, if I land in New York, before coming down to see you, I plan on running over to Conn., and seeing Coons for a little while. Got a letter from him today, and expects to be walking in another month. If so, should just about hit it right..sorta love that man, honey..more than a man should love a man...but except for him...I would probably not have been around to collect these points for awards. I'll just have to wait and see what the situation is.

Can't begin to tell you what it is like here. We had a brawl on Saturday night..I was thoroughly dis-gusted as usual at such things. Sunday night, we had a million point dinner with some Krauts. One of the Lts. shot a wild boar, and they fixed it for us. I ate till I'm still sick...had literally pounds of it smothered in excellent gravy; delicious salads, one of tomatoes, one of potatoes and one of cucumbers. Inevitably, beer wine and schnapps, whatever you like. I had some of the former, but Crawford was getting tight on the latter, and so I didn't indulge (not that I would have anyhow). The wine was fairly good, considering the war..and the hospitality was sickening, except for the old lady who I think was very sincere. She would not let a plate get empty, and neither would she allow the glasses to. I was amused, and on the whole enjoyed myself.

Last Thursday night (soon you will think we are social climbers, or something), we visited some of the local uppity ups, and between German, French, Polish, and a smattering of English by Anasthesia (well, her name is something like that) along with the exhaustion of the wine (which was about like our grapefruit juice at any drug store without the sweetening), I left at 11:15. At 3:00 in the a.m., the Capt. and Don came in woke me up, pulled me out of bed, and nothing would do them but that we play and sing for a solid hour. Poor neighbors. So, you see, we aren't exactly twiddling our thumbs at night anymore. The Old Man fired Boots today, Helena is getting over her nervous breakdown..her mother has been swell to us; the Vulture (alias the Mole, the Falcon and the Beast) has her George back, and doesn't pester us. The Communist cop was given the works, we got Freddie out of jail (Freddie was at Buchenwald for two years..and a character naturally, being slightly off, even yet...which is quite natural), Greene is back from Paris ("God, what a terrible place that is...but how nice it would be to die there!!") half alive, but very contented. Naturally. We figured up our accrued leave today, and I have 50 coming to me. (That's 50 days) Can't begin to tell you the odd number of

Eight. The Fatted Calf

characters that drop in and out all day long around us. If it isn't one, it is about three or four. The musicians who hounded us for a while have ceased upon request, and things are in good shape for a move to the field. If you can figure up a place to go, like Australia or Alaska or some place where the A. B. can't get to us easily, arrange for our passports with B. Carrol and we will head there on our honeymoon, er something. I'm still convinced America is beyond redemption, and I for one am ready to get out for a cooler looking sport. Wanna come along???

Must close for tonight...love and kisses and stupid of you..but I don't have any of your telephone numbers, and probably no chance of getting them now. Any how, love again, and by for now.

      Johnny

23rd August, 1945.
Dearest Annie,

Well, back in the field again..don't know for how long.. rumor has it that it will be for over a week and when that is up, that we may move on to another area for processing home. In the meantime we are still getting rid of a lot of junk here and there and some day I may get down to bare essentialities.

The oil on here is some that I put on for to prevent rust, and it seems to be splattering. [Goodin is referring to splatters on the original letter.] Hope that I can get this typewriter through, for it has grown to be quite an attraction. As well as a very nice little instrument for writing.

No other news than what I told you the last time I wrote. Got your August 17 letter last night. Can picture you running around Washington without no shoes..just what the H---? Must have been quite a celebration. Wish that I could have been in it with you..but at the same time, I am thankful to be alive to celebrate it instead of like a lot of kids I know of.

Sorry my letters haven't reached you. Gee, Crawford just got transferred to another outfit and it will probably mean a delay of about a month for him now. And I had sure hoped to go home with him, as things would have worked out beautifully with the two or four of us.

Luckily for me, I have over a 100 so didn't get transferred..but that is the army...you never know when they will make a screwy deal on you. The latest rumors are that we will be in Le Havre about the 5th of September... so that with about three weeks there...I still have a

Appalachia to Dessau

chance to make it by October some time...I want to take my Thanksgiving hunt again..although it may be something to see if I can go hunting again like I used to. At least, they won't be shooting back this time. I hope that maybe some of these days...if things work out, maybe you'll have to learn how to shoot a shotgun, too. I remember that you can shoot a rifle fairly well!!!

My Mom writes that WJ is having to get her out of trouble over some rental agreement with some of her high-priced tenants that live down in the rock house where we went shooting that afternoon. She laughed at the thoughts of her having to go to jail and make bail and all that stuff...she ain't lost her sense of humor by a darned sight!!

Well, honey, it is raining and the darkness grows, so guess I had better close for tonight...will try and keep you posted as near as possible on what is where with me. I might mention that my trek south may not be as scheduled as it would appear that I will be in charge of a group of men to report to Atlanta Ga. for discharge and instead of a southern route, I'll have to take a northern trek to get around to see the people that I want to and to finally wind up in Washington...maybe its best...only Fate can tell, huh?????

Love and kisses Baby, and take care of yourself....the time grows shorter and shorter......

Johnny

24 August 1945 Germany

Dear Folks,

Just a line to say hello..have gotten two letters from you all in the past couple of days but I still have no news to tell you.

Have been having right much of a good time around here. We have been to three parties lately, and then occasionally have our personal little parties here. We have a piano naturally, and there is usually some German beer and wine around. It grows more and more difficult to pass the time of days as we wait for the boat, and orders, and so on. There are two ducks here that I get quite a kick out of feeding..he gobbles up everything in sight, and she is so bashful she wont come and get what is hers. He eats out of my hand..and I feed them apples for as long as ten or fifteen minutes at times.

We are settled on the Main river, watch the kids fish sometimes, watch the girls swimming and........

Some time in the future you can look for a notice to

Eight. The Fatted Calf

stop writing to me over here. I don't know when it will come, or where..we are, as I have said, just waiting. And the old fever is getting hot now.

Tell George Swingle that I hope to go hunting with him about December some time, that I expect to be home by then, and to get ready for it. I don't expect to hear from him now..in fact we are waiting for all mail to be cut off most any day now.

Art Meyer sends his regards and love to you and hopes that you are well and happy.

       Love and kisses,
       Johnny

August 25, 1945 (Excerpt) Germany.....
Dear Folks,

Just a few notes to tell you everything is strictly as usual...doing nothing exciting, in fact doing nothing but reading a bit and writing a few letters in between times. Nothing else going on, a few poker games, which I haven't been into, and eating and sleeping. Night before last slept nearly 11 hours..a record for me...but I'm not getting fat on it...all of us are waiting to go home...and nothing else much matters, when or where....

Sis writes me that Reg is in New York now...wonder for how long he will be there ...don't look like as though I'll get to take off from there for home, otherwise he might be able to fly me home...

Well dullness forces me to quit..

Official photograph of John D. Goodin, 1st Lieutenant, 1945.

Appalachia to Dessau

think I'll go and see about the mail for tonight...take care of yourselves and maybe sometime within the next 60 days I'll be blowing in.

       Love and kisses to all Johnny.

Hope I can help eat Mr. Charles turkey.

 Same day...got another letter from you all tonight.. written Aug. 16th...not bad time at all, is it?
 Nothing new here, though they just came in with a report that a bunch of officers are getting transferred to another outfit in the morning, and we are all sweating it out..it is either the 99th Inf. division or the 9th Armored Divn....no one has the full information as yet... we all are pouting..cause it can be any one with over 85 points here..and all of us have over 85 points....
 Sorry to hear about the dog..but guess it can't be helped...sorry that I couldn't be there to break her of the habit..but then some of these days...maybe I will get back there and have me a few good dogs.....
 Celebration must have been quite something from all the reports that I've gotten from all over the company... glad that it is a relief to you as well as to me. Someone wrote me that it seemed impossible that only a year ago they worried their fool heads off, even knowing that only the good die young.... well. Death is no chooser...we have had boys to drown here, many killed in accidents...and one kid got drunk and fell out of a third story window the other night...only broke his arm and back...
 To ease your worry...don't think anyone will be coming home with me, but just me...I got enough worries on my mind without assuming the responsibility of a wife at a time like this..but don't be surprised......ha....

       Johnny.

Goodin wrote the following jubilant letter to his mother telling her to get the fatted calf ready sometime after October 1, because he was coming home!

28 August, 1945. Germany...Still.

Dear Mom,

 Haven't got any bracelets, beads, or other sentimental items...but I am bringing me home...and I'm still convinced that is the main thing to get home.
 In brief, honey dumplings... <u>I'MA COMING I'MA COMING</u>
 Sometime after 1st October, you can begin to have the

Eight. The Fatted Calf

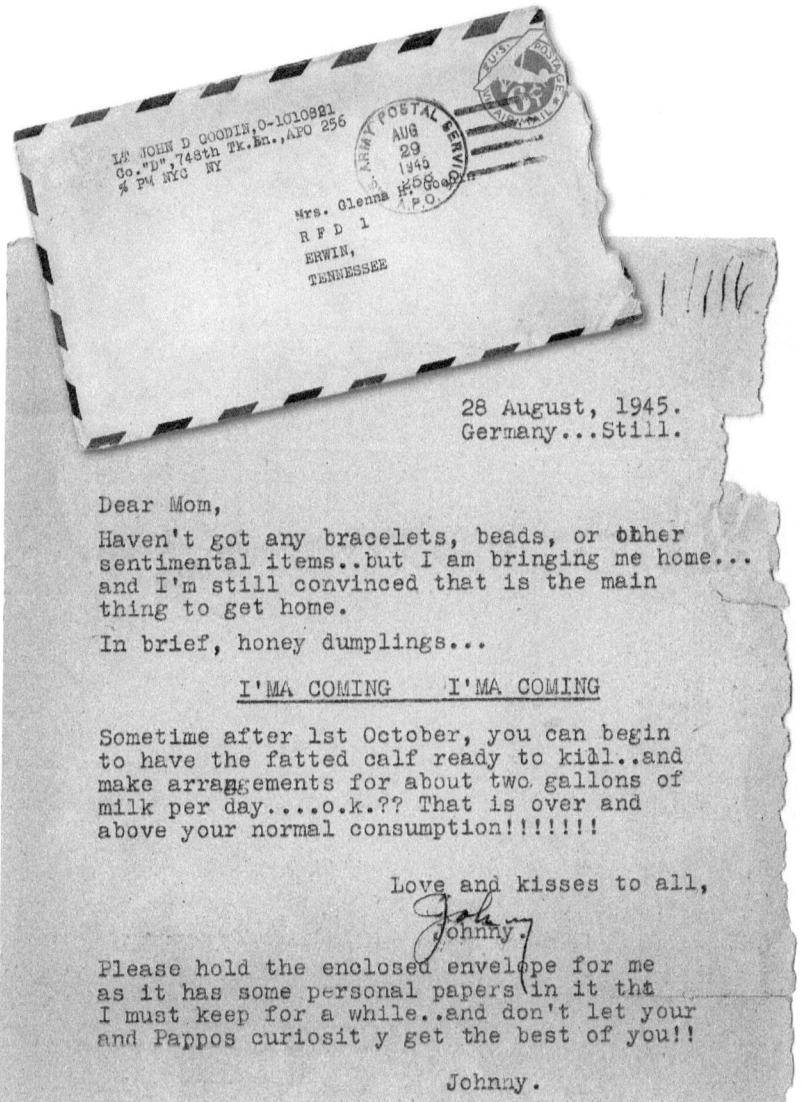

28 August, 1945.
Germany...Still.

Dear Mom,

Haven't got any bracelets, beads, or other sentimental items..but I am bringing me home... and I'm still convinced that is the main thing to get home.

In brief, honey dumplings...

I'MA COMING   I'MA COMING

Sometime after 1st October, you can begin to have the fatted calf ready to kill..and make arrangements for about two gallons of milk per day....o.k.?? That is over and above your normal consumption!!!!!!!

Love and kisses to all,
Johnny.

Please hold the enclosed envelope for me as it has some personal papers in it tht I must keep for a while..and don't let your and Pappos curiosit y get the best of you!!

Johnny.

In this last letter to his mother, dated August 28, 1945, Goodin excitedly tells her to "have the fatted calf ready, 'cause I'ma coming!"

> fatted calf ready to kill...and make arrangements for about two gallons of milk per day....o.k.?? That is over and above your normal consumption!!!!!!!
> Love and kisses to all, Johnny

Appalachia to Dessau

```
Love and kisses to all,
    Please hold the enclosed envelope for me as it has some
personal papers in it that I must keep for a while..and
don't let your and Pappos curiosity get the best of you!!
                        Johnny.
```

This series of photographs is titled "Return Home."

Top: Soldiers head toward the train that will take them to their transport home, 1945. *Above:* The S.S. *Coaldale Victory* transports soldiers home from the European Theater, 1945.

Eight. The Fatted Calf

The steam ship *Coaldale Victory* transports soldiers home from the European Theater, 1945.

Soldiers fill every available space on the S.S. *Coaldale Victory* in anticipation of their journey to the United States.

Top: Soldiers preparing to disembark. *Above:* The S.S. *Coaldale Victory*, 748th Tank Battalion banner proudly displayed, carries John Goodin and other soldiers who are all eager to step on American soil.

Eight. The Fatted Calf

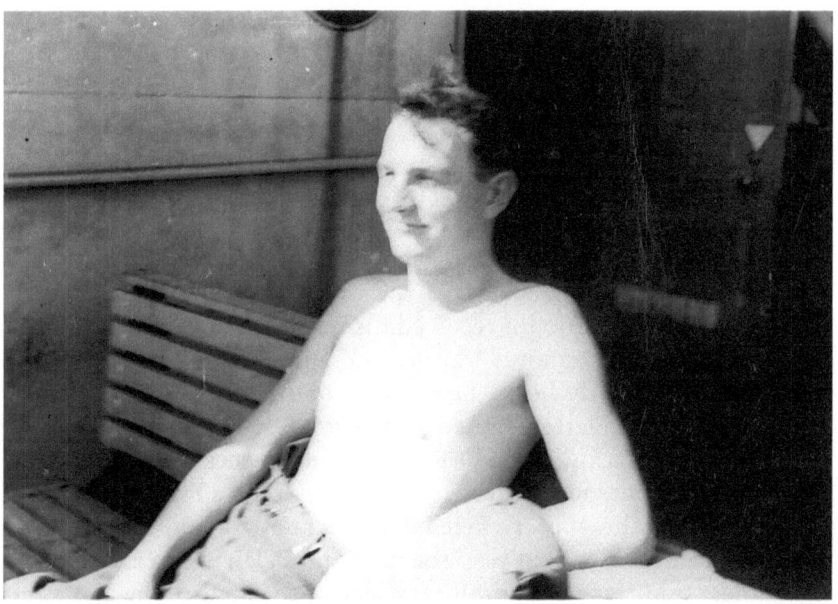

John D. Goodin, a little less formally attired and glad to be headed home, smiles, relaxes, and enjoys the sunshine.

Soldiers are greeted with the stars and stripes and a large sign "WELCOME HOME—WELL DONE."

Epilogue

Although John Goodin received his notification of official departure from the Third Armored "Spearhead" Division on June 30, 1945, it would be many months before he returned to the states.

The departure letter, signed by Doyle O. Hickey, brigadier general of the U. S. Army, lauded the efforts and success of the Division to "relentlessly pursue and destroy the enemy across France, Belgium, and into the very heart of the Reich. Day after day and night after night, without pause and without rest, the men of this Division carried on in the highest traditions of our military service to enhance the glory and reputation of this great fighting unit ... men like you have skyrocketed the name of the Third Armored Division across the entire world, and its deeds of valor and accomplishments have been equaled by only a few, and surpassed by none."

Goodin's last months were spent on cleanup duty and being moved from place to place with several delays of the final departure date. As an attorney, he was also a trial advocate judge, presiding over court-martial cases.

All correspondence ended after the last letter to his mother saying they could expect him sometime in October. As in many of the letters to his mother, John used the Biblical reference of the prodigal son in Luke 15 of "killing the fatted calf." He also asked her to "make arrangements for two gallons of milk per day." Goodin talked about milk throughout his letters emphasizing his longing for the comforts of home sorely missed on the front.

The final letter, written in the teasing tone he always used with his mother, is an appropriate ending to Goodin's long and difficult battle in World War II. His exuberance at the expectant return home is palpable and poignant. The undated Return Home photograph shows Goodin sitting on the boat, shirtless and smiling. From Appalachia to Dessau, he had served his country well and was ready to return to the home ground of East Tennessee.

Chapter Notes

Introduction

1. Watauga Association of Genealogists Upper East Tennessee. *History of Washington County Tennessee 1988.* Salem, Walsworth Press, 1988.

Chapter One

1. *Spearhead in the West, the Third Armored Division 1941–1945.* This book is an official project of the Third Armored Division, published under authority contained in Sec. V, ETOUSA Cir. 86, 25 June 1945, and mailed in accordance with the provisions of Postal Circular No. 38, Hq, U.S. Forces, European Theatre (Rear), 11 Oct 1945, p. 18.
2. "Camp Wheeler." U.S. Army Corps of Engineers Savannah District, https://www.sas.usace.army.mil/Missions/Formerly-Used-Defense-Sites/Camp-Wheeler/ Accessed 01 June 2021.
3. John Goodin Papers, Archives of Appalachia, East Tennessee State University. https://archivesofappalachia.omeka.net/exhibits/show/soldiersletters/fieldbook-and-map.
4. "Training the American GI." The National World War II Museum New Orleans, https://www.nationalww2museum.org/war/articles/training-american-gi, Accessed June 01, 2021.
5. Edward R. Feagins Memoir, Archives of Appalachia, East Tennessee State University, Box G, Folder 1, p. 6.
6. *Ibid.,* p. 12.
7. *Ibid.,* p. 4.
8. *Spearhead in the West, The Third Armored Division 1941–1945,* p. 40.
9. *Ibid.,* p. 43.
10. *Ibid.,* p. 44.
11. "Erwin Youth Graduates from Fort Knox School." *Johnson City Chronicle,* 16 June 1942, https://etsu.newspapers.com/image/587743231/?terms=erwin%20youth%20graduates&match=1.

Chapter Two

1. "Goodin Assigned to Armored Group." *Johnson City Chronicle,* 26 July 1942, https://etsu.newspapers.com/image/587423898/?terms=Goodin%20assigned&match=1.
2. *Spearhead in the West,* p. 45.
3. "Freedom's Desert—Rice Army Airfield and the Desert Training Center." *YouTube,* Donnenfield and White, 26 May 2022. https://www.youtube.com/watch?v=sK2rybDu3AM.
4. *Spearhead in the West,* p. 45.
5. Steinbeck, John. *Travels with Charley: In Search of America.* Franklin Watts, 1962.
6. *Spearhead in the West,* p. 46.
7. *Ibid.,* p. 46.
8. "Freedom's Desert."
9. *Spearhead in the West,* p. 45.
10. "Freedom's Desert."
11. "Fort Irwin, California." *U.S. Army Bases.* https://armybases.org/fort-irwin-ca-california/. Accessed 6 June 2023.
12. *Spearhead in the West,* p. 46.
13. *Spearhead in the West,* p. 48.
14. "Headline: With Erwin Boys in Service." *The Erwin Record.* 3 December 1942, https://etsu.newspapers.com/image/587743479/?terms=with%20the%20boys%20in%20service&match=1.

Chapter Notes

15. *Spearhead in the West*, p. 48.
16. *Spearhead in the West*, p. 49.
17. *Spearhead in the West*, p. 51.
18. *Spearhead in the West*, p. 52.

Chapter Three

1. *Spearhead in the West*, p. 52.
2. *Spearhead in the West*, p. 53.
3. *Ibid.*
4. *Spearhead in the West*, p. 54.
5. *Ibid.*
6. *Spearhead in the West*, p. 55.
7. *Spearhead in the West*, p. 56.
8. "Victory Mail." *Smithsonian National Postal Museum.* https://postalmuseum.si.edu/exhibition/victory-mail. Accessed 18 May 2022.
9. *Spearhead in the West*, p. 56.
10. *Spearhead in the West*, p. 58–59.
11. *Ibid.*

Chapter Four

1. *Spearhead in the West*, p. 60.
2. *Ibid.*
3. *Ibid.*
4. "World War II and the American Red Cross." *American Red Cross.* https://www.redcross.org/content/dam/redcross/National/history-wwii.pdf. Accessed 8 June 2023.
5. *Spearhead in the West*, p. 60.
6. *Spearhead in the West*, p. 61.

Chapter Five

1. *Spearhead in the West*, p. 62.
2. *Johnson City Chronicle* Newspaper Clipping, 16 July 1944. John Goodin Papers, 1872–1999. Archives of Appalachia, East Tennessee State University, Johnson City.
3. *Combat Trail of the 32nd Armored Regiment Third Armored Spearhead Division*, #3. Ravensteins Geographische Verlagsanstalt u. Druckerei, Frankfurt-Main.
4. *Spearhead in the West*, p. 66.
5. *Spearhead in the West*, p. 196.
6. *Spearhead in the West*, p. 66.
7. *Spearhead in the West*, p. 74.
8. *Combat Trail of the 32nd Armored Regiment Third Armored Spearhead Division*, #4.
9. *Spearhead in the West*, pp. 66, 196.
10. *Spearhead in the West*, p. 68.
11. *Ibid.*
12. *Spearhead in the West*, p. 69.
13. *Ibid.*
14. *Combat Trail of the 32nd Armored Regiment Third Armored Spearhead Division*, #5–18.
15. *Spearhead in the West*, p. 69.
16. *Spearhead in the West*, p. 70.
17. *Spearhead in the West*, p. 71.
18. *Combat Trail of the 32nd Armored Regiment Third Armored Spearhead Division*, #5.
19. *Combat Trail of the 32nd Armored Regiment Third Armored Spearhead Division*, #6.
20. *Spearhead in the West*, p. 71.
21. *Spearhead in the West*, p. 73.
22. *Combat Trail of the 32nd Armored Regiment Third Armored Spearhead Division*, #7.
23. *Spearhead in the West*, p. 73.
24. *Combat Trail of the 32nd Armored Regiment Third Armored Spearhead Division*, #8.
25. *Spearhead in the West*, p. 73.
26. *Spearhead in the West*, p. 73, 199.
27. *Combat Trail of the 32nd Armored Regiment Third Armored Spearhead Division*, #9.
28. *Spearhead in the West*, p. 73.
29. *Combat Trail of the 32nd Armored Regiment Third Armored Spearhead Division*, #10.
30. *Spearhead in the West*, p. 75.
31. *Spearhead in the West*, p. 201.
32. *Spearhead in the West*, p. 75.
33. *Spearhead in the West*, p. 202.
34. "Security on the March—Mechanized Units." Official Training Film T.F. 21 2035 War Department Army Ground Forces Signal Corps Production, 1943, https://www.youtube.com/watch?v=B3Qx8yPp7t0, 26 May 2022.
35. *Ibid.*
36. *Ibid.*
37. *Ibid.*
38. *Combat Trail of the 32nd Armored*

Chapter Notes

Regiment Third Armored Spearhead Division, #11.
39. *Spearhead in the West*, p. 77.
40. *Combat Trail of the 32nd Armored Regiment Third Armored Spearhead Division*, #11.
41. *Spearhead in the West*, p. 80.
42. *Combat Trail of the 32nd Armored Regiment Third Armored Spearhead Division*, #12.
43. *Spearhead in the West*, p. 80.
44. *Spearhead in the West*, p. 203.
45. "How to Destroy German Tanks." Training film 25804. Periscope Film LLC. https://www.youtube.com/watch?v=KqTZfBKw5Mc, 26 May 2022.
46. *Combat Trail of the 32nd Armored Regiment Third Armored Spearhead Division*, #13.
47. *Spearhead in the West*, p. 80.
48. *Spearhead in the West*, p. 82.
49. "Security on the March."
50. *Spearhead in the West*, p. 18.
51. *Spearhead in the West*, p. 82.
52. *Combat Trail of the 32nd Armored Regiment Third Armored Spearhead Division*, #14.
53. *Combat Trail of the 32nd Armored Regiment Third Armored Spearhead Division*, #15.
54. *Combat Trail of the 32nd Armored Regiment Third Armored Spearhead Division*, #16.
55. *Spearhead in the West*, p. 85.
56. *Combat Trail of the 32nd Armored Regiment Third Armored Spearhead Division*, #17.
57. *Spearhead in the West*, p. 85.
58. *Combat Trail of the 32nd Armored Regiment Third Armored Spearhead Division*, #18.
59. *Spearhead in the West*, p. 86.
60. *Combat Trail of the 32nd Armored Regiment Third Armored Spearhead Division*, #19.
61. *Combat Trail of the 32nd Armored Regiment Third Armored Spearhead Division*, #20.
62. *Combat Trail of the 32nd Armored Regiment Third Armored Spearhead Division*, #21.
63. *Spearhead in the West*, p. 91.
64. *Combat Trail of the 32nd Armored Regiment Third Armored Spearhead Division*, #22.
65. *Combat Trail of the 32nd Armored Regiment Third Armored Spearhead Division*, #23.
66. *Spearhead in the West*, p. 94–95.
67. *Combat Trail of the 32nd Armored Regiment Third Armored Spearhead Division*, #24.
68. *The Stars and Stripes*, 14 Sep 1944, Vol 1. No. 62. John Goodin papers, 1872–1999. Archives of Appalachia, East Tennessee State University, Johnson City.

Chapter Six

1. *Combat Trail of the 32nd Armored Regiment Third Armored Spearhead Division*, #25.
2. *Spearhead in the West*, p. 102.
3. *Combat Trail of the 32nd Armored Regiment Third Armored Spearhead Division*, #26.
4. *Spearhead in the West*, p. 98.
5. *Ibid*.
6. *Combat Trail of the 32nd Armored Regiment Third Armored Spearhead Division*, #27.
7. *Spearhead in the West*, p. 99.
8. *Spearhead in the West*, p. 100.
9. *Spearhead in the West*, p. 215.
10. *Ibid*.
11. *Ibid*.
12. *Ibid*.
13. *Spearhead in the West*, p. 103.
14. *Combat Trail of the 32nd Armored Regiment Third Armored Spearhead Division*, #28.
15. *Combat Trail of the 32nd Armored Regiment Third Armored Spearhead Division*, #29.
16. *Spearhead in the West*, p. 104.
17. *Spearhead in the West*, p. 106.
18. *Spearhead in the West*, p. 107.
19. *Combat Trail of the 32nd Armored Regiment Third Armored Spearhead Division*, #30.
20. *Spearhead in the West*, p. 108.
21. *Combat Trail of the 32nd Armored Regiment Third Armored Spearhead Division*, #31.
22. *Spearhead in the West*, p. 108.

23. *Spearhead in the West*, p. 114.
24. *Combat Trail of the 32nd Armored Regiment Third Armored Spearhead Division*, #32.
25. "Battle of the Bulge Remembered." *Elizabethton Star*. 16 Dec. 1984. John Goodin Papers. Archives of Appalachia. East Tennessee State University, Johnson City, TN.
26. *Spearhead in the West*, p. 112.
27. *Ibid*.
28. "Battle of the Bulge: The Greatest American Battle of the War." *National Veterans Memorial Museum*, 16 Dec. 2020, https://nationalvmm.org/battle-of-the-bulge-the-greatest-american-battle-of-the-war/. 15 Feb 2022.
29. *Spearhead in the West*, p. 119.
30. *Combat Trail of the 32nd Armored Regiment Third Armored Spearhead Division*, #33.
31. *Combat Trail of the 32nd Armored Regiment Third Armored Spearhead Division*, #34.
32. *Combat Trail of the 32nd Armored Regiment Third Armored Spearhead Division*, #35.
33. "Lt. Goodin Suffers Arm Wounds in Europe." *Johnson City Press*, 25 March 1945.
34. *Combat Trail of the 32nd Armored Regiment Third Armored Spearhead Division*, #36.
35. *Combat Trail of the 32nd Armored Regiment Third Armored Spearhead Division*, #37.

Chapter Seven

1. *Spearhead in the West*, p. 142.
2. *Combat Trail of the 32nd Armored Regiment Third Armored Spearhead Division*, #38.
3. *Combat Trail of the 32nd Armored Regiment Third Armored Spearhead Division*, #39.
4. *Combat Trail of the 32nd Armored Regiment Third Armored Spearhead Division*, #40.
5. *Combat Trail of the 32nd Armored Regiment Third Armored Spearhead Division*, #41.
6. *Spearhead in the West*, p. 145.
7. *Combat Trail of the 32nd Armored Regiment Third Armored Spearhead Division*, #42.
8. *Spearhead in the West*, p. 145.
9. *Combat Trail of the 32nd Armored Regiment Third Armored Spearhead Division*, #43.
10. *Combat Trail of the 32nd Armored Regiment Third Armored Spearhead Division*, #44.
11. *Spearhead in the West*, p. 145–146.
12. *Combat Trail of the 32nd Armored Regiment Third Armored Spearhead Division*, #45.
13. *Spearhead in the West*, p. 148.
14. *Spearhead in the West*, p. 150.
15. *Combat Trail of the 32nd Armored Regiment Third Armored Spearhead Division*, #46.
16. *Combat Trail of the 32nd Armored Regiment Third Armored Spearhead Division*, #47.
17. *Combat Trail of the 32nd Armored Regiment Third Armored Spearhead Division*, #48.
18. *Combat Trail of the 32nd Armored Regiment Third Armored Spearhead Division*, #49.
19. *Spearhead in the West*, p. 252.
20. *Spearhead in the West*, p. 253.
21. *Combat Trail of the 32nd Armored Regiment Third Armored Spearhead Division*, #50.
22. *Spearhead in the West*, p. 252.

Bibliography and Further Reading

Primary Sources

"Battle of the Bulge Remembered." *Elizabethton Star.* 16 Dec. 1984. John Goodin Papers, 1872–1999. Archives of Appalachia. East Tennessee State University, Johnson City, TN.

"Battle of the Bulge: The Greatest American Battle of the War." *National Veterans Memorial Museum,* 16 Dec. 2020. Retrieved from https://nationalvmm.org/battle-of-the-bulge-the-greatest-american-battle-of-the-war/. 15 Feb 2022.

"Camp Wheeler." U. S. Army Corps of Engineers Savannah District, https://www.sas.usace.army.mil/Missions/Formerly-Used-Defense-Sites/Camp-Wheeler/ Accessed 01 June 2021.

Combat Trail of the 32nd Armored Regiment Third Armored Spearhead Division, #3. 1945. 10×27; Ravensteins Geographische Verlagsanstalt u. Druckerei, Frankfurt-Main, John Goodin Papers, 1872–1999. Archives of Appalachia, East Tennessee State University, Johnson City.

Edward R. Feagins Memoir, Archives of Appalachia, East Tennessee State University, Johnson City.

"Erwin Youth Graduates from Fort Knox School." *Johnson City Chronicle,* 16 June 1942, https://etsu.newspapers.com/image/587743231/?terms=erwin%20youth%20graduates&match=1.

"Fort Irwin, California." *U.S. Army Bases.* https://armybases.org/fort-irwin-ca-california/. Accessed 6 June 2023.

"Freedom's Desert—Rice Army Airfield and the Desert Training Center." *YouTube,* Donnenfield and White, 26 May 2022. https://www.youtube.com/watch?v=sK2rybDu3AM.

"Goodin Assigned to Armored Group." *Johnson City Chronicle,* 26 July 1942, https://etsu.newspapers.com/image/587423898/?terms=goodin%20assigned&match=1.

"Headline: With Erwin Boys in Service." *The Erwin Record.* 3 December 1942, https://etsu.newspapers.com/image/587743479/?terms=with%20the%20boys%20in%20service&match=1.

"How to Destroy German Tanks." Training film 25804. Periscope Film LLC. https://www.youtube.com/watch?v=KqTZfBKw5Mc, 26 May 2022.

John Goodin Correspondence, 1941–1945. John Goodin Papers, 1872–1999. Archives of Appalachia, East Tennessee State University, Johnson City.

Johnson City Chronicle Newspaper Clipping,16 July 1944. John Goodin Papers. Archives of Appalachia, East Tennessee State University, Johnson City.

"Security on the March—Mechanized Units." Official Training Film T. F. 21 2035 War Department Army Ground Forces Signal Corps Production, 1943, https://www.youtube.com/watch?v=B3Qx8yPp7t0, 26 May 2022.

Spearhead in the West, The Third Armored Division 1941–1945. This book is an official project of the Third Armored Division, published under authority contained in Sec. V, ETOUSA Cir. 86, 25 June 1945, and mailed in accordance

257

Bibliography and Further Reading

with the provisions of Postal Circular No. 38, Hq, U.S. Forces, European Theatre (Rear), 11 Oct 1945.

The Stars and Stripes, 14 Sep 1944, Vol 1. No. 62. John Goodin Papers, 1872–1999. Archives of Appalachia, East Tennessee State University, Johnson City.

Steinbeck, John. *Travels with Charley: In Search of America*. Franklin Watts, 1962.

"Training the American GI." The National World War II Museum New Orleans, https://www.nationalww2museum.org/war/articles/training-american-gi, Accessed 01 June 2021.

"Victory Mail." *Smithsonian National Postal Museum*. https://postalmuseum.si.edu/exhibition/victory-mail. Accessed 18 May 2022.

"World War II and the American Red Cross." *American Red Cross*. https://www.redcross.org/content/dam/redcross/National/history-wwii.pdf. Accessed 8 June 2023.

World War II Field Notebook. John Goodin Papers, Archives of Appalachia, East Tennessee State University. https://archivesofappalachia.omeka.net/exhibits/show/soldiersletters/fieldbook-and-map.

Further Reading

Combat Trail of the 32nd Armored Regiment Third Armored Spearhead Division may be viewed at https://s3.amazonaws.com/omeka-net/4141/archive/files/3468eb6aca16dd8115ba3723c709a469.jpg?AWSAccessKeyId=AKIAI3ATG3OSQLO5HGKA&Expires=1692230400&Signature=B6HO9OftkrKwwOMd%2BuhC6N5Apk%3D.

More information about John Goodin and WWII may be found here: https://archivesofappalachia.omeka.net/exhibits/show/soldiersletters.

Postcards may be viewed at: https://archivesofappalachia.omeka.net/exhibits/show/soldiersletters/postcards.

Index

Numbers in ***bold italics*** indicate pages with illustrations

ack-ack 77, 125, 135, 136
air raids 77, 101
American Red Cross (ARC) 73, 96, 110, 112, 186, 188, 219, 238, 239
American Red Cross Mostyn Club 99, 112
Anderson, Shep ***78***, 91
Arnold, Henry H. 214
artillery 29, 38, 52, 90, 120, 122, 124, 125, 126, 129, 130, 136, 141, 146, 148, 153, 158, 164, 170, 176, 186

Baker, Lou 5, 17, 89, 90, 96, 102, 107, 109, 110, 112, 114, 115, 117, 118, 119, 121, 124, 126, 131, 133, 134, 135, 138, 143, 145, 163, 166, 231
Baker's Beau 115, 130, 173, 176
Barrett, Sgt. Horace 39
basic training 9, 13, 14, 17
Battle of the Bulge 172, 175, 176, 179, 184, 201, 223, 224
Beachum, Capt. John C. 229
Belgium 120, 140, 151, 167, 168, 172, 173, 174, 175, 176, 181, 222, 225, 228; Ardennes 64, 151, 172, 178, 179, 229; Gouvy 175; Langlir 176, 177; Lierneux 175; Luxembourg 175; Manhay 172; Marche 172; Mons 136, 146; Soy 178
Bilotte, Sam 132
Blanchard, Gen. William H. 159
bombers—*Fortress, Liberator, Mustang* 136, 157, 159
Briscoe, Jean 5, 22, 27, 29, 51, 53, 61, 74, 80, 83, 84, 88, 91, 96, 98, 102
Brooks, Hubert 210
Buchenwald 230, 237, 242
Byrd, Sen. Robert C. 218, 219, 220

Cabonias, Col. 108
California 26, 37, 38, 41, 42, 44, 53
Camp Kilmer, New Jersey 70, 71
Camp Pickett, Virginia 9, 58, 61, 184
Camp Polk, Louisiana 9, 32, 34, 36, 56
Camp Wheeler, Georgia 9, 14, 16, 224
Capetown Castle 71
Carpenter, Captain 108
Carter, Anne 5, 20, 26, 30, 31, 36, 40, 46, 55, 127, 133, 164, 166, 168, 17, 173, 174, 179, 180, 181, 209, 218, 229, 233, 241
Carter, Bill 5, 25, 203
Carter, Margaritte (Marg) 5, 26, 46, 53, 54, 55, 56, 60, 70, 82, 98, 127, 231
church 1, 7, 21, 29, 37, 80, 96, 122–125, 127, 134, 145, 153–154, 158, 161, 171, 214, 218
Clinchfield Railroad 3, 6, 96, 121–122, 162, 169
Coaldale Victory ***248–250***
Combat Trail of the 32nd Armored Regiment, 3rd Armored Division 4, 118, 254–258
Coons, Walter H. 76, 186, 204, 207, 242
Corlett, Gen. Charles H. 134
Crisp, Zack ***78***

D-Day 115, 118
Dad 5, 18, 25, 27, 29, 55, 63, 82, 89, 92, 94, 95, 105, 110, 130, 153, 163, 164, 165, 179, 184, 185, 186, 188, 196, 203, 207, 209, 212, 235; *see also* Goodin, Thomas Elliott
Departure, Letter of 226
Desert Training Center 37, 38, 49; *see also* Freedom's Desert-Rice Army Airfield
Dewey, Thomas E. 124, 164, 206
Dixon, George W. ***78***

Index

Doan, Col. Leander L. 137, 159
dog biscuits 38; *see also* hardtack; rusk
Dragon's Teeth 147, 148, 149, 151
Duncan, Liz 5, 24, 25, 29, 82, 85, 93, 120
Duncan, Paul 5, 24, 25, 29, 82, 85, 93, 120
dynamite 27

East Tennessee State Teacher's College 3, 13, 34
Eastern Theater of Operations ETO 92, 97, 103
Edwards, Capt. George B. 38
Eisenhower, Dwight D. 214
Elizabethon Star 175
England 74, 76, 77, 80, 86, 95, 99, 102, 107, 108, 196, 207, 212, 215, 233, 240, 241; Bath 106; English Channel 118; London 83, 88, 99, 100, 101, 113, 221; Salisbury Plains 83; Somerset 113; Southampton 113, 116; Weymouth 113, 116; Wiltshire 9, 74, 113
English Channel 116
Erwin, Tennessee 9, 36, 127
The Erwin Record 58, 82, 104, 119, 154, 162, 208, 213
Europe 72, 107, 118
Exher, CWO Joseph H. 229

Feagins, Edward R. 15
Feldman, Ben 77
Fisz, Gene 78
Ford, John A. 78
Fort Erwin, Barstow, California 52
Fort Knox, Kentucky 9, 23, 27, 32, 36, 107, 224
Fort Oglethorpe, Georgia 12, 14, 31
France 84, 117, 118, 120, 169, 214, 218, 219, 225, 227, 238, 240; Aisne River 146; Ambriéres 138; Belleau Wood 227; Braisne 146; Canisy 137; Cannes 196; Cerisy La Salle 137; Chateau Thierry 227; La Ferte Sous Jouarre 145; Fromental 141, 142, 143; Gavray 137; Le Havre 209, 243; Joue du Bois 141; Liége 146, 222; Marne River 145, 227; Maubeuge 136, 146; Mayenne 138, 141; Melun 145; Mortain 137; Nice 196; Normandy 113, 116, 118, 126, 136, 140, 143, 218, 229; Omaha Beach 113, 116, 118, 138; Paris 145, 187, 188, 190, 196, 201, 211, 213, 220, 221, 224, 227, 242; Ranes 141, 143; Reims 211, 227, 233;

Roncey 137; St. Jean de Daye 123, 126, 132, 136; St. Lô 136, 137; Sée River 137; Siene River 137, 142, 145, 151; Soissons 227; Versailles 193; Verviers 147, 171, 222; Vire River at Airel 125, 126
Freedom's Desert-Rice Army Airfield 38; *see also* Desert Training Center

German Infantry Divisions: Scharnhorst 201; Von Hotten 201
Germany 120, 154, 165, 173, 184, 187, 207, 211, 216, 224, 228, 233, 237, 244, 246; Aachen 153; Asbach 193; Aschaffenburg 204, 230; Berlin 153; Bernberg 201; Bettingen 238, 239; Bonn 191; Cologne 186, 188, 198; Dessau 193, 201, 207, 208 (*see also* prison camps); Dill River 193; Duren 213; Elbe River 207, 229; Eppertshausen 206, 215; Erft Canal 186; Frankfurt 221, 230; Gieboldehausen 198; Greifenhagen 208; Hachenburg 193; Hanau 230; Harz Mountains 198; Herborn 193; Herzberg 198; Honnef 190; Hoven 170; Könnern; Jessnitz 201; Langfeld 147; Langerwehe 170; Lippstadt 194; Main River 244; Marburg 199; Mösbach 204, 24; Münsterbusch 151; Nordhausen 198; Nothberg 170; Nütheim 147; Obergiech 170; Oberpleis 199; Osterode 198; Paderborn 193, 194, 200; Remagen 190, 192; Rhine River 188, 190, 191, 194; Roer River 170, 185, 186, 213; Ruhr 194; Saale River 201; Veckerhagen 195; Weser River 195, 200
Gilboe, Ronald D. 118, 119, 171
Goodin, Betty 24, 57
Goodin, Glenna E. Hall 3, 18, 57, 81; *see also* Mom or Mother; Witch of Endor
Goodin, Jean 24, 57, 80
Goodin, J.R. 5, 19, 65, 133, 197, 205, 207; *see also* Goodin, Tom, Jr.
Goodin, Thomas Elliott (T.E.) 3, 17, 34; *see also* Dad
Goodin, Tom, Jr. 5, 24, 88, 105, 131, 160, 163, 164, 196, 203, 212, 213, 214; *see also* Goodin, J.R.
Goodin, Tommy 5
Goodwin, Arthur E "Pop" 26

Hall, Pyott 5, 17, 79, 164, 217
hardtack 38; *see also* dog biscuits; rusk

Index

Hearne, Coye F. 118, 119
hedgerow 123, 137, 139, 173
Henry, Maj. Gen. John 38
Henry, Brig. Gen. S.G. 28
Hickey, Brig. Gen. Doyle O. 90, 149, *159*, 194, 195, 211, 226, 252
Hitler, Adolf 72, 198, 201
Hittler, Lt. Harry 189
"How to Destroy German Tanks" 142

Indiantown Gap, Pennsylvania 9, 62, 64, 68
Italy 71, 73, 84, 217

Japan 239
Johnson City, Tennessee 3, 13, 34, 36, 57, 73
Johnson City Press Chronicle 12, 33, 34, 51, 104, 187, 205, 210, 213, 223, 228

Kafrewaz, Larry S. "½" *78*
Keirick, Park C. *78*
King George VI 102
kitchen police 8, 16
Knoxville News Sentinel 164
Krisle, George M., Jr. *78*

Land Army Girls 95
lawyers 14, 17
Legnini, Ron P. *78*, 107
Levy, Meyer L. 76
Lewis, John L. 105
Limestone, TN 105, 130, 202, 212–213
Liverpool 74
Louisville, Kentucky 5, 23, 25, 26, 28
Luftwaffe 137, 154

maneuvers 39, 41, *47*, *49*, 50, 52, 54, 56, *76–77*, 83, 99
marches 38, 97
Margie 51, 53
Martin, Maj. Bill 189
Mathew, Chester *78*
Mattox, George 5
McKee, Maj. Gregg 147
McKellar, Sen. Kenneth D. 113
Melton, Robert L., Esq. *78*
medals 216; Bronze Star 154, 161, 163, 186, 216, 228; Distinguished Service Cross 146; Distinguished Unit Badge 147; Oak Leaf Cluster 147, 187; Purple Heart 161, 185, 189, 201; Silver Star 134

Meyer, Art 5, 13, 26, 47, 62, 96, 129, 222, 245
Mojave Desert 9, 37, 38, 39, 53
Mom or Mother 5, 18, 19, 26, 29, 30, 35, 50, 55, 57, 59, 63, 65, 74, 77, 80, 84, 86, 88, 90, 91, 92, 93, 95, 99, 102, 104, 110, 113, 115, 118, 120, 124, 129, 131, 133, 138, 142, 155, 156, 157, 158, 161, 162, 164, 165, 170, 171, 177, 188, 192, 201, 211, 212, 213, 222, 231, 244; *see also* Goodin, Glenna E. Hall
Montgomery, Field Marshall Bernard Law 221
Moore, Herbert G. 222
Morgan, Kat 5, 17, 22, 25, 168, 177, 231
Moss, C.D. (Charlie) 53, 56, 145, 163, 169, 176, 208, 211

National Veterans Memorial and Museum 184
Nazis 72, 139
Newsweek 167
9th U. S. Army 194
notebook, field 14

Officer Candidate School 28, 31, 32, 34, 36
Owen, Capt. John B. 189

Pacific, South 203, 207, 209, 212, 214, 225, 227, 234
Panzer Divisions 193, 200; 1st SS Leibstandarde (Adolf Hitler) 141, 175; LEHR 126; 9th Panzer Division 148; 105th Panzer Brigade 148; 2nd SS (Das Reich) 141, 175; 12th SS Hitler Jugend 175
Patton, Gen. George S. 38, 234
Pearson, Drew
Pearson, Herman A. *77*
Pearson, Roy L. *77*, 118, *119*, 128, *190*
Phetteplace, L.H. 5
plane(s) 38, 102, 136, 153, 164, 186, 224
Poland, Poles 201, 220
Pop or Pap 18, 19, 21, 29, 35, 57, 59, 71, 73, 81, 84, 88, 93, 96, 104, 123, 130, 131, 133, 134, 142, 152, 176, 183, 239; *see also* Goodin, Thomas Elliott
Prague 220
Prince Henry, Duke of Gloucester 102, 103
prison camps 201; *see also* Dessau

261

Index

Readers Digest 218
Reg 16, 92, 102, 214, 217, 245
Reich 225
Rhineland 151; Siegfried Line 147, *148*, 149, 151, 152, 210, 229 (*see also* Dragon's Teeth); Stolberg 136, 151, 152, 153, 185, 189
Rice, California *36*, 37, 39, 40, *41–42*, 44, 56, 57, 58; *see also* California
Richards, Robert, United Press War correspondent 147
Richardson, Lt. Col. Walter B. 189
Roosevelt, Franklin D. 106, 124, 164, 206, 210
Rose, Gen. Maurice *120*, 138, 146, 147, 157, 159, *172*, 193, 194, 195, *199*
rusk 38; *see also* dog biscuits; hardtack
Russia, Russians 201, 208, 220, 237, 241

Sawyer, Ellene Goodin 5, 69, 10, 1071; *see also* Sis
Sawyer, Glenna 5, 29, 30, 80
Sawyer, Reginald P. 5, 16, 19, 48, 50, 51; *see also* Reg
Scotland 91, 100, 102, 105, 112, 116
"Security on the March—Mechanized Units" 139, 143
Shields, George B. *78*
Shoopla, David (Pencil) *78*
Signal Corps 181
Sis 19, 20, 23, 24, 29, 30, 31, 42, 47, 48, 50, 51, 53, 55, 56, 59, 65, 69, 73, 74, 79, 85, 87, 89, 91, 92, 93, 94, 98, 104, 107, 109, 110, 112, 114, 120, 131, 133, 134, 143, 154, 164, 165, 166, 176, 179, 183, 185, 207, 216, 217, 231, 233, 235, 238, 240, 245; *see also* Sawyer, Ellene
Smith, Al "Snuffy" *78*
Spearhead 3–4, 118, *119*, 120, *123*, 136, 138, 141, 146, *148–149*, 171, 211, 215, 225, *226*, 229, 252
"Spearhead in the West" 77, 144, 151, 175, 176; *Spearhead History Official Record of Combat* 141, 153, 208
Spitfires 74, 77
Stars and Stripes Newspaper 125, 134, 137, 138, 147, 222
Stein, Gertrude 237
Steinbeck, John: *Travels with Charley* 38
Stettinius, Edward R., Jr. 206
Stuart, Wilburn A. *78*
Swantko, Stephen *78*

tank(s) 29, 38, 39, 50, 77, 90, 95, 118, 120, 124, 136, 137, 139, 141, 142, 143, 151, 152, 155, 161, 170, 175, 185, 186, 194, 201, 202, 204, 206, 208, 219, 229, 230; American M24 Chafee *141*; Destroyer *199*; German Panzer IV *145*; SS Panzer *200*; Sherman *123*, 137, 144, *180*, *197*; Tiger 146
Taylor, Bob 132
Ten Commandments 154, 155
Tennessee 132
tents 38, 42, *43*, 53, 108, 111, 113, 116
Texas 39
Tomasello, Theron *78*
Towne, Capt. Hollis L. 180
Trial Judge Advocate 234, 240
Truman, Harry S. 213
23rd Armored Engineer Battalion 145

University of Kentucky 3
University of Tennessee 7, 13, 34, 36

Victory Mail 88
V-J Day 239, 240
Von Kluge, Field Marshall Günther 139
voting 124–125, 132, 152

Waddell, Mayer, PFC 198
Wade, Frederick J., Jr. *78*
Wales 102
Walker, Maj. Gen. Walton H. 34
Wallace, Henry 213
Washington and Lee University 3, 34, 47, 50, 65
Waters, Lt. Col. E.E. 33
Wehrmacht 137
Whitlaw, Nathaniel O. 159
Wilkie, Wendell 106
Wilson, Woodrow 220
Witch of Endor 5, 106, 107
Women's Army Corp WACS 221
Women's Auxiliary Air Force (WAAFs) 95
World War II War Department training film 143; *see also* "How to Destroy German Tanks"; "Security on the March—Mechanized Units"

Yarborough, Major 108

Zhukov, Georgy 221